Kirk—

I am sure Dennis would have wanted you to have one of these. Thanks for your thoughts, help, & communication. Would be really cool if this comes to fruition... long overdue!

Your signature printer

This book printed by
McNaughton & Gunn, Inc.
960 Woodland Drive
Saline, MI 48176

Printed in Saline, Michigan, USA

SHIPWRECKED:

REFLECTIONS OF THE SOLE

SURVIVOR

AN UNBELIEVABLE TRUE STORY OF SURVIVAL

ON THE GREAT LAKES

AN AUTOBIOGRAPHY

BY DENNIS N. HALE

Dennis Hale
P.O. Box 104
Rock Creek, OH 44084
dennishale@windstream.net
greatlakessurvivordennishale.com
Copyright 2010

1

ISBN 978-0-692-00930-7

Additional copies may be purchased from:
    Dennis N. Hale
    P.O. Box 104
    Rock Creek, OH USA 44084
    Email: dennishale@windstream.net

Front and rear cover: Photographs by Chris Winters.
Front cover layout: Lexie Nieszczur.
Artwork: Steve Witucki and Robert McGreevy

2

Dedication

I would like to dedicate this book to my twenty-eight shipmates and friends who lost their lives in the sinking of the *Daniel J. Morrell* on Lake Huron November 29, 1966. You are forever in my heart and on my mind.

Dennis Hale

ACKNOWLEDGMENTS

First and foremost, I would like to thank my family for all the help and encouragement. Without them this book would not have been written.

Brian Morgan, a good friend and fellow boatnerd. Helping him to write an article about me encouraged me to continue writing.

Chris Winters and his wonderful talent with a camera for the front and rear cover photos, even though it almost froze me to death again.

A special thanks to Robert McGreevy, a friend I've known for a least 20 years. I have many of his paintings and I cherish his artwork. His fantastic color print of the *Morrell* is on the back cover.

Steve Witucki, someone I cannot praise enough. Not only did he do the artwork within these pages, he also did a mural of the *Daniel J. Morrell* on my van and other numerous pieces of artwork. All I had to do was ask.

Ric Mixter, a man of many talents, for reviewing and doing the layout of this book.

Tom Farnquist and Pat Labadie for their expert and professional guidance over the years.

Bill Forsythe, for knowing how to make connections and connecting me to the right people.

Lexi Nieszczur, a very intelligent and talented young lady of 13, for doing the layout of the front cover of this book.

4

Tim and Julie Nieszczur, for letting their daughter spend time with me doing the cover and encouraging Lexi's interest in Great Lakes history.

Randy, my psychologist, along with Nancy Clark and the support group at IANDS (International Association on Near Death Studies) for making me feel "normal" and not the only one to experience something out of the ordinary.

So many others, such as Frank Frisk, Dan Hall, Lee Murdock, Andy Sikora, the crew of the Great Lakes Lore Museum in Rogers City, Michigan, and all the others who have encouraged, promoted and gave me moral support over the years, or have contributed photographs and pieces of information pertaining to the *Morrell*.

To all of you people out there that I've met along the way who said to me throughout the years, "Man, you should write a book."

PREFACE

I shouldn't even be alive to have written this book, and for many years I have labored over the thought of doing it. I really didn't think it would be possible for me to sit down and bare my feelings and thoughts on a subject that's very tender, loving and emotional for me. As all of you are aware, there are some subjects that are entirely too private to share with the whole world. To speak of these subjects publicly would be opening my soul for public scrutiny. I thought it would be difficult to share my inner feelings. However, time and temperance is the great healer, and the time has come to share my fears and feelings and to accept how other people perceive me.... I know what I experienced.

After being rescued from the raft I was taken to Harbor Beach Community Hospital and treated for hypothermia and dehydration. I also received the last rites of the Catholic Church. At that time I talked to the priest and told him about (what I found out later) was an after-life experience. His response was, "Oh, Dennis, I don't think I would be talking about that." I was crushed. I had more to tell him about the strange things that happened to me, but when he said that, I listened to him and didn't say another word. He made me feel ashamed and unclean and that people might think I was a little deranged. So I didn't talk about it for some 25 years, and then only to close friends.

For years people have told me, "Man, you should write a book."

So here it is. Everything I didn't say to the priest, and more. Now it's up to you, the reader, to judge whether I was just having follies of the mind or not. Before you judge me, keep in mind after reading this story that there was a pattern and meaning to incidents that occurred to me. So, judge me as you will. I hope you find this book interesting and informative.

THE POEM

All night the wind raged viciously
Around Lake Huron's shore,
It hurled the snow in piled up drifts
And hammered at our door.
It felled the power poles and broke
Their wires by which we live,
In modern comfort, all alone
It made up primitive.
This night no radio voice came in
Nor phone call could go out,
The wild wind taught us violently
What winter's all about.
Our candles guttered in the drafts
On electric blanket spilled
The congealed wax on its thin nap,
Where we lay huddled, chilled.
Within the lulls of shrieking wind
Faint whistles came from ships,
Off course, and blinded by the snow
With all that force at grips.
At sometime, when we shivered cold
A doomed ship staggered by,
The *Daniel J. Morrell*, out there
Was readying to die.
Six hundred feet of tortured steel
Proved not by sixty years,
Was breaking, like the seas around
No time to send up flares.

No time to call the nearby shore
Scarce time to launch the boats,
Scant time to lift and drop the rafts
Or pull on heavy coats.
And some got off and some were left
The difference, it was slight,
For only one lived through it all
That murderous, bitter night.
Just one was spared to tell the tale
Of how she broke in two,
Just one to live, by fate was picked
Of all the *Morrell*'s crew.
Just one was saved on one small raft
Part sheltered by the dead,
He lay and clung with frozen hands,
Scarce feeling left, from dread.

Chapter 1

" What the hell am I doing here?" I said out loud to myself. It's a cold wet rainy April morning in 1964 and I'm standing at the foot of Cherry Street in Erie, Pennsylvania. Looking straight ahead of me I see Erie Bay, beyond that is Presque Isle Peninsula and beyond Presque Isle, the open waters of Lake Erie. Off to my right is this rickety old dock where the ancient rusting hull of the Great Lakes steamer *Daniel J. Morrell* is tied up. I wonder if this old piece of crap is sea worthy. Am I putting my life at risk? I don't think so. These lakes have been sailed for years. As true as that is, every once in awhile you hear about one of these big freighters going down. The things you have to do to get a job and support your family! I've been out of work long enough, so I'd better climb aboard and take this one.

As I'm walking towards the ladder I'm still debating. Damn it's a long way up there. I don't know if I can make it up a ladder with all of my stuff. Someone just threw a rope over the side of the ship and hit me in the head. Looking up, I see another face looking down at me. "Tie your stuff off and I'll pull it up for you!" he shouts. Well, it looks like I'm going to try out sailing!

The *Morrell* was built in 1906 in West Bay City, Michigan, six years before the *Titanic's* maiden voyage, seven years before construction started on the current Welland Ship Canal, eight years before World War I, and well before the Golden Gate and George Washington Bridges were built. At the time, she was the largest vessel built at West Bay City and was named after Daniel Johnson Morrell (1821-1885) who was from Philadelphia, Pennsylvania. In 1855 he became general manager of the Cambria Iron Company. Specifications for the *Daniel J. Morrell* are as follows:

Built by West Bay City Shipbuilding Co.
Triple expansion steam engine (2,000-hp) and two boilers (both built by Detroit Shipbuilding Co.)
Fuel: coal
Length: 586.5'
Breadth: 58.2'
Draft: 27.4'
Gross tons: 7,763
Pilot house, crews quarters forward, 18 cargo hatches center, engine room galley and crew quarters aft.
Constructed of riveted steel.
Hull Number: 619
Official Number: 203507
Owners: Cambria Steamship Company
Operators: 1906-1926: M. A. Hanna Company
Operators: 1927-1966: Bethlehem Transportation Div. of Bethlehem Steel, Cleveland, Ohio.
Additions later on:
1919- The Sperry Gyro Scope Company installed on the ship the first Gyro compass used on the Great Lakes.
1930- The double pilothouse was replaced.

1945- Two new Babcox and Wilcox boilers were installed.
1956- A three cylinder 3,200-hp Skinner Unaflow Steam Engine
 replaced the current one, along with a larger shaft and five-blade
bronze propeller.

Morrell underway

The *Morrell's* primary cargo was coal, iron ore and stone. She sailed for
many years with only one major incident. In 1919 she sideswiped her
sister ship, *Henry Phipps*.

Good jobs were still hard to come by, and since I lived in
Ashtabula, Ohio, and it is on Lake Erie, I figured that sailing would
be a good way to make money. I wanted to work in the galley, but as
things turned out I was an ordinary seaman working as a deckhand. As a
deckhand I did a lot of dirty work getting the ship ready to sail, and I did
my share of painting. That was okay with me, for the food was great and
the pay was even better! I could always go to the galley and get one of
my favorite meals, smoked chubs. (Chub is a Great Lakes fish.) One thing
I quickly discovered was how everyone worked together and how they

watched out for each other. The comradery was something I had never known. It was like we were all brothers with the same common goal. I learned from them and was taught by them how to become a better man as well as a better seaman, someone that could be depended upon and someday looked up to.

While sailing the Great Lakes there were many ports to visit and many things to see. Any night of the week was a good night if we were in port. Unfortunately, as a deckhand, I had to work almost every time we were in port. However, I didn't plan on being a deckhand all my life. If we didn't have to work, the first thing we would do was change our clothes, then climb down the ladder and head to town. I never saw a bar I didn't like. If one of us would get into trouble on shore the others would come to his aid. "If you messed with one of us, you messed with all of us" seemed to be our motto.

I quickly learned to love this lifestyle and the new family I had found. I saw many new places and a lot of new faces, but too soon the season was over and I would return home to my family. Christmas was just around the corner and I had made pretty good wages that year, so it would be a good Christmas.

Our last trip of the season took us to Duluth, Minnesota, to load grain and we would then return to Lackawanna, New York, to a grain elevator to unload it. The unloading process would take place after the ship was laid up and the crew was gone.

Before arriving in Duluth, the cargo hold had to be cleaned

spotless and it had to be dry. It also had to be inspected before it could be loaded. It would take us three days to go from Lackawanna to Duluth. The entire cargo hold from stem to stern, top to bottom and side to side was hosed down. For a day and a half, around the clock, we worked in the cargo hold. Every nook and cranny, every crease and even the overhead steel beam were hosed down. Everyone worked their butts off.

Upon arriving in Duluth the temperature was hovering around zero. After tying up the ship the inspectors came aboard and inspected the cargo hold. We failed to pass inspection, but the area that needed to be cleaned we could clean without using water. The cargo hold had to

Morrell at the locks

be dry before loading grain. If not, the grain would swell and cause other problems.

Soon after we started loading, the first mate came around with a shot of brandy for everyone hoping it would help fight the cold. After we were loaded with grain the lines holding us to the dock were let go, and we finally headed south to Lackawanna and lay-up.

I felt really bad that I had to leave the *Morrell* and return home. The future was uncertain. I would return home with no job and I could not get unemployment. At that time sailing was considered a seasonal job and you were not eligible for unemployment if you worked seasonally. I was quite concerned about the welfare of my family. In spite of this worry, we did have a very nice Christmas. My wife and children received many presents, some were the things they wanted, others were things they needed.

The country was just starting to come out of a recession and jobs were still scarce. I found out that anyone that was hiring would not hire me when they found out I was a sailor off of the boats. They knew that come spring I would be gone, and they wanted full-time employees. They would tell me, "I don't want to train you for a few months just to have you walk off the job when springtime comes." After looking for work for some time, my next-door neighbor, Bob, who also sailed, told me that they were hiring at the Pittsburgh and Conneaut Dock Company in Conneaut, Ohio. He told me they were working on U.S. Steel boats replacing the ballest tank/cargo hold walls and that there would be enough work until spring. Bob said he worked there every winter after he finished sailing.

I went to Conneaut looking for a job, was hired and started the following day. I had to dress warm because it was really cold work. The ship we were working on, the name I don't recall, was tied up next to the dock sitting in frozen Lake Erie. While working in the hold, the cargo loading hatches were kept open. That would allow the smoke from the welder's rod to escape. Down below, in the cargo hold, the men would burn wood in two fifty-five gallon drums, but the only time you could feel heat coming from the fire was while we were on break. Most of the time we were working too far away from the drums to reap the benefits of the burning wood. I enjoyed working there very much. Most of the men that I worked with were also sailors. I worked there until the end of March, at which time I was called back to the *Morrell*.

I couldn't wait to climb aboard the *Morrell* again. However, it was tempered by the fact that I had to leave my family once more. We had a real nice winter together and some good times, but I had to leave and make a living. I couldn't continue working at the Pittsburgh and Conneaut Dock Company, for we had finished the cargo hold jobs.

In 1965 when I returned to the *Morrell* for fit-out, I was promoted to deck watch. My new duties included sounding the ballast tanks and keeping track of how much water was in each one. I would then mark the different depths of water in the ballast tanks on a chalkboard in the pilothouse and engine room. Water is used as ballast when there isn't any cargo in the boat. It helps to lower the boat in the water and makes it safer to operate.

Morrell loading

Sometimes while unloading, the buckets of the unloader would puncture the walls of the cargo hold and water would leak out of the ballast tanks and into the cargo hold. Until they could be properly repaired I would go into the cargo hold with the watchmen, and we would drive wooden wedges into the punctures. As soon as the wooden wedges swelled up the leak would stop. Of course, I would still have to chip and paint and do the same work as I did before. In my opinion, I worked one of the best watches on the ship. It was the four to eight watch, four o'clock in the morning until eight o'clock in the morning and the same hours in the evening. The four to eight watch was the first mate's watch and was referred to as the "mate's watch."

That year I met the nicest man a person could ever meet. His name was John Rutherford, and he was the head cook. If you really have to like someone, it should be the head cook. The meals he would prepare were beyond belief!

I would awaken John around four thirty in the morning to start breakfast. At five o'clock I would go back to make sure he was awake. John would be waiting for me with a double shot of liquor, and he would insist that I drink it in front of him. At six o'clock in the morning I would go to the pilothouse and relieve the wheelsman at the wheel so he could take his break. When he returned I would go back to the galley and take my break and again John would hand me a double shot of liquor. There were times that, it seemed to me, he was just watching for me and every time he would see me he would hand me a glass of liquor. Sometimes after my watch I would walk into the galley a little wobbly. John would then fix me four slices of French toast, a half dozen slices of Canadian bacon, and all the coffee I cared to drink. John really knew how to take care of the crew!

That same year my roommate was Harvey Hayes from Erie, Pennsylvania. He is frightened to death of bats, thus his nickname is Harvey "Batman" Hayes. It must have taken all of a day for him and I to become great friends. Harvey and I always seemed to find trouble, be it on shore or on the boat. It was a sure thing to find us at some bar stirring up a little bit of mischief and trying to pick up the women. Occasionally some of the other crew would go out with us and we all would have a really good time.

Harvey Hayes, Brian Morgan, Dennis Hale (Morgan Photo)

I could, and probably should, write a book just about Harvey. What a colorful person he was then and still is! We certainly did a lot of crazy things together, Harvey and I. Even nowadays we sit around and talk about the fun we had sailing together.

That year, while tied up in the slip in Lackawanna, the U.S. Coast Guard came aboard and we had an inspection and safety drill. The drill included uncovering the lifeboats and lowering them into the water while we were in them. Then we rowed the boats a little ways, just to see if we could, and then returned to the *Morrell*. We passed inspection and the drill, which made me personally feel really good about it. What a confidence builder!

Something that I did notice was that boat sinkings were never talked about very much. The *S.S. Carl D. Bradley*, *Cedarville* and the *Steinbrenner* were brought up in conversation, but no one dwelled on it. Perhaps it was because everyone sailing on the *Morrell* felt secure. I know that I felt secure.

I recall hearing at some point that sometime back in the 1920s the *Morrell* was in a collision with the steamer *S. H. Robbins* as they were both entering Whitefish Bay. It was snowing very heavily and visibility was very poor as the *Robbins*, ahead of the *Morrell*, entered Whitefish Bay. The *Robbins* passed astern of several anchored vessels in the bay before deciding it would be foolish to go any further. She fell in line with the other vessels and dropped one anchor that dragged a short distance before it held. With poor visibility, the *Morrell* was passing the bow of the *Robbins* when it came in contact with her. The *Morrell* rubbed a considerable part of the bow before the vessels were cleared of each other. The Morrell was found to be at fault.

It was another great sailing season. I found out that sailing on the

Great Lakes is quite an experience. You really run into some whacked out people. Don't get me wrong, they're really good people, just a little different. I wouldn't trade my time with them for anything in the world. I don't know, maybe this was the season in my life that I really started to grow up. For men, I think the growing up process takes a while.

This was the year the meteor lit up the sky in Buffalo, and it could be seen in a large area of New York and Pennsylvania. It must have been about two o'clock in the morning when this event occurred. We were coming into Lackawanna, and I was working on the deck with the deckhands unclamping the hatches so as to unload after making the dock. All of a sudden it looked just like daylight! It was as if someone turned a light switch on. I recall chuckling to myself and thinking, didn't I read this in Genesis? Looking skyward we could see this large ball of fire with a tale streaking across the sky. It was quite an amazing sight!

At the end of the season we laid the ship up in Toledo, Ohio. It took us about three days to make the bow section ready for winter. Normally we would leave after making her ready. However, the stern section was shorthanded and they had to tear down the engine, so Harvey and I volunteered to stay over and work the extra two weeks. Harvey and I had a great time for those two weeks. We were in town and in different bars every night.

Harvey and I talked about sailing together the following year. We had been talking about it for the past month. We also talked about our families visiting with each other through the winter. However, while laying up the stern of the ship, Harvey said he was uncertain as to whether he would be back or not. He said that while we were laying up the bow section, he and another man were sent into the ballast tanks to check for leaking rivets on the hull. That kind of frightened him because there were entire steel plates with leaky rivets. He also stated that the leaking rivets in the section of the ballast tank they were in were too numerous to count. I found that hard to believe. I said to him, "If that was true, how would it stay afloat?" He responded by saying that he was told that the incoming water would freeze and stop the leaks.

The *Morrell* was dry docked February 18, 1965. Various rivets and steel plates were changed or repaired. During a ship's life, it was not uncommon for rivets to be changed along with sections of the hull. I couldn't begin to list all the repairs the *Morrell* had had in the sixty years she sailed.

In the1966 season, Harvey didn't return to sail. I feel certain he was concerned about the integrity of the entire ship. He said that he talked it over with his family and decided it would be best if he stayed ashore and found a job. His daughter did not want to see him return to sailing. She was about five years old at that time. I really felt bad that he wasn't coming back with us that year. We had such a good time together the year before, and he was the best roommate I had ever had.

The demand for steel products in 1966 was at a sharp increase. The Vietnam War was escalating, American autos, especially the hot muscle cars, were in demand. Also, a project called the World Trade Center, consisting of five buildings and two office towers, was started in lower Manhattan in August. By the end of that year, Great Lakes carriers would have hauled 85,273,676 gross tons of iron, (the most since 1957) the key ingredient for making steel. Bethlehem, the number two steel producer at the time, had orders to fill. The now 60-year-old *Morrell* would sail another season.

The sailing season began uneventfully. We primarily sailed between Taconite Harbor, Minnesota, and Bethlehem Steel in Lackawanna, New York. In August, Captain Bill Hull was replaced by Captain Arthur Crawley, age 47, from Rocky River, Ohio. It was his first command, but the crew was not concerned. Captain Crawley started as a deckhand and worked his way up. Some of the older crew had worked for him when he was a mate. They nicknamed him the "bull of the woods." I never asked anyone how he got this nickname. Everyone knew that he was experienced and knew how to sail.

The ship sailed over the Thanksgiving holiday, not uncommon on the Great Lakes. While on what we thought would be our last trip of the season, we were told that after we off-loaded iron ore in Lackawanna we would have to make one last trip, the thirty-fourth of the season. Another vessel, I think it was the *Bethlehem*, was to make that trip, but she developed engine trouble. Needless to say, the crew was pretty well bummed out. They were looking forward to their off time, but the *Morrell* had to sail again.

Sailing from Lackawanna, with water for ballast, her course would

21

take her across Lake Erie, up the Detroit River, across Lake St. Clair, up the St. Clair River and into Lake Huron. From there we would sail north through Lake Huron to the St. Mary's River, pass through the Soo Locks into Lake Superior, then straight across to Taconite Harbor. This would take about three and a half days traveling at thirteen miles per hour.

By the time we arrived in Lackawanna the crew had resolved themselves to this one last trip. As we arrived at the dock I noticed two ships were ahead of us waiting to unload. Unless there are problems, it takes eight hours for the machines, called Hulett unloaders, to off-load a ship.

Living only three hours from Lackawanna, I kept my car there in case I had the opportunity to go home. This, I thought, would be a good chance to take my belongings home before the last trip. I found someone to stand my watches, checked with a mate and decided to leave. Before leaving I checked with John Groh, a shipmate, to see if he wanted to be dropped off on the freeway near Erie, Pennsylvania, close to where he lived. He said yes, so off we went! I dropped him off as planned and continued on to Ashtabula. I spent that evening and the next day in Ashtabula then picked up John at about eight thirty that night.

Before even arriving at the dock at Bethlehem Steel in Lackawanna, I could see the lights of the *Daniel J. Morrell* as she was clearing the break wall. It was eleven thirty, and we had missed the ship! The date was November 26, 1966. We went to the Coast Guard station and I called Captain Crawley on the ship to shore radio. He told us to meet the ship at Consolidated (Mullen) Coal Dock in Windsor, Ontario. There the *Morrell* would take on 221 tons of coal for fuel. If I didn't catch the ship I would forfeit vacation pay, extended vacation pay and an annual bonus, all totaling about $6000-$7000.

We returned to Ashtabula to spend the night before leaving the next day for Windsor. Upon awakening I called a friend of mine named George Burguard and asked him to go to Windsor with us and then drive my car back to Ashtabula. He agreed, so off we went again. We arrived in Windsor around eleven o'clock in the morning only to find that the *Morrell* hadn't come in yet. That was a good thing, because I don't know what we would've done if we had missed it again! John and I found a restaurant and had a bite to eat and then went back to the coal dock to wait for the *Morrell* to come in. We were then informed that due to high winds in the Detroit area, the *Morrell* dropped anchor just south of Detroit at 1800 hours on November 27th. Captain Crawley notified his dispatch in Cleveland of the delay at 0615 hours on November 28th.

That evening several boats came in to load coal for fuel. John and I went aboard and raided their refrigerators for dinner. That night we stayed below the fuel dock in the locker room and slept on wooden benches. The *Morrell* heaved anchor and docked at the coal dock at 0705. The *Morrell* did not have a bow thruster. As the ship approached the dock they lowered two crewmen over the side with a landing boom to handle lines. Great Lake ships would usually dock unassisted by tugs, and the *Morrell* was no exception.

When John and I boarded the ship in Windsor we were teased by our shipmates for missing the ship. They said things like, "Couldn't you get out of bed and leave your woman?" To make matters even worse, that wasn't the first time I had missed it. I don't know about John, but I was pretty tired. We had been waiting for about sixteen hours for the boat to dock. We departed from the dock at 7:30 A.M. and I was told I could go to bed and the other watchman would finish my watch. John had to work, but I could have just laid around and relaxed as I was on my own time. I could have watched TV or listened to CKLW, a rock 'n roll radio station in Detroit. It was a cold raw day November 28th, so there were no ladies to watch sunning themselves on the decks of the Chris-Craft, Lyman, or

Morrell at the Locks- Steve Witucki

Owens power boats, which was a great pastime in the summer months. Instead, I went to the galley, got some grub and went to bed.

The *Edward Y. Townsend*, the sister ship of the *Daniel J. Morrell* and also owned by Bethlehem Steel, was sailing on the same run as we were. She had anchored in the St. Clair River below Stag Island, up river from St. Clair, Michigan. The *Morrell* passed her at 1300 hours on November 28th. Both masters communicated to each other about the condition on Lake Huron. At 1453 hours the *Townsend* heaved anchor and started sailing about an hour and a half behind the *Morrell*.

Fighting eight-knot currents under the Blue Water Bridge that connects Port Huron, Michigan, with Point Edward, Ontario, the *Daniel J. Morrell* entered Lake Huron. This lake is the second largest of the Great Lakes. At 750 feet deep, covering 23,000 square miles, it is the fifth largest fresh water lake in the world. November weather on the Great Lakes is something that sailors take very seriously. They have great respect for the November gales. Late that afternoon the winds at the south end (Port Huron) were at six to twenty-eight knots and freshening.

I was awakened around three o'clock in the afternoon to stand my evening watch. I noticed that we had just passed the Huron Lightship. Built in 1920 in Morris Heights, New York, she is the only lightship in the world painted black. WAL526 was assigned to mark Corsica Shoal on lower Lake Huron from 1936-1970. Little did I know that this would be the last time the crew and I would see the Lightship. After taking a shower I walked to the stern and went into the galley for something to eat before starting my watch. I talked to some of the guys and then I walked forward to start my watch, but first I stopped in the crew's work hall and talked to some of the guys. We joked around a little and talked about this being our last trip. While walking forward I noticed that we were now in Lake Huron. That was good because it meant that I would stand my watch in the pilothouse. If we had been in the river, I would have to stand on the bow in the cold. I was looking forward to four hours in the nice warm pilothouse.

In the pilothouse was Captain Art Crawley, First Mate Phil Kapets and the wheelsman, Stu Campbell. The Captain was on the ship's phone when I came into the pilothouse. He was talking to someone about the weather. Captain Crawley was a real good man and always had time to say a few words to you. It didn't matter if you were in the pilothouse or walking down the deck. After finishing his conversation on the phone, he turned to me and said, "I see you made it back. You lost a lot of money, missing the boat. I hope it was worth it." I responded by saying that I would have lost more if he wouldn't have let me get back on board. I thanked him. He said a few words to the mate and then went below to his cabin.

As soon as he was gone the mate and the wheelsman tore into me half joking, half serious. Things cooled off soon and we got back to doing our jobs. Everyone was in a good mood. At six o'clock Stu went back to the galley to eat dinner, and I relieved him at the wheel. While he was gone the mate and I talked. I had brought back two bottles of liquor for him, as he had requested, when I went to the galley earlier. I told him that when I got up to stand my watch I stopped by his cabin and knocked on his door, but when he didn't answer I put the suitcase with the liquor in it inside his door. He thanked me and said he would pay me in the morning.

When Stu returned I headed to the galley to have a bite and talked to the deck watch for a while along the way. I did notice that the wind seemed to be a little brisker and perhaps freshening. When I got to the galley the guys razzed me about missing the boat again. When I walked back from the galley, I noticed that ice had formed on some of the bulwarks and hatches where spray was coming over the port bow. I walked down the starboard side to keep from getting wet and returned to the pilothouse the same way. I arrived back at the pilothouse around seven thirty.

It seemed like a normal watch. There was weather coming in, but I didn't hear anything that alarmed me. There weren't any warnings, just a normal watch. No one was standing around the radio listening to it. At one point Stu made a comment to the mate about the weather and the mate said something to him about some weather that was north of us but not in the area we would be in. When the watch was over, I asked the mate and Stu if they wanted anything from the galley. They said yes, so off to the back of the boat I went once again.

In the galley the guys were watching television and bullshitting. I had some chicken and chocolate milk to eat as I talked to Art Fargo, Nick Homick and Sam Grippi. We just talked about general stuff, getting the boat loaded and getting back to Lackawanna and laying up. I talked to a couple of the other guys as well, Don Worcester and Joe Mahsem. It was the same conversation - load, unload and lay-up. Everyone just wanted the trip to be over and lay the boat up. Laying-up the ship means to shut it down for the winter, putting everything away and covering most of the stuff on the deck. The men working in the engine room tear down the engine and clean out the boilers. All of this is done annually.

Sam was from Ashtabula. He and I were real good friends. His nephew Vince and I went to school together and I knew a lot of his family. In the winter Sam and I would go rabbit hunting together and then in the spring before it was time to sail again, his wife Sarah would fix a spaghetti dinner with rabbit. It was delicious! My wife and children also loved it. Sam would make a quick trip to Ashtabula with me when there were boats ahead of us unloading if he could find someone to work his watch. This last time I went home he had said, "We will be home soon after we lay-up. I don't think I'll go home with you this time."

At last I got some chicken from the galley for the First Mate and Stu and went forward. Again I walked forward towards the bow of the ship on the starboard side. There was still spray coming over the port side of the bow. I gave the mate his chicken and had a short conversation with him. I then went to Stu's cabin and did the same. Stu and I talked for a short while. I said something about the weather being so shitty with the wind being so brisk and there were waves coming over the bow. He reassured me that everything was okay. He said, "It may get a little worse, it may get a little choppy, but everything is going to be okay." I told him that I didn't hear anything about that in the reports on the radio. He said, "Were you listening?"

I responded with, "Kind of. Well, maybe I wasn't." I talked to him briefly and then walked down the companionway past Al Wieme's cabin to my cabin.

I had the cabin to myself. We were one watchman short and he would have bunked in my cabin. I washed up a little and decided to shower in the morning. I took a book off of my bookshelf so that I could read before going to sleep, undressed down to my undershorts and jumped into bed. I turned on my bunk light and then turned off the the overhead light. My sister Jean had suggested that I read *Sandburg's Lincoln*. Whew! Was that some dry reading! I read for about an hour or so before marking my spot in the book, turning off my bunk light and going to sleep. It must have been around ten o'clock or ten-thirty by then. A dreamless sleep found me fast.

Chapter 2

Ah, what the hell is that? A loud bang just woke me up. It must be the anchor bouncing on the bow, I think. I'll roll over to my right side and go back to sleep. After rolling over, almost at once, I hear another loud bang. Whew! It sounded like a cannon going off. Oh, man! My books are falling off the shelf and that has never happened before. If it's going to get that bad I'd better get up. I reach up to turn on my bunk light. Oh, damn! The light isn't coming on. Something's got to be wrong. I'd better get up. I don't recall the boat rolling or pitching a lot through the night.

I start to slide the curtains from around my bunk. Oh! Shit! Oh! It's the general alarm. I can see small sparks as the hammer strikes the bell over and over again. Whew! What's going on? Oh, man. Maybe it's just a stand-by or something. After jumping out of bed, I reach overhead to find my life jacket and put it on. Now I'm opening the door to the companionway. Stepping out and into the companionway, I turn left towards the opening to the deck. As I start down the companionway towards the opening Al Wieme is coming out of his cabin. He is right in front of me as we race for the main deck. He stops at the entrance to the spar deck. He yells, "Oh, my God!"

I ask him, "What do you see? What's happening?" He doesn't answer, just pushes past me and goes up the companionway and back into his room. I step out onto the deck and I cannot see the rear of the boat. I can see where the deck ends. There are lights shinning upwards from where it ends. Now I see the stack starting to rise. The lights are illuminating it and giving it a creepy, eerie glow. I can't believe this is happening!

Oh, man, I've got to get to the crew's work hall on the port side. When I get there just three of the crew are standing inside talking. I see Norman Bragg, John Groh and John Cleary. "What's going on?" I ask. Norman Bragg tells us that the ship has buckled and most likely the bottom is gone. We talk about what is happening now and what was going to happen and what our chances are of coming out of this alive. It doesn't look good. Norman was on the *Steinbrenner* when it sank in 1958 on Lake Superior. I think we respect him and look to him for guidance because he made it through that sinking. The other two guys are really upset and keep asking him questions - what's next and what's happening? It seems like the same questions over and over. I think I even ask him several times what is going on and if we can save ourselves.

He explains to us that the bottom of the boat had hogged (buckled) and cracked. The bottom is gone and it won't be long before we will be in the water. Oh, man, why is it that I'm not afraid? Why am I so calm? Finally Norm says, "It's time to get on the raft fellows. Grab some heaving lines so you can tie yourself to the raft. You don't want to be separated from that raft. It's been good to know you guys." He steps onto the spar deck and starts walking aft towards the raft. John Groh and John Cleary follow.

Typical liferaft

The raft is located on the spar deck between number three and number four hatches. The raft itself is too big and heavy to pick up and throw overboard. It is constructed of steel drums, perhaps eight feet long, connected by a steel superstructure. The drums are approximately five feet apart. Placed on top of this assembly are two by fours that make the deck on the raft, with two by fours on the outside edge to help hold you in. The raft sits in its own stanchion on the deck. It also has a carbide light on rope that is tied to the raft. The canister, with the carbide in it, is connected to the deck by means of a pin that goes all the way into the canister. The pin is welded to the deck. The idea is to sit on the raft and wait for the boat to sink and the raft to float away. At this time the pin will come out of the canister and the carbide light will ignite when it gets wet.

I need more clothes. I wonder how much time I have? I have to go back to my room. It's pitch black out. Walking back towards the starboard side I reach the companionway that leads to my cabin. I wonder where Al Wieme is? I haven't seen him come out of the companionway yet. I walk to the rear of the companionway to my room in the darkness. While walking down the companionway towards my room, I extend my right arm and count the doors until I come to my room. Once inside my room I feel my way around, looking for more clothing, but I can't find any clothes. I've never known this type of darkness! Finally I find my Navy peacoat. Whew! My life jacket, my peacoat and boxer shorts is all I have on. That is it. I can't spend more time looking. I must hurry back to the raft!

I leave my cabin and walk out to the spar deck and start walking towards

Steve Witucki

the raft. Ah shit! It's cold and it's been snowing. I can feel the ice and snow coming up between my toes as I walk down the deck to the raft. I reach the raft and climb aboard and sit down behind John Groh. He has a heaving line (rope) and is tying himself to the raft in the sitting position. I don't want to do that. What will happen if I have to be free of that line real quick? I jab John and say, "John, give me a cigarette." He ignores me because he is too busy tying himself down. Al Wieme is sitting in front of John. We are all facing the port side. The bow (front) of the boat is to my right and to my left is the stern (rear.) Seated to my left is John Cleary and in front of him is Norm Bragg. Norm is also tying himself down to the raft. It doesn't take long until most of the crew from the forward end is either on the raft or around it. Oh, the noise! The noise! The engine is laboring. It sounds like it's crying. I can hear it cry. I can hear the sound of steam escaping, and I can see it in the air. The wind is screeching through the wires and I hear the crunching of steel. "God, don't leave us now."

As I look towards the bow, I see someone on the foc'sil deck. It looks like the second mate, Duncan MacLeod. He has a flashlight in his hand and is fumbling with something in his other hand. Why isn't he coming down to the raft? Why is he just standing there messing around? "Get down here, MacLeod!" Together we all stand a better chance.

Captain Crawley is telling us, Henry Rischmiller, Charles Fosbender, Stu Cambell and everyone else on or around the raft, that he didn't get off an SOS. He's saying that the electrical cable broke when the ship cracked and everything just happened so fast they didn't have a

34

chance. The only way he got the general alarm to sound was by taking the battery out of the directional finder and touching it to the lead wires for the general alarm. Then I wonder if the men in the stern of the ship got a general alarm. He's saying that we shouldn't have even been out here in this storm, that he didn't know that it was coming. Captain Crawley also states that the sister ship to the *Morrell*, the *E. Y. Townsend*, is within fifteen miles of our location and that there are other ships in the area. Now he's telling us that once the raft gets into the water we have to get into the safety compartment and fire some parachute flares as soon as we can. This will make the other ships that are in the area aware that we are here.

Such noise, I can't believe the noise! Everything seems so crazy because of the situation we're in. It's so weird the way the ship is bending, the noise the engine is making, the wind, the lights in the back and none forward. There's a look of disbelief on the faces of my shipmates! In this dim light their faces look yellow and waxy. I'm saying to myself, we can do this. We can do this. Everything is going to be okay. Waiting to see what's going to happen next and not knowing what awaits us is unsettling. God save us!

I hear a noise to my left towards the stern. I can see Oiler Don Worchester in front of the port side after cabins. He has an oilcan in his hand, and he is looking forward. He looks so very calm. My God, does he know what's happening? I can see no one else from the stern of the ship. Did they get a general alarm? They must know something is wrong because they can't keep steam pressure up and with all of this noise they must have some inkling.

What the hell was that? Oh shit! I'm looking over my left shoulder to the starboard side of the deck. The spar deck is starting to tear at the starboard gun wall. (Where the main deck meets the starboard side.) I can feel my heart rate increase. Whew! That's one inch steel plate and it's tearing like a piece of paper! I can hear it scream, and I see sparks and puffs of smoke every once in a while. That must be smoke or dust every time it hits a rivet. It's screaming! The tear is now between the hatches. I hear it screaming as it tears across the deck. I hope that if the rivets are flying out of the steel that we will be safe. (I later found out, no one was injured by flying rivets.) I don't know how long it takes to tear from starboard to the port side. It seems like it's taking forever, but I really don't think it's longer than a minute. The deck is now tearing on the port side. Soon the two sections will separate. The boat is separating into two sections, with the stern section still under power and both sections still afloat. Now, as I'm looking over my left shoulder, I'm looking into Lake Huron as it whips and dances below us. When I look straight ahead over the port side I see the stern section of the *Morrell* coming straight for us while still under power. The water hasn't reached the boilers yet, as there hasn't been an explosion. The deck and cargo hold lights are still on and I can see into the cargo hold.

The wind wails as it throws frozen drops of water in our faces. It feels like needles hitting us. It tears at our clothing as it whips past. I can hear someone far away talking, "Hang on, it won't be long. It won't be long now. Soon we will be in the water!" I can hear another voice saying, "God help us." Everything is happening so fast now that my brain doesn't seem to know what my eyes are seeing. My heart is beating so fast it feels like it's trying to come out of my chest, and my breathing is so rapid I can hardly catch my breath. Everyone is just watching and waiting as the stern section advances toward us. I'm thinking, God I hope the stern section doesn't run over the bow and kill all of us! I close my eyes and hang on to a steel bar that's under my legs and wait for the next thing to happen. "Hail Mary full of Grace. The Lord..." How I pray God is here tonight and can see what's happening to us. He has always been with me in the past.

Ah, it's cold! The damn water is so cold and it's all around me. It feels like my whole body is contracting. Which way am I, face up, or face down? It's pitch black in this water. I'll let some air bubbles out to find out which way is up. I start swimming to the surface. My lungs feel like they are going to explode before I can take a breath of air. God, it's cold! Finally I'm on the surface, and I can't see anything or anyone around me in the water. I'm starting to panic. I don't want to be alone here. God, please don't let me be alone! Then from between the waves I see a raft bobbing in the water. The carbide light did ignite. It was almost as bright as daylight around the raft. I don't see anyone on the raft or near it. What happened to everyone? Where are they? I can no longer see the raft. It must be in the low section between two waves. It's so very cold! As I look at the raft it seems to be drifting farther away from me. I don't know if I can swim. My body is starting to feel tight and hard to move. I'd better try before I lose sight of the raft again. It's so hard to swim! It's as though someone is holding me back. I know! It's because of the wet peacoat. Should I stop and take it off? No, I'd better not. Every now and then I catch sight of the raft as it bobs between the waves. Sometimes it looks father away than other times. I don't know if I can catch up to it.

God, why have you always made life so hard for me? I have never found joy in being me.

Dennis on the bow of Morrell

Chapter 3

I was born on Amore Avenue in Cleveland, Ohio, on January 23, 1940. My birth took place at home in the house we lived in. I was the fourth child born to Claytor and Ruby Hale. I had two older brothers and an older sister. From what I've been told, the entire family was looking forward to my birth. There was a drawer in the dresser where they put my baby clothes in preparation for the big day. I was to be named Dennis Neal, but I was nicknamed Fritz. I don't know where the name Fritz came from, for I am told I was actually named after a radio announcer, Dennis O'Neal.

Five years earlier my family had migrated from a small town in Virginia called Lebanon. My parents were looking for a better life with more opportunities. As things turned out, my father opened his own auto mechanic garage in Cleveland. Business was good and he was successful. Often my family would make trips to local attractions just to go picnicking or to go fishing. Several times during a year they would venture to Virginia to see family and visit with them for a short while. Everything was done as a family. This was before my birth.

On the night of my birth, my mother's sister, Pauline, was visiting from Virginia. My Aunt Pauline had given birth just two months earlier to a healthy boy who they had named Preston. I was born at approximately two o'clock A.M., a healthy child that weighed about 11 lbs. 2 oz. My family said I was just too big of a baby, for my mother hemorrhaged that night and passed away shortly after my birth. Aunt Pauline breastfed me for several days until she went back to Virginia. (Until the day of his death, Preston swore I owed him a meal.) After she left I was fed what they called a "sugar tit" along with bottled milk. A sugar tit is simply sugar wrapped in a cotton towel for a baby to suck on. I don't know where this idea came from. I don't know how often I had this fed to me, but I guess I liked it.

My family, being from Appalachia, relied heavily upon other family members during difficult times of need. My father was not capable of raising four children and running a business, so the four of us children were farmed out to live with relatives. My Aunt Carrie took care of my older brothers and my sister Jean. They lived in Novelty, Ohio, quite a distance from where I was living with my Aunt Inez and Uncle Vern in Cleveland. Aunt Inez already had five children, one son and four daughters. Their son's name was Harold. He was in the

Grandma & Grandpa Hale

Navy, and I didn't meet him until I was five years old. My aunt and her four daughters, Helene, Joyce, Louise (she was called "Love") and Betty, were wonderful towards me. They played with me as if I was a toy doll,

40

always doting over me and seeing to it that I had everything I wanted. The girls treated me like a brother and I looked upon them as my sisters. I even called my aunt "mom."

I can still recall, when I was around three or four years of age, riding my tricycle on the sidewalk in front of the house and my Aunt Inez called for me to come inside. She said she needed to talk to me. My three cousins were there as well. She told me that she wasn't my mother and that my mother had died during my birth. I can recall going back outside, once again riding my tricycle, and wondering if she knew what she was talking about. I was thinking, of course she is my mother, as I had no other mother. Her telling me

Dennis age three

about this didn't change things. I still felt very loved and I loved all of them very much. They played with me, gave me my meals and clothed me. At that time everything seemed to be just great.

The house I lived in, with my aunt, was right next door to the house where I was born. What a great neighborhood this was! All the neighbors called me Butch. This is the nickname that stuck with me until I was a teenager. I don't know what happened to the nickname Fritz. I knew all of our neighbors and I recall that Halloween was a really special time of year. The neighbors were so friendly towards me as they talked to me and laughed and made remarks about my costume. I was always dressed as a bum for Halloween.

Just before I turned five years old I was told that we were going to move to a different house. I hated leaving the old neighborhood and I would often return there when I was old enough and knew how to ride a bike. Our new address was 9725 Parkgate Avenue. Parkgate is located between St. Clair and Superior to the north and south and East 105th Street and Liberty Boulevard east and west. The house was a duplex and the owners lived on the other side of the house. Their last name was Kurlander. It was located about four blocks from where we lived on

Amore, and the school was only a block away to the west. When moving day finally arrived there was excitement in the air! Several of my other cousins helped us move. It seems as though no matter where I was or what I did I was in the way. So, I decided to see what the new neighborhood looked like.

It was an old Jewish neighborhood, now infiltrated with many ethnic and black families. A block down the street

Dennis and friends 1946

42

to the west was Miles Standish School and just beyond that approximately one block was Cleveland's Cultural Gardens. The gardens were beautiful in the spring when all the crabapple trees were in bloom and majestic in the winter after a heavy snowfall. These gardens soon became a wonderful play area. In the summer neighborhood children and I played on the trails and in Doan Creek. We also ran through the water in the fountains throughout the park. Hide and seek in the park was the best and then there were the crabapple fights. In the winter we went sled riding down Snake Hill, had snow ball fights and made snowmen. My best friends were Peter Dale and Linda and Gary Gorchester. Being with them was the only sane time in my childhood. I was now nearing the age of five and I would soon be going to Miles Standish School.

Living in the house next to ours was an old Jewish woman named Goldie. She was a wonderful woman, always feeding me things like homemade soups, kafilta fish and lots of homemade baked goodies. Our landlords, the Kurlander's, were equally as good to me, and they also fed me. In the next house on the Kurlander side of our building lived the Fosters, a black family. What lovely people they were! They also gave me things like candy and toys that their grandchildren had finished playing with.

As I was growing up so were my cousins. It wasn't long before three of them married and moved into their own homes. By the time I was five the only one home with me was Betty. She and I were very close, very good friends, and I knew she loved me. She too was engaged and it wouldn't be long until she married and moved into her new home. I started missing her long before she moved.

Mrs. Macy and Mrs. Minor were my kindergarten teachers. (I can't remember what I had for lunch today, but I can remember the names of my kindergarten teachers 65 years ago!) School was really great and I absolutely loved it. I made friends with the neighborhood children, and I would visit them at their houses or they would come to my place to play.

After Harold came home from the Navy I could not have my friends over to my house. It was all right for them to be there before he came home from work, but they had to be gone before he came home. Harold would be rude to them and belittle me in front my playmates.

I didn't get to see my father or my brothers and sister very often. My father didn't visit my brothers and my sister much either. Often I would wonder if he was really my father, and if he was, he should visit me more frequently because I was really a nice kid. My sister Jean would visit me once in a while and she would always bring me a book to read. I recall one time she brought me the book *Black Beauty*. It was usually late evening when she arrived, just about my bedtime. She would come up to my bedroom with me and read to me. She told me that if I fell asleep she would finish the book another time. I did indeed fall asleep, but she never did finish that book.

Sometimes when Jean would come to visit me, I would tell her how unhappy I was living with my aunt. I would tell her how I would love to live with her. She would tell me that her apartment was too small for the two of us, but maybe someday. Jean always told me to pray and she would recite with me the "Now I Lay Me Down to Sleep" prayer. Within six months to a year after my fifth birthday she taught me how to kneel and talk to God.

Dennis and Jean

Jean had a rheumatic heart from the age of thirteen. I knew that her health was a problem for her, and in my own mind I used to think that was the reason she didn't come over and visit me more often. At night when I would kneel and pray I would always ask God to help make Jean well again.

After graduating from high school she worked as a dental assistant for a number of years. Following that she was pretty much housebound most of her life due to her heart condition. She had a love of books and reading and that was how she spent a lot of her time. She also enjoyed writing poetry and even had some published. Several of her friends were literary junkies that had been published as well. I didn't feel comfortable around any of them. Another thing she enjoyed very much was telling me what to read and what music to listen to. However, that was better than her making the dental appointments for me every few months to have my teeth cleaned and checked. Jean was a strange woman. The more time I spent

45

with her, the stranger I found her to be.

I very seldom saw my brother Ed. My brother Robert, his nickname was Gay, was named after the family doctor that delivered me. Gay would hang around with Harold every now and then, so I did get to see him once in a while. However, we really didn't talk often or very much. Maybe we just had nothing to say to each other. We really didn't know each other as brothers. Perhaps my brothers and my sister and I just had nothing in common because we hadn't been raised together as a family. I don't know what happened to my father after my mother died. Life seemed to change for my whole family. That is what my siblings would tell me. My father never took us on picnics, fishing or trips out of town like he used to do with them. It was like we lost both of our parents. After I grew older I really felt bad, and also guilty, about the life changes that came about in my family after my mother died.

Aunt Inez and Uncle Vern were starting to have problems. Uncle Vern liked to drink and often he would come home drunk and they would argue. He didn't seem to spend much time at home anymore. I really liked my Uncle Vern. I recall his eyeglasses because they had clear plastic frames. Vern also had his own garage and his glasses were always covered with grease, black grease. It was stuck in the frame around the lenses. You could say it was the first thing you would notice about him. He was always nice to me and treated me very well.

The thing I remember most about Uncle Vern was his sternness around the dinner table. He would say some type of prayer before the meal and then there was absolutely no talking until after we were finished eating. I was always in trouble because of this and would be sent away from the table. I missed a lot of meals because I didn't know how to shut up!

It wasn't very long before my aunt and uncle separated and then divorced. Uncle Vernon would still come to the house now and then and visit with us. One day I received a phone call from him and he asked me to meet him at his garage because he had something for me. I walked over to his garage and there before me was a brand new bicycle that he had purchased for me. He even took the time to teach me to ride it. I had a hard time understanding this because Harold was always telling me that no one really wanted or loved me.

Sometimes things happened at home that I just didn't quite understand. Although I felt like part of the family, there were times that things just didn't seem to be right. Whenever we had company over for dinner I was told I had to stay in the kitchen while everyone else ate in the dining room. After everyone else had eaten their fill, I could eat whatever was left. Most of the time there wasn't much, maybe a potato, some milk and cornbread or a chicken wing or back. I couldn't understand why there was nothing for me. If I asked one of my cousins why there was no food for me, I was told it was because we had company.

Another thing I remember happening, usually on Saturday nights, was family and friends would come over to the house with guitars, mandolins, banjos and various other musical instruments. They would all play music and sing and have a good time. I was not allowed to participate in any of this. I was always sent upstairs to bed even if it was a get together in the afternoon. Often I would sneak downstairs and hide under the dining room table and watch them make music and sing. Someone would always find me hiding there, then I was punished and sent back to bed.

As a child, I was seldom sick. I did have the chicken pox as a baby, but no measles, mumps or any other childhood illnesses. I very rarely had a cold, but when I did, it didn't last very long.

At or around the age of seven I was electrocuted. The bathroom was located on the second floor next to my bedroom. When you walked into the bathroom, straight ahead was the claw-footed cast iron bathtub. To your left, next to the bathtub, was the toilet, and the sink was next to the toilet. Across from the sink, on the right wall was a medicine cabinet with a mirror and a small table was standing beneath it. There was a radio on the table so that you could listen to music while you were in the bathroom. One night, after my Cousin Love used the bathroom, I was told to take my bath. She asked me if I would like her to leave the radio on. I said yes. I very seldom used the radio because I was never in the bathroom that long. I filled the bathtub pretty close to half full and then jumped in.

The water was warm and comfortable that night as I bathed and played around in the water. I decided to see if the Lone Ranger or the Green Hornet was on the radio or some other children's program. As soon as I touched the selector knob to change the station I felt the electricity pulsing through my body. The water in the bathtub was dancing up and down and I couldn't release my hand from the selector knob. I started yelling and screaming for help, hoping someone would come soon and save me. In no time Love was there and unplugged the radio. Aside from having the hell scared out of me, there were no ill effects. I did have some strange things happen to me afterwards, but that is a whole other story.

I did do some weird things as a child, mostly in the winter. While living on Parkgate my bedroom was on the second floor at the rear of the house. On the rear wall, in the back of my bedroom, was a door that led to a balcony that ran the entire width of the house. (Now, I find the following very strange.) In the winter I would play a game. I would block the backdoor open about two inches and then open the window next to the bed about one inch. I would then take all the blankets off the bed and just leave the sheets on it. I had pajamas on, and I would crawl under the sheet and gather it all around me and tell myself I had to learn to keep warm. As a child, I thought this would toughen me up, and who could tell, someday I may need to keep warm. The follies of a child's mind! Little did I know what the future held for me.

Harold was discharged from the Navy several months before I started school. Aunt Inez, Uncle Vernon and the girls planned to have a large celebration for him. At last, the war was over, and the entire family was happy to see him come home. It was a very joyous time. Friends and family from all over the state of Ohio, even from Virginia, came to visit with us and celebrate Harold's return. A new and prosperous time was upon all of America... Harold was my hero.

I had no way of knowing that my whole life was about to change. Having a hero meant I wanted to be around him all the time and learn what he could teach me. Yes, I wanted to be just like Harold. Maybe I tried to spend too much time with him. Maybe, as a young child, I asked too many questions. Harold was annoyed with me all the time. He never played with me or even talked to me unless he was drinking or around other people. If no one else was around he would talk to me with annoyance and disgust in his voice. His eyes would even show anger or hatred, but nonetheless, Harold was my hero.

It must have been when I was around the age of six years old when Harold really started physically abusing me. If I got out of line just a little bit, he would severely punish me. He would spank me with a belt or a switch or squeeze the muscle on my legs just above my knee. Other things he would enjoy doing was grabbing the muscle between my neck and shoulder and squeezing hard or putting his fingers in my arm pit and lifting up. Sometimes he would grab my hair and shake my head or pull the hair on the back of my neck. Of course, these things would happen when no one was around.

He also told me that my father, brothers and sister didn't want me because I killed my mother. Harold said that his family didn't want me either and that I would have to move as soon as I was older. He always reminded me that his mother, Aunt Inez, wasn't my mother and that nobody wanted me. Of course, that explained to me why my family never came around. I was totally confused, and just didn't understand why I was such an outcast. Many nights I cried myself to sleep thinking that absolutely no one wanted me.

There were many times I talked to Aunt Inez about Harold's treatment towards me and how mean he was to me. She would tell me that he was just trying to teach me the difference between right and wrong, and he was trying to make a man out of me. She would say, "Now Butch, you know how good he is to you when you're not being bad." No, I didn't know how good he was to me. Talking to her about my feelings never did do any good.

Needless to say I soon became very frightened of Harold, more so when he was sober than when he was drunk, although he always seemed to have a beer in his hand. Often Harold would tell me that I killed my mother and he wasn't going to let me kill his mom or hurt his family.

It was also about this age that Harold started abusing me in other ways. He would tell me that if I were to tell anyone, or if anyone were to find out, I would be in a lot of trouble, and he would have to beat me or maybe even kill me. For days following an encounter he was very mean and cruel to me and threatened me a lot. He was always very cruel. Every night after going to bed I would think about Harold's cruelty towards me, and I would pray and hope that something would happen to him so that my next day would be better. I always prayed that something would happen to Harold. I hated Harold! He was no longer my hero.

I can recall one time when I had done something wrong, or

something that Harold didn't like, and he came after me and I ran to try and hide from him. To avoid him I ran into the basement and into the coal pile in the coal bin. He was smiling and coming towards me like a hunter after his prey. I was very frightened. Just as he started to grab me I looked toward the stairway that led down into the basement, hoping to find an escape route. My brother Gay was sitting there on the stairs and laughing. I yelled at him to help me, to save me, and he just sat there laughing. It's hard to talk about all the feelings that washed over me at that moment, and how I feel now as I write about it. Why was there no one there to save me? I felt so alone and deserted.

As I look back at this time in my life, when I was a young boy, I really think the physical abuse and Harold's hatred and meanness towards me affected me more than any other abuses. As an adult, whenever I would look back and think of him and the way he treated me, I would get very angry and upset. Oh, how I wish that just once I would have reached out and knocked him on his ass! At the time of this writing I am sixty-nine years old. It was just about three years ago that I decided to let this thing with Harold go and try to stop being angry and try to have a better understanding of the things I cannot reverse. Certainly, this has not been an easy undertaking.

Chapter 4

I hope I'm not misleading you into thinking I was an angel of a child. It seemed like I was always in trouble. I can recall my buddy Pete and I playing on the top of our neighbor's flat garage roof. The woman that owned the garage was throwing flowerpots at us trying to chase us away. There were many nights I would be out playing and having so much fun I just didn't want to go home. I caught hell when I finally did get home though. There were times my playmate's parents would call my aunt and ask if I could stay later. Most of the time she would say yes I could stay. There were other times, when Harold was home, I would tell my friend's parents that I talked to Aunt Inez about staying a little later that night to watch television, and she said it would be alright. Their parents always bought my little untrue story. Television was new then and we didn't own one, so they thought it was okay, nothing unusual. It seems to me that the longer I stayed away from home any night, the more frightening going home became. I guess this is true with all children of any age. I caught a lot of hell when I did get home, and most of the time I was grounded for a week. Somehow I managed to get out of the grounding after a day or so.

When I think back to those days of playing on and jumping off of garage roofs, it was a big thrill for all of us kids. It was almost as though we were cheating death. Now let me tell you why I stopped doing it.

Every once in a while we would go to my Aunt Carrie and Uncle Bob's farm in Novelty, Ohio. It was just a day to visit on the farm, hayrides and a nice dinner in the evening. Whenever I was involved with these things, I was exploring the farm and looking for roofs to jump off of. Everyone always warned me to be careful about what I was doing and not to jump off of any buildings. Did I listen? What do you think?

There were many buildings on the farm. The chicken house that they kept the chickens in seemed like a good prospect. It was rather high, and on one side someone had stacked some lumber. I thought this was the ideal spot to jump. I climbed up onto the roof and viewed the lumber pile to see where I could jump on it. When I thought I had the right spot, I jumped. The first thing I felt was pain as I landed on the woodpile due to an unseen nail going completely through my left foot. It even went through the large bone that led to my big toe. I tried and tried but could not remove my foot from the nail.

Crying, I started yelling and screaming until several of my cousins arrived. It took two of them to pull my foot off of the nail. I thought I was going to pass out before they finally released my foot! I was then taken to the nearest hospital where I was given a shot to numb my foot and then a drainage tube was inserted. Three people held me down, as well as a doctor, while this procedure was done on me. I was also given a shot to prevent tetanus. After a few weeks the drainage tube was removed and I was back to being the old me. I guess you could say my last jump was the most memorable.

Another incident that really scared the hell out of me happened when I was learning to play baseball. I couldn't have been more than six or seven years of age. All of us neighborhood children were good friends, and for the most part we all went to school together. One Saturday afternoon there was a bunch of us kids playing in the schoolyard at Miles Standish School. Someone suggested that we play a game of baseball and we started choosing sides. I think this was the very first time I ever played baseball. I don't recall which side I was on. I just remember playing center field.

We soon retired the opposing team and it was our turn to bat. I was given all kinds of instructions by the other players on how to hold the bat and how to hit the ball. The first time up at bat I struck out. I was instructed not to swing at every ball that the pitcher threw at me. They showed me how to measure the distance from the ground to the bat and where the ball should be so I could hit it. I was really nervous my next time up and I let the first two balls go by. The third ball the pitcher threw I took a swing at. I could feel and hear the ball as it came in contact with the bat. I watched as the ball went all the way out into left field. I started running to first base, but I didn't make it that far when I started hearing a big commotion behind me. I stopped and turned around to see what had happened. One young black friend of mine named Pinky was sitting on the ground bleeding from his head, and there were people all around him. I started running towards him, and when I got to him I found that he was hit in the head by the bat that I had thrown after hitting the ball. He was unconscious and bleeding very badly. There was a flap of skin hanging from the wound. Terrified, I started running home. I didn't know if I killed him or if the other kids were going to jump me and beat me up because I had injured him.

Once I got home I didn't say anything to anyone about what had happened. Maybe I was hoping that no one knew it was me that caused Pinky's injury, and I wouldn't hear any more about it. That night Pinky's parents came to the house and told my aunt and cousins what had happened. I guess that I almost killed Pinky. If the bat had gone in any deeper it would have hit him in the temple and he would have died. I caught a lot of hell over that and rightly so. I guess that's why I never really cared for baseball. If you need more proof that I wasn't an angel, read on.

I tried to stay away from home as much as I could, just to avoid Harold. I recall very few instances that I participated in family activities because there weren't very many. I went to Euclid Beach Park maybe once with my cousins and maybe one or two picnics.

When I was seven or eight years old I spent a lot of time with Pete Dale and his mother. Pete's mother took us to Cedar Point Amusement Park once, or maybe twice. She also took us to Euclid Beach Park and the

Cleveland Zoo. I think I learned to love her, for she was such a sweet, kind and caring person. Often I had wished that she was my mother or that I had a mother just like her. Almost all of my free time I spent with Pete. We would take streetcars and travel all over Cleveland by ourselves or just go to the movies. Aunt Inez saw to it that I had a little money for the movies and sometimes enough for candy or popcorn.

At home, at this point in my life, I didn't really have very much supervision. I came and went as I wanted, within reason, and only had to explain where I was once in a while. Usually when I came home late.

I don't know if children six, seven and eight years of age talk to God. I know that I did. I believe Jean was instrumental in forming my belief in God. She didn't visit me often, but when she did she would always tell me to have faith and trust in Him and He would always be there to answer my needs. There were many nights I would ask God to make me a better child or just to take my life. I would also pray to my mother. I would ask her why she left me when I needed her the most. I would beg her to please help show me the right path so that I might be strong and knowledgeable and teach me the right way to take care of myself. I would tell her, "Without you I will always be alone." Then I would wonder what my life would be like now if she were here with me.

I knew in my heart that my friends were treated differently by their parents than I was treated by mine, and I really felt that I was just in everybody's way. There were many nights, as many as there are stars in the sky, when I thought everyone would be better off if I just wasn't around. There was not much joy and laughter in my family. On the nights that I was sad and depressed like this, I would try to think of ways to end my life. In my mind I could see my heart, and I would picture it beating. With my ears I could hear it beating. I would count the beats and when I got to ten or twelve I would slow down my count, and as I slowed down the count my heart rate would actually slow down. My breathing would become shallower as I slowed the count down. It would get slower and slower, so slow that it would frighten me, and that was all it took to make it start beating its regular rhythm again.

At this time in my life, I would wake up early Sunday mornings and put on my finest clothes. The rest of the family was still sleeping, so I quietly let myself out of the house. I would then look for a church to go to, but living in a Jewish neighborhood there were no churches to be found. I have to admit I did knock on a lot of the Synagogue doors, but to no avail. I did this for several Sundays, each time venturing further away from home, but there were still no churches to be found. On several Sunday mornings I would see Pete and his mother outside walking towards the bus stop. I asked Pete where they were going and he told me he was going to church with his mother. I thought that perhaps he and his mom could help me in my search for a church and some type of faith. It was a time and place in my life that I really needed God.

Somehow, I managed to talk to Pete about my search for a faith and I told him what I thought I was looking for. He said I was welcome to go to church with him and his mother. The next Sunday morning I was

58

dressed and ready to go to church with Pete and Mrs. Dale. We had to take a streetcar down East 105th Street to Euclid Avenue and then another streetcar west on Euclid to East 55th Street where the church was located.

There was a Catholic church, very old and very Gothic looking. It almost looked forbidding. When we went inside, he put his fingers in a dish of water and then crossed himself. Prior to going into the church Pete told me to just to do whatever he did. As I reached to put my hand into the water, his mother grabbed my hand and told me I was not allowed to do that. I wasn't in church five minutes and I was already in trouble and very much confused!

The church was gorgeous inside and the priests were dressed and adorned with beautiful clothing. Another thing that confused me was that they didn't speak English. I guess I thought that was really cool, so every time I had a chance to go to church with Pete and Mrs. Dale, I would go. I found the Catholic church quite fascinating and intriguing. I don't know what it was, but as a young child, I became hooked on the Catholic faith. All I know is, I really needed to have God in my life.

I was still very vigilant of Harold when I was about seven years of age. I tried to stay away from him more than ever, but that was very difficult to do at times. Being extremely frightened of him didn't help either. I tried to stay away from home as much as I could. I would be out every night until it became dark, even knowing I would be in trouble when I got home didn't seem to matter. Aunt Inez would yell at me and give me hell and Harold would chime in with her. This seemed to be the maximum punishment and I learned to deal with it. Harold didn't have too much to say to me when she was around. As I look back now, I think maybe Harold was afraid to say too much in front of my aunt for fear I would say something to her about what he'd done to me.

When I was eight and a half or nine years old I found my first job. I had a paper route with the Cleveland Plain Dealer. I only had it for about two months until something better came along. I was offered a job with the Checker Ice-Cream Company selling ice-cream from one of their three-wheeler bicycles. On the front of the bicycle, on a platform, was a large cooler, and it was packed with ice-cream bars, ice-cream sandwiches and drumsticks and then covered with dry ice. I would ride my bike down residential streets ringing a bell and selling the ice-cream novelties to all that were interested.

There was one day I made a lot of money because I sold a lot of ice-cream. However, by the time I got back to the ice-cream company it was pretty late in the evening. I went inside the building to unload the cooler of ice-cream and dry ice. Inside the building a man was standing with his wife and two children. They also worked for the ice-cream company. I remembered seeing and talking to them a few times. This time the lady asked me what I was doing working so late. She also said I shouldn't be on the streets that time of night as it wasn't safe. When I started to argue with her, she offered to let me stay at their house for the night. I was really tired and the thought of riding all the way home made me decide to stay with them. I would call Aunt Inez when I got to their house. I was never warned about strangers as a child, so I thought it would be alright to go with them. After arriving at their house we all had a bite to eat and then went off to bed. I was to share a bed with their son who was about my age. He and I went upstairs to his bedroom and we started talking and eventually fell asleep. I never did get a chance to call my aunt.

I couldn't have been asleep very long when I heard a loud noise and people running and doors being slammed shut. All of a sudden the bedroom door jerked open and a policeman was standing there. I can remember saying to myself, what did I do now? Did my aunt send the police to find me? We were all taken to the police station and Aunt Inez and Harold had to come and pick me up. I really did catch hell over that but not real bad. I was kind of surprised. I thought it was going to be a lot worse because I didn't come home, and I hadn't phoned them to let them know where I was. Needless to say, I no longer worked for the Checker Ice-Cream Company, and some new rules were made for me to follow.

Some years later, while talking to Jean, she informed me that the house had been raided by the police because it was a house of ill repute. She told me that the house had been watched for quite some time. Whenever she had a chance, or was around some of her friends, she would never let me live it down. She would introduce me to her friends as her younger brother that was pulled out of a whorehouse at the age of nine!

After a while when all this died down I received some really good news. Harold would be moving to Los Angles, California, within the next few weeks. I couldn't believe it! This had to be the best news I ever received in my whole life. The plan was for Harold to move to California, find a job and get settled in, and then Aunt Inez and I would move there with him. They said it might take a year or better before we could move depending on how fast Harold found a job. I was hoping Aunt Inez and I would end up not going to California to live with him. Life would be so much better without him around. I felt at last, there is a God, and He did hear my prayers!

Chapter 5

I'm struggling to swim in the water during the storm, and finally after several minutes I arrive at the raft. Art Stojek and John Cleary are already aboard. I'm pulling myself up and they've got a hold of my coat or my life jacket, and they're helping to pull me onto the raft. Whew! I'm tired and it's hard for me to breathe. As I try to take deep breaths, the bitter cold air being pushed by the wind is stinging my face and gets into my lungs. After a short time I regain my strength, and I briefly start to wonder how I got into the water. There must have been a huge wave that swept everything and everybody overboard and into the icy cold water. Looking around and searching for other people in the water, I can see the bow section as it slowly starts to slide beneath the surface. It is being silhouetted by the lights from the stern section, which is still under power and moving away from us.

I look up at John Cleary, and he is just staring at me with a blank expression. There's only the three of us on the raft, and I don't see anyone else in the water. As I start to try and open the safety equipment compartment, I notice Art and John leaning over the end of the raft and pulling someone aboard. It's Charles Fosbender, who we call Fuzzy. I hope we can find others to bring aboard the raft. Once again my eyes scan the darkness of the water in search of other crewmembers, all the while listening for someone to call out. Once again I neither see nor hear anyone. There could be someone out there between the waves that's not noticeable at this time. I will have to keep an eye open for them.

John Cleary

Once Fuzzy is aboard, I tell all three of them, "We have to get into the safety compartment in the middle of the raft. We have to fire off some flares." The lid to the safety compartment has been damaged from when the raft was swept overboard. It is kind of pushed in. It takes the four of us to force it open by sticking our fingers in the slats and tugging on the lid until it finally breaks free. By the time it opens, our fingers are numb, and we all stick our fingers in our mouths to warm them up.

Once the compartment is open everyone starts reaching into it for something. I don't know if they even know what they are looking for, but I am searching for the flare gun and flares. Reaching into the compartment I find the flare gun. I load the gun and fire off a parachute flare, making sure that I aim and fire directly overhead. To my amazement the flare doesn't seem to go very high. It lights the sky pretty good, but it doesn't seem to stay up for very long. I load a second flare into the gun and fire it again. I know we had six parachute flares in that compartment. Now we only have

64

four, and I will have to keep track of them.

I'm having a hard time understanding Art Stojek. When he talks he's not making much sense and is also talking with a whiny voice. He's complaining about being there in his pajamas and asking me over and over again, "What are we going to do now, Denny? What are we going to do now? Why did this happen? What are we doing? I only have my pajamas on. What are we doing now?"

I'm telling him, "You're better off than I am. I only have under shorts, a life jacket and a peacoat that I'm wearing. We're going to stay alive until someone finds us." Damn it's cold!

I think that Art must be going into shock. He's just not acting right, and yes, he only has his pajamas on. I will have to try and look after him. This is Art's first year of sailing, and I really don't know him that well. It is also John Cleary's first year of sailing. He is clad only in a sweatshirt and jeans. Fuzzy was standing watch at the time of the sinking, and he is fully dressed. He has been sailing for a number years.

Damn it's cold! I can hardly feel anything and my hands are so numb. I'm looking into the compartment because I want to find the storm oil. It's not there and neither is the sea anchor. "Did anyone see the can of storm oil? Where is the sea anchor?" I yell. Please, God, be here for us. Don't make us suffer before we die.

The sea anchor is a tapered canvas bag and into it fits a metal tapered can of oil. The metal can has a screw at the narrow end that, when opened, will allow a slight flow of oil out of it. The metal narrow tip sticks out of the narrow end of the bag. When used together, the sea anchor is supposed to hold the raft in place, and the oil will come to the surface and calm the water around the raft. However, it is virtually useless under the conditions we are in.

While swimming to the raft I thought about spreading the oil on my legs and all other exposed surfaces of my body. I was hoping that this would help hold my body heat in. Fuzzy said, "I saw Art throw some things overboard."

I asked, "Art, did you see the storm oil?"

"What was it in?" he questions.

"A metal can with a big taper to it" I reply.

"I didn't know what it was and I threw it overboard," he tells me.

John Cleary has the sea anchor, and I really see no point in using it if we don't have the storm oil. It went over the side as well. I didn't complain to them about it. I don't think any of us are thinking quite clearly, and really, who knows what lies ahead of us. I certainly wanted that storm oil badly, though.

I'm taking a hand-held flare out of the compartment and trying to light it. It doesn't seem like my fingers want to work because they are so numb! I lay down on my right side. The other guys gather around me, and we place our hands around the flare to try and get some warmth. If it's giving out any heat, I don't feel it.

Fuzzy said, "Don't let that stuff bubbling out of the tip of the flare drip onto your leg. It will burn a hole through it."

Like I really care at this point! I reach down and touch the side of my thigh. It is numb. I doubt very much if it could have been more than fifteen minutes since the boat sank. For some reason, at this time we don't have much conversation. Myself, I'm always thinking of anything or any way to save our lives and every minute, how to keep warm.

As soon as the last flare goes out, I get back onto my knees and start looking into the compartment again for anything we can use. I'm taking out all the flares and the hand-held flares and placing them on the deck next to where I will lay down. I notice Fuzzy at the end of the raft with a flashlight. He seems to be signaling some lights on the water. I ask him, "What are you doing?"

He says, "I'm signaling that ship over there."

As I look at the lights on the water, the bow section is still slowly sinking into Lake Huron. The lake water is almost up to the pilothouse. The bow section is still being silhouetted by the lights from the stern section. I tell him, "Man, that's no ship. That's the stern of the *Morrell*. Can't you see by the angle of the lights? Please don't signal it anymore. Try to save our batteries for when we really need them."

"Okay, I'll shut it off. Are you sure?"

"Yeah, look at the angle of the lights, Fuzzy. Are you okay, Fuzz?"

Fuzzy says, "Yeah, yeah I'm just cold."

By now, everyone else is lying down. I'm on my knees trying to get anything out of the compartment that I think we will use, including the last of the flares. It takes a little while because John and I are talking. He asks me, " What do you think our chances are?"

"A lot better than the guys that didn't make it to the raft with us," I tell him. Now he's telling me about his father and the problems between the two of them. He says that the reason he is sailing is due to disputes with his father. He also talks about his girlfriend, Kathy, and if anything happens to him to let her know he loved and cared about her, and that she was the last thing on his mind before he passed away. I tell him, "No John, were going to make it! Just keep hanging in there. Don't lay on your stomach, get on your side. Bring your knees up toward your chest. Try to keep as little of your body exposed to the elements as possible." He makes a kind of grunting sound and just continues to lay there. John has started talking really slow and I notice that he is starting to slur words. I gently jabbed him with my fist several times and ask him if he's okay.

"Yeah, yeah, just really cold."

I have to get back into the compartment. I tell John, "Don't go to sleep, if you find yourself starting to fall asleep let me know."

As soon as I get everything out of the compartment I lay the items on the deck of the raft next to where I am going to lie down. Then I reach up to close the lid on the compartment. As I do this I see something twinkle or glitter out of my left eye.

Oh, my God! Oh, my God, it's a wave! I can't believe what I'm seeing. It has to be at least twenty-five to thirty-five feet high. I can see the foam on the crest of the wave being blown off by the wind. It looks like a large wall of water. Unbelievable, totally unbelievable! The glow from the carbide light is illuminating it. It's going to crash down on us and kill everyone! Without even thinking I slam the lid to the compartment shut, falling forward onto the lid and deck of the raft, at the same time rolling over to my left side. Holding onto a steel bar to keep me from being washed overboard, I wait for the wave to come crashing down on us.

I don't have enough time to warn anyone else about that huge wave. There is no way we can prepare for it. Surprisingly the wave doesn't crash down on us. Instead, we go right through it. Ah, the water is so cold! The force of the wave is almost pulling me off of the raft. I've been under water so long my lungs are starting to burn. I need air! I need air! When will this ever end? I don't want to live through this anymore. I wish I were dead!

As we break through the back side of the wave, I can hear everyone gasping for air and then I hear our screams as the wind hits us at sixty miles an hour, raking our bodies, hurting, burning and stinging our skin. It almost feels like my skin is being peeled off. I am very cold and I can see everyone else is just shivering with cold, also.

John starts talking to me. "What the hell happened? Why did we go through all that water?"

I tell him, "We went through a huge wave."

John replies, "I don't know if I can go through another one."

"I don't want to go through another one either." He wants to know if I can see them coming. Catching my breath I say, "Right now I can't. I don't know how far away they are from each other. I don't know. I don't know, John."

"Let me know so I can get a breath of air first," he says.

Now I notice that the carbide light is out and it's total blackness. I can't see. I can't see the waves coming. Again, I am underwater, and again the long wait until we come out through the backside of the wave. My lungs are burning! My lungs are burning! Ahhhh...we gasp for air and moan as the cold air hits us. Oh, no, another wave! How long before we're out through the backside? God, but it's cold! Where are you, God? Please save us!

Pain. Pain and cold, mountainous waves, one after another. It is actually warmer going through the water, but there's no warning, no chance to get a breath of air before the next wave hits us. When there isn't another wave there is the wind, and it makes my skin just burn like fire. The burning only lasts a short while and then my skin is numb. I am numb all over. I reach down and touch my thigh. My skin is so numb I can't tell if I am using my fingernails or closed fist. It's just numb. Damn!

It's cold, it's so bitter cold. I don't want to do this anymore. I just want to die. Dying would be so much easier. I'm certain that just a few minutes in the water and I will be gone and this will all be behind me. Ah! Now I'm under another wave. I'm just going to let go of this raft. I don't care. I hope this will wash me overboard. This will put me in hell, but I don't care. I want this to be over. The wave is lifting me up off the raft. I'm floating above the raft and I can feel the water rushing past me. I'm not moving with the wave though. I'm being held in place by the way my shipmates are positioned around me. I keep bumping into them as I float just above the surface of the raft. The wave isn't lifting me high enough to clear myself of the other guys. I'm through the wave again. Ah, shit! It's so cold and it's windy and I just don't care. I just don't care anymore. Oh, God! Why are You making me suffer like this? Why must You make me suffer before I die?

I find myself talking to God often. Not praying, just talking. Asking Him to save us and not let us die. Why is He making us suffer like this, why is He making us an example? Is He thinking about how this will affect our families? Often while talking to Him I get very angry, especially when I think about our families.

It's just a continuation of disappearing into the wave and popping out the backside. Eventually, the waves and gasping for air subsides. Whew! Another wave to go through. Just when I think the waves are stopping, even though the wind is still brisk. I find myself in another wave. Now everything is calm for a while, but once again another wave hits us. The wind, the wind is always there as we come out of the wave.

I'm keeping my hands warm by putting them in my mouth, or sticking them inside the life jacket against my chest. If left in the cold it wouldn't take long for them to become numb and unusable. I use my hands to do a variety of things so I will have to keep them warm. I'll rub my feet together to try and keep them warm. Every now and again I raise my right leg, bend it at the knee and rotate my ankles just to keep the blood circulating. I'm sticking my right arm into the air, moving it around, bending it at the elbow, and flexing my fingers as well. With my hands, I rub my face and ears. I find that doing this helps to keep me a little warmer. Here we go again, through another wave! I will have to start all over, moving, rubbing, and flexing. Repeating this also helps to keep me thinking and challenges my mind.

Before dawn the storm finally subsides. I'm lying on the raft and I'm praying. I'm telling God that we did nothing bad enough to deserve this type of punishment, and if He could, please spare my shipmates. Perhaps they thirst for life more than I do. I just don't want any more of this. Whew! Pray, I'll pray for all of my shipmates. I have an image of them in my eyes and in my thoughts and I pray for them. I pray for their families and their children. I pray for all of my shipmates, forward end of the boat and the after end of the boat. I soon start to wonder about all of them.

Sam Grippi is from Ashtabula. He and I started sailing together the first year I was on the *Morrell*. I went to school with his nephew, Vince, and I knew other members of his family as well. I just.... what will I say to his wife, Sarah, if I make it and he doesn't? Could it be that Sam and the rest of the crew have already been picked up, and

Sam Grippi and Dennis on Morrell

we are the last ones out here waiting to be found? What happened to the third mate and the rest of the forward crew? They were either on the raft or around it before it went into the water. John Groh had tied himself to the raft along with Norm Bragg. What has happened to them? Where are they now? The men on the stern of the ship, did they make it? The last glimpse I had, it was under power and sailing down the lake. Did the men in the stern of the ship try to steer it? There was steerage on the upper deck, the boat deck. Was there anything I could have done differently to help save lives? Would I have been better off if I had panicked, or did being calm get me to where I am now, on this raft? Well at least my body will be found.

(I later found out that we were going through 30 to 35 foot waves, the wind was 65 miles an hour with a water temperature of 44° and the air temperature was 33°).

Throughout the balance of the night, everyone is pretty quiet. There isn't very much conversation. I know I spend most of my time in prayer or in conversation with God and I'm certain the other fellows are doing the same. I kind of think we all need this time to be alone within ourselves and to be in touch with ourselves and to make peace with our maker. At least that's what I'm thinking. The storm has pretty well subsided, I'm guessing, about five o'clock A.M. There is wind, gusty wind, but not really big waves. It is dark, terribly dark. I am still wet from the waves. It has not snowed or anything, it is just very, very cold.

As it approaches morning, I can see a thin layer of daylight between the clouds and the horizon. That opening, that little space, doesn't increase much as the sun continues to rise. However, it does get a little lighter and brighter as dawn approaches. The sky is still very overcast and it looks like it wants to rain or snow. I think to myself that it won't be long before daylight. Hopefully someone will start finding wreckage by then and the Coast Guard will probably start looking for us. Maybe we'll be rescued by two or three o'clock in the afternoon.

It is now about seven-thirty or eight o'clock and daylight. John Cleary is lying in front of me on his stomach. I look at him, and I notice a small amount of white foam coming out of his mouth. I wonder if perhaps he may have been sick. I jab him with my fist and I ask him, "John, are you all right?" He doesn't respond to me. I jab him a few more times and said, "John, wake up man. Are you okay?" I'm shaking him as hard as I can with my right hand. "Are you okay, man? Wake up!" I finally stop shaking him. Oh, he is gone! Oh, no! John is dead. The reality of John's death is like someone reaching into my chest and pulling out my heart. You can't die like this....I just can't believe it! It was like someone silently took him through the night. All of a sudden I become very frightened. Whew! I'm alive, why isn't he? God, why am I alive?

Everybody on the raft is so quiet. I have to check on everybody. I just have to know. Behind me is Art Stojek. I reach around with my elbow and kind of jab him with it. I ask him, "Art, are you all right?" He doesn't respond either. I said, "Man, are you okay? Art, wakeup! Are you all right?" Once again, he does not respond to me. All of a sudden tears start to swell in my eyes, and I feel this terrible loss. I...... Whew! I don't want to be all alone, I don't want to be alone! Charlie is lying behind my knees.

74

I kick him with my right leg hoping he will respond to me. "Fuzzy, are you okay?"

He says, "Yeah, I'm hanging in there. Did Art and John pass away through the night?"

"Yes, they're both gone," I replied. "I thought they were sleeping. I tried shaking both of them. You heard me. They didn't respond to me. Are you sure you're okay?" I ask again.

He answers with, "Yeah, I'm all right."

I ask him, "Have you been doing a lot of praying?"

"Yeah, that's all I've been doing is trying to pray."

I then ask him, "What do you think our chances are?"

He says, "I don't know. They didn't get off an SOS. We'll have to wait until somebody finds out we are missing, then they will start searching for us."

I answer with, "Perhaps another boat will find wreckage and the Coast Guard could find us sometime this afternoon." There is no further response from Fuzzy, and once again we grow silent.

I start thinking about Art and John. It's hard to believe that they're gone. They were both really nice guys. I had sailed with John a little bit longer than I sailed with Art, so I knew John much better. John seemed a little more open to conversation than Art did. I really feel the loss. I also feel despair for our situation.

No one knows we are missing. Nobody will be looking for us. Well, they will know when the boat fails to report in to the dispatcher at

Bethlehem Steel. I believe they report in every eight hours, but then again they may think we have antenna problems. Nobody is going to be looking for us. I guess when they find wreckage floating and bodies wearing life jackets that say *Daniel J. Morrell,* they'll know what has happened.

I lie here and I pray. It is so bitter cold. I just want to die and end this. I keep praying: The Our Fathers, Hail Marys and the Act of Contrition. I am praying for my shipmates that just passed away. I pray for my family and myself. I pray for Fuzzy and his wife, Jan. I pray for the men who didn't make it to one of the two rafts, each one of them individually.

After all of that, I don't want to live anymore. Do you hear me, God? I can't take the bitter cold anymore. It is just too much! I don't want to live anymore. It's so much harder to live than to die. Dying would relieve all my pain, suffering and mental anguish that I am going through, along with the unknown. It would take all of that away and just.... Whatever is next can't be any worse. No! I'm not going to die like this! All of my life I've had to fight to stay alive, and I'm not going to die now! Not like this! God, if you can't help me now, just stay the hell away from me! I can make it on my own!

Once I'm over being angry I calm down some. I start thinking about being someplace else that is warm. Maybe Hawaii, or the South Pacific. All of a sudden I feel like I'm moving, as if I'm floating through the sky at a rapid speed. It seems as though I am actually there. Oh, yes! I am there, lying in the sun on a towel. I can feel the sun's rays hitting my body, and I can feel the warmth just radiating all the way through me. There are a lot of people around me in bathing attire. I hear them talking and laughing. There are also children laughing and playing in the warm water. I see palm trees swaying in the warm breeze and the white sandy beach. No one notices me or talks to me, but it is such a good feeling to be here and to hear the laughter and feel the warmth!

There is something like cabanas on this beach. There's beach sand and trees on a peninsula that goes quite a ways out in the water. As I look out onto the peninsula all I can see are palm trees, some other flowering tree, people and cabanas. The people have dark skin like they have been lying in the sun for several days. I even have dark skin. The water is calm and slowly lapping the beach, making a very relaxing sound. I have no idea how deep the water is. I'm not going into it. I see people in the water, but I'm really not paying too much attention to them. I'm just sucking up the heat. It warms me thoroughly.

The water's color is bluish green. The beach is a whitish tan. Now I see a border of shrubs and flowering bushes and bits of green grass coming up. This is located back a ways from the beach. Everybody is so very happy. I am not having any conversation with anyone. It is like no one knows I am here. I don't really care about conversation. I find happiness in the other people's faces that are around me. The beach is very crowded and....immediately I am back on the raft. I am just back, just back.... just like that!

I seem to be taking stock of myself. Am I still on the raft? Am I alive? Am I cold or hurt and am I bleeding? Has anything changed? No, I'm on the raft, and it's still cold. I feel even colder. I'm trying to move my right leg. It feels very stiff when I try to lift it. I bend my knee and wiggle my ankle. I move both of them a couple of times and then go back to rubbing my feet together, trying to get them warm. My hands are in my mouth, both of them. I have to keep my hands warm. Every once in awhile I take them out and stick them between my skin and the life jacket on the upper part of my chest. This will also help keep them warm. Keeping them in my mouth seems to dry my mouth out.

Oh, God, why are you doing this to me? Why are you making me suffer like this? I pray you'll take my life. I can't do this anymore. Maybe I haven't been a good person. Maybe You're right in taking my life, so please take it now! Please, please, please let me die now!

I don't know what time it is. I don't know where I am. I know it's cold, it's overcast, and all I can see is water. The water is calm, maybe a little choppy but not much. There's no water coming over the side of the raft. I'm no longer getting wet. My clothing is starting to dry out from the wind. There is a little bit of wind, but nothing to be concerned about. It's still dark. It's cloudy. I guess the right word is gray. Yes, it's gray out.

Ah, ah, I can feel Fuzzy starting to move around. I can feel his hand on my hip as he lifts himself up. "I can see land," he says.

"How close are we, Fuzz?"

"Were not even close. I can see land," he says. "We are quite a ways from it, but I think we're drifting in that direction."

"What time is it, Fuzz?"

"Two o'clock."

"How long ago did the *Morrell* go down?"

"About twelve hours ago."

"Are you okay Fuzz?" He is laying back down and he's silent. "Fuzzy, think we'll be home for Christmas? Man, I'll bet our wives are going nuts if they found out about the ship sinking."

Fuzzy's silent for a minute, but then says, "I've been thinking a lot about her. What will she do without me in case I don't make it?"

I tell him, "We will make it, man. We are both in pretty good shape. We can hold out until someone picks us up. I don't want you to leave me, Fuzz. We need to keep each other going. Just think of how nice it would be to be home for Christmas. First we would go to a nice warm hospital and have those sexy nurses waiting on us. Geeze, you can't beat that!"

"Yeah, I know," Fuzzy says. "I just want to be home."

I am really upset and grieving for Art Stojek and John Cleary. They were such nice guys. I can't bear the thought of losing Fuzzy, too.

"Where in the hell is the Coast Guard?" I ask. "They should've found us by now." I am constantly looking skyward for a helicopter and scanning the water for a Coast Guard cutter. Where are they? We need them right now!

Once again we both grow silent. Damn, it's cold! I'm wondering what to do, how can we save ourselves? Maybe we should try rowing the raft. I can't get to the oars. (I mentioned earlier about the raft being damaged when it was thrown overboard. The lid to the safety compartment was pushed in and we had to pry it open. When I laid down on the raft, I laid down on the lid for that compartment and it fell in with me. My left armpit and my left leg, just above the knee, were laying on metal rods, and my hips were in this compartment.) If I can get out of this hole, where will we row to? There's just no way I can hold an oar. It's just too cold, way too cold.

I can't move, I just can't move right. My body doesn't seem to want to move like it should. The cold is getting into my joints. I'm figuring that they are starting to freeze. It won't be long now. Somebody will find us or we'll both die. It really doesn't matter much which one, I just want to be past this and get it over with. God, I hope I'm home for Christmas. I don't know what my wife and kids will do if I'm not there. I don't want to disappoint my family, or myself. I want to be home for Christmas. I need to go home, I guess I just want to be home for Christmas. I can't see my wife and children getting along without me. Christmas is an important time for everybody. It's strange that I am praying to die, but I set myself a goal to be home by Christmas. Home by Christmas. I need a goal. I have to have a challenge. I need to reach out for something. I guess I'm playing both sides of the fence. I definitely want to be home, and I want all the cold and pain to go away. I just want all the pain to leave. I could.....

Whew! Yeah, you know, as much as I pray to live, I pray equally as much to die. I don't care. I just don't care anymore.

I'm even making jokes with God. Well, I know You're over in Ethiopia, You're feeding the multitudes and You probably just haven't the time right now to help us, but if You're done by dinner time there, and You don't have anything else to do, come on by and take a look at our situation. Get us out of here! We've got a lot to live for. I kind of laugh. Oh, the promises I make to God! I promise Him everything and anything. I tell Him how sorry I am for all the things I've done wrong in my lifetime. I really do need Him now. Dear God, you know I've tried to be a good Christian, but life just gets in my way.

I no longer have physical pain. Everything just feels numb and cold. I'm not certain if I would have pain if I try to move, I've been fairly sedentary. I do have mental pain. I guess that's the best way to explain it. The only thing my mind wants to think about his being rescued and being home for Christmas. These thoughts seem to consume my mind.

Oh, oh! I'm being lifted off of the raft and I'm traveling at a high rate of speed. What the hell is going on? I'm home now, and it's Christmas Day. My wife and children and I are all around the tree, and we are starting to open presents. It's nice and warm and I can smell the turkey in the oven. Everyone seems so happy. I've been awake since three o'clock in the morning fixing dinner. Son of a gun! I got a brand new Ted Williams double-barreled shotgun for hunting rabbits with Sam. It's just what I wanted.

Wait, what happened? Where is everyone? I'm in my house alone.

There is no ceiling or roof to the house. As I look up I can see blue skies. There are clouds, and they are purple in color. I can see three faces in the clouds. People I don't know and they're all looking at me and talking amongst themselves. I think it's about me. I don't recognize these people. They are older men, and they look a little different. I think perhaps they may be Jewish. Their sideburns are long and curled and they all have beards. They're wearing what appears to be black felt hats with some type of design on them. They whisper to me, "Stay warm, stay warm." It's like I can feel the warmth of their breath on my body as they whisper, "Stay warm, stay warm." They whisper to me several times and warm me up before they just seem to fade into the sky.

Ah, in the blink of an eye I'm back on the raft. Shit! I was hoping that I had died. I don't understand. I don't even question myself about what just happened. I'm very disappointed that I haven't died.

I still can't see anything but water. I'm looking for the flare gun so I can stick the rope into the water and suck the water out of it. I'm thirsty and I need something to drink. I can't fire off a flare this time of day because it wouldn't do any good. I've got to move just a little bit. Ah, I can move my right arm and my right leg very slowly. I have to keep the blood circulating. That's what I was told when I was a kid. You've got to keep your blood circulating when you're cold. Ouch! It hurts. My left armpit and knee ache from laying on the steel rods. Whew! Man, I have to get this left armpit off of this steel rod. The pain is killing me, but there is nothing I can do about it.

God, why are You doing this to me? Just let me die. Let it be over with! I'm going to pray that You let me die or let me live, but let this be over now. I will soon be losing my faith in You.

I feel Fuzzy moving around again. He puts one hand on my hip and the other one on the deck of the raft. "Are you all right, Fuzz? Can you see anything yet? How close are we?"

Fuzzy responds with, "Oh, man, we're close. We are going to bottom out on the shore pretty soon. I can see a lot of large boulders and rocks in the water along the shoreline. We will be able to feel the bottom of the raft bouncing on the bottom of lake."

I can't see the shoreline, as I am facing out to sea. I ask him, "How close will we be? Ah, can you see any houses, any people? Can we get up and walk to the beach?"

"Yeah." Fuzzy sounds a little strange.

"How you doing, man? You all right?"

"Yeah, it kind of feels like my lungs....they're heavy and there's something in them," he says.

I ask him what he means. No response. "Well, can't you just cough that stuff out and get rid of it?" Fuzzy starts coughing and oh, he fell on me! He fell with his arm around me. I try to talk to him hoping he will respond to me. He is gone. Oh, shit! Did I cause his death by telling him to cough? Why did I tell him to cough? I may have just killed him! If he wouldn't have coughed maybe he would still be alive!

My eyes are wet, I'm crying. Art's gone, John's gone and now Fuzzy's gone.... I am alone now. I'm the only one left. Maybe soon I will die. Perhaps in an hour, maybe two, and all my pain will be gone as well. I can't last much longer. I feel good about passing away but at the same time there's a great sadness about me. I want to live, I just can't stand the pain and waiting....keep waiting for the end to come. My thoughts are of my family and Fuzzy's family. When he was alive he gave me hope, you know. He said we'd be bottoming out pretty soon. He said it was around three thirty in the afternoon. Ahhhh! Maybe there still is a chance that I can make it. I'm so tired of fighting, though. All of my life I've fought and struggled to stay alive. Well, no point in feeling sorry for myself. What's going to happen is going to happen. It's not in my hands. Maybe I should just take these clothes off, this life jacket and peacoat.

Oh, what was that? I think I felt the raft hitting on the bottom. The waves are pushing us towards the shore. They are also starting to turn the raft around to where I can almost see the shoreline. Yeah, we're on the bottom, just bobbing along. It's getting towards dusk, and soon there will be darkness. Ah, Ah, yeah. I can see the shoreline. It seems like maybe we're hung up on the rocks some two hundred yards from the shoreline. I can see the trees. It's a woods or a forest. I start yelling and screaming. "Help! Help! I'm on the water!" No one responds but still I'm waiting to see a light coming through the woods. I start yelling and screaming once again. "Help! Please help me! I'm on the water!" Again, no response.

Damn! It's cold! I'll rub my feet together, that always works. They do feel numb. Well, shit, they ought to be! The rest of me is numb. I feel extremely cold right now, maybe because the sun is setting. Maybe that's when I'll die, sometime through the night. Maybe sooner. God, can I make it through the night? I won't be able to see anything at night so I've got to make it. I've just got to make it. I have to let everyone know what happened to the *Daniel J. Morrell*.

Morrell 1966

Chapter 6

My mind drifts back to my childhood when the day to move to California has come. My Aunt Inez and I climbed aboard a train in Cleveland that would take us to Chicago, Illinois. There we would board the *City of Los Angeles*, which would be the longest of the two train rides to Los Angeles. Aunt Inez told me that it would take three entire days to reach Los Angeles. As we traveled, I thought of what was ahead of me and began to reflect on my situation.

The last three months had been wonderful with just my aunt and I at home. We had no problems at all. Thank God! What a wonderful difference not having Harold at home made. In the evenings Aunt Inez would make peanut butter crackers with hot chocolate and we would sit around and talk about our new adventures in California as we ate our snacks. She would tell me of Hollywood and Griffith Park, swimming in the Pacific Ocean and all the special attractions there were to see. I was very excited.

As I think back, it seems as though Harold was in charge of my discipline, when he was around, my aunt and I didn't converse very much at that time. It's totally impossible to think that I was that much of a problem child. I thought I was only trying to be a normal kid. It was hard for me to imagine that soon things would be back to normal again, with Harold in charge of my life and the continuing brutality and abuse. I just didn't know what to do. If only there was some way I could fight back, but I was too frightened of him. I thought that dying couldn't be any worse than what I was going through. I often wondered why God was taking me down this unhealthy path. I thought more about this later in the trip.

The train ride was great. At first it was very interesting for there was a lot to see and a lot to do. The scenery was very beautiful and there was a new adventure around every bend in the railroad tracks. My aunt would point out different highlights as we traveled along. All of the passengers seemed very friendly towards me. There were also other children aboard the train, and I made friends with them and we played together as we traveled. The hardest part of the trip was going through Texas. It took about twenty-four hours to cross it. It was so plain and rather barren, and there wasn't much to see that kept me interested during this part of the trip.

When we arrived in Los Angeles, Harold was there to pick us up. He took us to his sister Joyce's house, and we visited with her for a while before going to our new house. Joyce lived about a block away so that meant it would be easy to visit with her. We lived in West LA between Pico and Washington Boulevard on West Avenue. It was a nice three-bedroom stucco house. The neighborhood was absolutely beautiful with lots of palm trees and lovely homes with flowering gardens. In the darkness of night there was a fragrance of night blooming jasmine everywhere. Each house was a different color, salmon with a brown tile roof or green with a red tile roof, all were of southwestern Spanish design.

Soon my attention comes back to my present situation. It has been about fifteen hours since the ship went down. As the evening turns into nighttime, I see less and less of the shoreline. However, I can hear the gentleness of the waves slapping on the shore. After it gets totally dark, I can see the sweep of a lighthouse beacon and lighted navigational buoys that are off of the shore. Wow! Buoy lights. I wonder where I am? Certainly not Harbor Beach. Am I perhaps close to a shipping channel? My hopes rise. My eyes scan the horizon for the lights of a freighter but there are none to be seen. Disappointed, I turn my thoughts to shore and the sweep of the lighthouse beacon.

Lying on the life raft facing the shoreline, I can see the sweep of the light when I look towards my feet. That doesn't help me, I don't know which lighthouse it is or where it is located. I know that with the darkness comes colder temperatures. The skies have been gray throughout the day. Maybe there will be snow tonight. Maybe I won't see the dawn. I have to think more positive. I am just going to talk to myself from now on and be me inside. I can't let go of me. I can't become something else. Somehow, I will have to find some humor in the situation to know that I'm still in here. Damn, how can I do that?

I'll try to make myself shiver. I always heard that shivering is a good response when you're cold, and it's supposed to be automatic and help keep you warm. For some reason I just can't make myself shiver. Damn, it's cold! Ah, damn!

Looking toward shore, all of a sudden I see some lights coming from beyond the trees. Wow! It had to be a house, a farm, or maybe a barn and the farmer is inside milking his cows. Could there be children outside playing in this cold weather? "Help! Help! I'm on the water!" I shout with all the strength I have left in me. Where is the flare gun? I have to fire off a flare. Loading the flare gun, I fire one round straight overhead. As soon as the round is airborne the barrel of the flair gun breaks off, falls and hits me in the head. Quickly I grab the hot barrel. I rub it in my hands and then I rub my hands all over my face and ears. The heat feels absolutely wonderful! It seems to temper the coldness throughout my body. Damn, what else can go wrong? "Help! Help! On the water!" I shout again. Please, God, let me see a flashlight come through the woods. "Help! Help! On the water!" No one comes...... I wait, and still......no one comes.

What am I going to do now without that flare gun? I have three shells left. Maybe there's some way I can hold the gun together and fire it. Carefully loading one shell into the chamber, I try to line up the gun barrel with the handle of the pistol. I point it overhead and pull the trigger. Ah! Whew! It worked! What a rush of heat to my left hand from holding the barrel! Without hesitation, I rub my face and ears, trying to warm them up. I start yelling and screaming as I had done before. I just want to see a flashlight coming through the woods, but again, nobody comes...... I wait and again......nobody comes. Could those have been headlights from a car? No, I don't think so. They didn't move. Whatever it was, they didn't see my flares. Is there anything else I can do to help people find us? It's important to me that when they find this raft that there are four people on it.

Now I only have two flares left and I don't want to waste them. What will I do if I don't make it until morning? Well, nothing I can do about that. I can make it! I'll make it till dawn. As soon as I see those lights come on, I will wait a while and then fire off another flare. It would make it so much easier if I could hear a car starting up. Then I would know when to start yelling. It could be that someone is milking their cows or feeding their chickens before they go to work. It could be that children are outside waiting on their school bus. Maybe they will see the flare or maybe they'll hear me yelling. If I only knew, if I only knew. If I can just make it through the night. I want to pray.

It feels as though someone just laid down next to me. I can hear a whisper, no there's more than one whisper. "Move. Move." Is that a whisper? What is that noise? What the hell is going on? I don't care. Nothing can hurt me because soon I'll be dead anyways. Ah, man, my eyes must be going. I can see real dirty, funky-colored yellow lights and green and orange lights as well. I don't know if it's a buoy on the water or in the sky. Whatever.

"Move over," I can hear a voice say. Unable to move, I continue to lay in the same position. Whoever is lying next to me is warming me up.

90

Looking skyward I can see the lights more plainly now.

Ah, the voices have stopped and the lights are gone. The voices, if they were voices, sounded very strange and they seemed to be talking to each other, not to me, but like I was right between them. Maybe there were three or four different voices. Very low voices, almost a whisper. It seemed like they were talking a different language. All I could understand was "move over." I have to question why they didn't help me or help save me.

I wonder what time it is. I have to keep looking towards the lake. I can't let myself sleep tonight because it would be just my luck to fall asleep and a boat would go by and I couldn't signal it. I've got to stay awake. "I can make it! Yes, I can make it!" I have to stop thinking negative thoughts. I have to think about making it through this and about coming out of this alive. I have to challenge my mind. I have to find something to keep my mind active. Money, I think I'll count money. I'll add it and subtract it, divide it and multiply it. I soon grow bored with this and I start playing solitaire. It is a very interesting game and a real challenge to play in your mind. (I never lost a game!)

After morning comes, if no one finds me, I will try to sleep. Chances are a boat will see me better in the daytime than it will at night. I have always heard that when you freeze to death you just go to sleep and never wake up again. Is it possible that is what I am hoping to achieve? The thought has crossed my mind more than once. Yes, yes, what an easy way to go. No pain! What the hell am I talking about? My body is numb, and I can't feel pain or anything else.

What a terrible night this is. It's bitter cold and there's a slight breeze. Although my shipmates are gone, I still talk to them. I ask them for advice and confirm to them that we will make it. "Just hang in there, fellas, you'll never be forgotten." I guess I want to hear a voice, even if it's just my own. I think about a variety of things to keep challenging my mind. I plan on the dental work I need and the amount of work I should have done. I debate on whether to have novacaine or have nitrous oxide. It is a long, rough night. Every once in awhile I can see buoys and the light coming from the lighthouse. I look on the beach to see if lights are on in the house yet. I try to cry and I can't muster up any tears. I guess I'm feeling sorry for myself.

It's a bad night and very cold. Once again I try to force myself to shiver, but for some reason that response in me doesn't seem to work. So I try and do it on my own. I think about the strange things that happened to me that first night and wonder if I'm losing my mind. My thoughts always return to dying and how I could help this process along. Tonight, when other things are not happening, I pray to God to take my life. Why must you make me suffer before I die? Am I that bad of a person? I'm going to lay down and put my hands in my mouth and pray. It seems to me that praying is a catalyst for other things to happen to me, and they do.

Once again I'm moving at a very rapid speed. Things just seem to zoom past me. My sister Jean is holding my hand and smiling at me. We are walking on the sidewalk in front of this large Tudor house that had what appeared to be a basement greenhouse. I am thinking to myself that

92

this looks like the big Unitarian Church just off of Route 90 in Concord, Ohio. Jean used to attend the Unitarian Church when Farley Wheelwright was the pastor. As we start to walk into the building, Jean is clinging to me. It's almost as if she is afraid to go inside. I feel apprehensive about being here, and I really don't want to be here either.

Once inside the building we are escorted to what I first thought was the greenhouse area. It really isn't a greenhouse, it's more like a sunroom. There are tables set up with fruit, cheese and wine on them. There seems to be some type of party going on. People are standing around talking while eating cheese, crackers and fruit and sipping wine. Naturally, I don't know too many of the people that are here. Jean's friend Ruthie is here and I recognize a few of her weirdo girlfriends.

After looking around a bit I do notice my half sister, Linda and her husband, Dick along with their daughter, Rita. I stop to talk to Linda and Dick for a few minutes. We don't even bother to ask each other what we are doing here. By this time Jean has almost draped herself over my body. I can't move without her being right close to me. The mood is rather somber with a lot of people casting suspicious or curious eyes upon Linda and I. About this time a woman walks up to me and introduces herself as Judge Sarah Hunter. She's telling me that she wants to keep Jean's book of poetry by Tagore, an Indian poet. I look at Jean and she doesn't object. I say, "That's fine." Jean doesn't talk to anyone while we are here. She seems to shy away from her friends.

While I am in this building the sunroom is warm and I can feel heat all around my body. Everything is so nice and warm. I'm dressed in casual slacks and a dress shirt with the sleeves rolled up one time. Everyone else's attire is just about the same as mine.

I find myself, once again, back on the raft. Loneliness and despair overcome me. I try to cry, but no tears will fall. What will become of me? Why is it taking so long to live or die? Is anyone looking for us? What about my family? I've all but given up on the Coast Guard. Perhaps they will never find us.

Damn it's cold! Death is the window to my mind now. What can I do to precipitate my death? I doubt I can take off what few pieces of clothing I'm wearing. My joints don't seem to work. Any movement is very difficult. I pray that death will come soon.

I wonder if I can stick my hands down my throat far enough to stop me from breathing? If I can do this, maybe I can position myself just right to where I would pass out and, more or less, impale myself on my hands. It's worth a try because anything is better than this. There, I lifted myself up onto my left elbow. I will put my left hand down in my throat as far I can. I'm supporting my left wrist with my right hand around it. It's choking me, and I cough repeatedly and gag. I think I'm going to throw up. Whew, boy, this is crazy! Whew! Nah, it's not going to work, but what a rush of heat that caused! My whole body warmed up. I'm going to do it a few more times just to warm up. Whew! My throat is getting sore and so is my stomach. Ahh......That made me tired.

The sky looks like it's starting to get light. Soon the sun will be coming up. No lights anyplace yet except for the buoy and the light from the lighthouse. I've got to remember to stop praying and look ashore once in awhile. I have to watch for the lights on shore to come on. After they come on, I will wait a while before I fire my last two flares off. So far I've had no use for hand-held flares. I don't know if they are still on the raft, and I don't want to look for them.

I haven't had anything to eat since about eight o'clock in the evening on the twenty-eighth and this is the morning of the thirtieth. I could really go for some hot consommé or maybe even some orange juice. My, what a strange thing to want. It's not something I've ever had a craving for before.

Maybe I should have listened to myself earlier in the year when I thought about getting a plastic bag and putting some cans of tuna fish in it. I would've also needed a can opener and cigarettes, a lot of cigarettes, and a lighter. I could have sealed the bag with melted wax or something like that. I thought about doing that often. I wanted something around just in case the boat went down. I could always drink lake water. The only big problem would be getting off the raft and back onto it. I wish I would've listened to myself and made that plastic bag with everything in it.

Well, son of a gun, I made it through the night! Why am I alive? Why am I still here? I just don't know why. I guess now isn't the time to think about that. It's been about fifteen hours since Fuzzy died. That's almost twice as long as he survived. I don't understand why I'm still alive!

It's been over twenty-four hours since the boat sank. I'm sure that when we didn't lock through at Sault Ste. Marie the Coast Guard must have started looking for us. I know someone out there will see the flare when I shoot it off this morning. I think I'm putting a lot of faith in the last two flares and my ability to yell. I really thought someone would hear me or see the flare last night. It was really difficult to make it through the whole night, though.

The lights are coming on! I just saw two lights come on! Well, two windows are lit. That's got to be a house. Maybe they got kids going to school or maybe they have to go to work. I think the sun starts coming up maybe around seven or seven thirty in the morning. Ah, maybe I'll wait until the lights go out, when they are leaving. That's when I'll fire them off. This is the last chance I have. If I can't make anyone aware I'm out here now, I'll never get another chance. I know I can't make it through another day.

It looks like it's about time to shoot off another flare. I don't know how I know that. I guess it just feels like it's time. I just want to be found soon. Please, God, let this work. Let's see if I can hold this together just right again. Pow! That's the sound I hear as the flare travels towards the sky. I made it work again. It looks like it's right over the house. Shit! I hope I don't catch the house on fire, and I laugh. Yeah, got to keep up my sense of humor. I'm going to rub the barrel of the flare gun on my face to see if I can warm my face up a little. I'm yelling and I'm yelling, "Help, help! I'm on the water." After doing this several times I grow tired and weak. I can't seem to yell as long as I did last night. I'll wait a short while and see if I can see a flashlight coming through the woods. God, I really need Your help right now. Please send someone to help me!

It's been about fifteen minutes. I can't wait any longer. I have to fire another flare. Pow! Please find me. Please find me. Looking towards the forest I watch for someone and listen for footsteps in the woods. It's been fifteen or twenty minutes since I fired off my last flare. No one saw the flare or heard me calling and yelling. No one comes, nobody. All hope is gone. I feel depressed. My last act of desperation sealed my fate. Maybe I didn't wait long enough, maybe I should have waited for something else to happen. I am so cold. I just want someone to find me. Even if they just stand on the beach and yell at me, that would be fine. Just find me, please. Now, if I do see someone on the shore or on the water, I have no more flares to let them know I'm here. It's just a matter of time. Now it's starting to snow.

Morrell in the storm- Steve Witucki

Chapter 7

I have never had to deal with death. I never lost anyone close to me before. Now I'm alone with the three bodies of my friends, but I try not to think about it. I avoid looking at them and ignore the fact that they are even here with me on the raft. I'm very frightened, and I know that death is waiting on me.

I've just given up. I don't think anybody's looking for this raft, but if and when they do find it there will be four dead bodies on it. I'm praying and praying and praying. I'm praying to die. I don't understand...... The waiting and not knowing is terrible, just terrible. Every moment I'm looking for something, a sign, somebody, anything. With every passing second I feel more and more doomed. I'm praying to die. It's snowing very heavily as I drift off to sleep.

I'm waking up now. I fell asleep while praying. Damn, you're not supposed to fall asleep when you're freezing because you won't wake up. Damn! Damn! Why in the hell am I alive? It looks like I'm still in the same place, the same situation.

I have my eyes closed and I'm talking to Fuzzy, John and Art and challenging them to do something. "Can you talk to me even though you're gone, even mentally? Can you send me some type of message? I'm going to concentrate on you sending me a message. Tell me how I can help myself. Can you give me a message?" No, all I can hear is "keep warm," and I think I'm telling myself that.

Opening my eyes I see John Cleary in front of me. I can't believe what my eyes see. John's hands and face are all glazed and covered in ice. All of his clothing is frozen to his body. I am suddenly filled with such hatred and love at the same time. John was such a nice kid. I have feelings of love, sadness, empathy and envy. How could God do this to him? Whew! Man, that was like the final insult. Crying, I lift myself up on my left elbow and I raise my right fist to the sky, shaking it, and cursing God and the Holy Family. "You can all go to hell! I don't need you! I'll make it on my own! I don't need your damn help!" I can feel the heat going through my body as I yell. Laying back down on the raft in silence for a few moments, I'm trying to collect my thoughts. That wasn't me that just did that. I'm not that type of person. I don't give way to anger. I've always been so nonviolent. What's happening to me? Who is inside of me? I feel so sorry for what I have just done and I am afraid of losing the "me" that I know is inside. Lifting myself up again on my left elbow and extending my right fist to the sky, yelling and laughing at the same time, I tell God, "Don't send your son! This is a man's job!" Laying on the raft laughing, I know the "me" is still here. I hope God understands. I start to wonder why He chose this hard life for me, and my thoughts return to my younger days.

100

The Monday following our arrival in Los Angeles I started to attend Alta Loma grammar school. The school itself was a beautiful, all stucco building. It was newly painted inside, very clean, and it smelled very fresh. The fenced in playground was at the back of the building with palm trees and olive trees that bordered the surrounding area. In the front of the building there were shrubs, loquat trees and guava bushes. I loved eating their fruit when they were in season. I guess maybe all of us kids loved to eat it.

The teachers and the other students were very friendly towards me and right away I made a lot of new friends. My teacher's name, that first year, I can't recall. After being in school for about one week they moved me up one grade. I was told that the schools in the east were a little more advanced. It seemed to me that things they were teaching me, I had already been taught. I did well in my new grade.

The second year in school my teacher's name was Mrs. Horner. She was young, attractive and not much older than most of us kids. She seemed to like me an awful lot and would spend a little more time with me if I needed it. My grades were always good in school and I fit in well with the other students.

While I was in Mrs. Horner's class, Art Linkletter's show, *House Party*, was looking for children to participate on his program. Art Linkletter was the star on this weekly syndicated television variety show. In one portion of the show they had children from a variety of schools in the Los Angeles area as guests. Mr. Linkletter would interview them and ask them questions about their school and about their private lives. Sometime the answers were really funny. Mrs. Horner came to me and asked me if I would be interested in going on the show and representing Alta Loma School. She also informed me that I was the only one from our school that would be going, but there would be other students from other schools in the area. She reassured me that all of the teaching staff thought I would represent the school best, so I did participate in the TV show.

It was really exciting and very interesting to see how television shows were produced. The television staff was extremely nice to all of us. They even took us to a nice restaurant for lunch, and after the program Mr. Linkletter gave us gifts. The best part for me was meeting Mr. Linkletter. At that time, in the early 1950s, he was very famous.

For the very first time in my life things seemed to be going just great for me. I was doing well in school, I had made a lot of friends and I felt as though I was really liked and was finally a part of something.

Harold was working a second shift so I very seldom saw him, which was a blessing. While on the train coming to California I had made some decisions. I planned to stay away from Harold as much as possible. The only time I would be around him was on the weekends and I would try to avoid him then. I also started thinking that I had the upper hand on Harold, and I had something over his head. At different times I would mouth off to him in front of Aunt Inez and all he would do is shoot me dirty looks. However, I would pay for it when alone with him. After arriving in California all he did was brutalize and assault me. All the other punishment, if that's what you want to call it, stopped.

I wanted to help Aunt Inez as much as possible around the house and in the house. I did love my aunt very much, and I wanted our relationship to be even closer. As far as I was concerned she was my mother. I also wanted to become more self-reliant. I wanted to learn things that would make me more independent. Something inside of me told me I was the only one that cared about me, and if I wanted to survive, I'd have to learn to survive on my own. I guess at this point you're wondering how a ten or eleven year old kid came to that conclusion. It was from watching other families and noticing how they interacted with each other and the love they shared with one another. If you look back to your childhood you may see that you also judged your family by watching other families. I could see by watching other families what I was missing in my family. It didn't feel permanent, everything felt temporary.

Not long after being on Art Linkletter's show there was a parent and teacher conference at school. My aunt did go to school and attend the meeting by herself. Mrs. Horner told her that I was a great student and my grades were very good. However, I was hanging out with a bad bunch of boys that were always in trouble. As soon as Aunt Inez arrived home from the meeting she sat me down and talked to me about my friends. She wanted to know what we did when we went out together and why I was coming home so late at night. Most of the time I was home by ten o'clock in the evening, ten-thirty was the latest. I told her we were shooting hoops or playing pool or maybe watching television in the basement of one of my friend's homes. Of course that wasn't the truth. I also started smoking about this same time in my life. I enjoyed hanging around with my friends and I knew nothing would change the bond we had.

Soon Christmas would be coming upon us, and the following June I would be leaving Alta Loma for junior high school. The name of my new school was George Washington Junior High.

Alta Loma was like all other schools, they had a Christmas pageant every year and yes, it was the reenactment of the birth of Christ. My part in the pageant was to narrate the entire reenactment. I recall studying very diligently because I wanted to get my lines right. I was telling the story of Christ's birth and that was very important to me. I think I did fairly well telling the story, although I did have to be coached a few times during the program, but all in all I did fairly well. At the time I didn't think much of being asked to be the narrator of the story, it was what I had to do. Aunt Inez and Harold were in the audience that night. I didn't tell them the part I was to play because I just knew they wouldn't be interested. God and Christ were never mentioned in our home unless it was in vain. After the pageant, to my shock and surprise, my aunt said I should feel very honored for being the narrator and praised me for studying so hard to get it right.

Summer soon arrived and I put my last days in at Alta Loma Grammar School. This would be a special summer for me. I wanted to spend as much time as I could at the beach and Knott's Berry Farm, and I wanted to go to Catalina Island again. I had gone there once as a Boy Scout and ever since then I wanted to go back. As it turned out, I did spend a lot of time at the beach and at Knott's Berry Farm, but I never did go back to Catalina Island. The summer flew by and before I knew it, it was fall and time to return to school. My friends and I really had a good summer.

Just before it was time to go back to school, my friends Gary and Linda from Cleveland, Ohio, stopped by the house to visit. They had moved to Orange County, California, about six months before we left Cleveland for California. It was nice to see them, but I had changed a lot and so had they. It would have been nice to visit them at their home but nobody would take me to see them.

Going to school at George Washington Junior High was pretty cool. I liked recess the best because the students could buy warm, fresh baked cinnamon rolls. There was always a long line of kids waiting to buy them. I'm certain they had other baked goods, but the cinnamon rolls were always my favorite. Another thing I did at recess was work out on the parallel bar. Even though I wasn't good at it, I still enjoyed it. A lot of the older boys worked on them, too, and I learned from watching them.

I was going to George Washington for about a week when I ran into an old friend, Freddy Clark. He was a black friend of mine from Cleveland and we used to play together often when we both lived there. It was great finding Freddy at my school in Los Angeles and renewing our friendship. While living in Cleveland we had a couple of sleepovers at each other's houses. Mrs. Clark and Freddie were true friends of mine. There were many times I had no place else to stay and they would hide me in their home. Sometimes I did things that I shouldn't have done, like staying out all night and not going to school the next day. Harold was just waiting to get his hands on me. I knew if I just waited a couple of days and then went home, when my aunt was there, things wouldn't be so hard on me. I would still catch hell from Aunt Inez for not telephoning or coming home, but if Harold had been there the punishment would have been many times worse. Somehow he would have had his hands on me hurting me, and he would've been extremely cruel to me for two or three days. I think Freddy was at my house a few times when Harold went off on me, and he was in one of his mean moods. Freddie must have said something to his mother about Harold and that's why she was so nice to me and let me spend a few nights there once in a while.

There were five of us guys that ran around together all the time. We were the best of friends. If you could find one of us you would find all of us. The other four guy's names were Richard, Jim, Bob and Pete. Bob and Pete were about three years older than the rest of us and Bob attended a different school. Pete was a little slow minded and went to school with the rest of us guys. The five of us got along real well together. We would cover for each other whenever it was necessary. At times we had to hide what we were doing from our parents. The truth is, most of the time we were out of our neighborhood.

My friend Jim's father was a bookie and he also had a newspaper stand on one of the main corners in LA. The newspaper stand was a cover for his bookie business and it gave his clientele somewhere to place their bets. Several times a day his father would have to come home and drop off uncounted money to Jim's grandmother. His grandmother would take the money, uncounted, and put it into her purse. From there Jim would help himself to the money. He would take anywhere from forty to one hundred and sixty dollars, that I know of. I have no idea why they never caught him taking the money. If any of us ever needed a few bucks, Jim would give it to us. He was better than having a rich father.

As I look back, we were just punks trying to have a good time at everyone else's expense. There were times we just walked the streets or stayed home and smoked a little pot. Pot wasn't always available so we didn't smoke it very often. We even started to dress alike and comb our hair the same way, a flat top with a DA. We wore Levis, a T-shirt with the sleeves rolled up and argyle socks. Yes, argyle socks! If we weren't wearing T-shirts we were wearing button-down the front shirts with the collar up in the back. The five of us must have looked a little strange walking down the street together. I suppose that was what we wanted at the time, to look and act a little different than the norm, but then again, everyone in California looked a little strange.

Jim would take us out for a dinner of hot dogs or hamburgers and then maybe to a show. We never needed our own money, Jim always had plenty. Another place we would go is Griffith Park for horseback riding or just walk around the observatory and watch people. Sometimes we went to Santa Monica beach or Muscle Beach. I learned to box at Muscle Beach and I became pretty good at it. If we couldn't be located at one of these places chances are we were in Hollywood. Quite often Jim would pick up the taxi fare and we would go to Long Beach and just bum around on the boardwalk.

For some reason we became bored with the things we had been doing and started looking for new adventures. Smoking dope was fun, but we just couldn't get it all the time. One day Jim and I were walking down Rampart Street near Alta Loma School when Pete pulled up in a pickup truck and asked us to get in. We both got in the truck and asked him where he had gotten it, and how did he get his driver's license. He told us that the truck belonged to his brother and that he was working on getting his driver's license. He claimed that he had his temporary, but he didn't offer to show it to us.

Several days later while we were talking to Pete, we found out the truck he was driving was stolen. Jim and I knew that his brother didn't own a truck and we had to wonder where the truck came from. We kind of figured Pete stole the truck. Pete said he had found the vehicle parked on the street with the keys in it, so he jumped in, started it up and took off. That night he parked it in the alley behind his garage.

Bob had said to us that he wanted to become a police officer after he graduated from high school. When he found out Pete had stolen a truck, Bob went nuts. The five of us got together and talked about what we should do. Bob felt we should go to the police department and have Pete turn himself in. Richard, his family was from Mexico, felt it would be wrong to turn in one of our friends. He said if anything, we should protect him. Jim wanted to think about it for a few days. I didn't think it was right to do nothing, but I also didn't want to turn him in, and Pete didn't want to turn himself in. Pete told us how exciting it was to jump into that truck, turn on the key, hear the engine start and then go speeding off. What he told us was that he went all over town and into Hollywood and then down to Long Beach and any other place he wanted to go. I remember that gas was only about twenty-seven cents a gallon in those days. On the second day Pete had the stolen truck, he skipped school and went to the beach and stayed there all day. When he was ready to leave he got on a bus and went home, leaving the truck in the parking lot at the beach. We talked it over and decided to do nothing. We would wait and see if the police would catch him.

I know that having a friend like Jim taught me one thing, that having money is very important. So I started looking for someplace to work and found two jobs. My first job was at the Culver City Speedway. One night I went there to watch the races and I saw kids my age selling popcorn, peanuts and programs. When I applied for a job they told me I had to have a Social Security card. I found out where the Social Security office was and went there, applied for my card and within a few days I had it. I then took it to the speedway and they told me to come to work on Friday evening. Working there was great. I met a lot of new people and made many new friends. The best part was I got to watch the races for free and I made a few dollars, too.

My second job was working at the Los Angeles Coliseum during football season. I did the same thing there that I did at the Culver City Speedway. The crowds were much bigger and I made quite a bit more money.

Sometimes it was late at night when I finished work. I really didn't feel like going home on the bus, but I had no other options. Aunt Inez didn't say anything about me coming home late because she knew that I was working. Occasionally I would run into Harold. He also knew that I was working at the Coliseum or at the Speedway. Still, Harold always asked me the same questions, "Where have you been? Why are you getting home so late? Don't let me find out you lied to me! Go to bed, you're not staying up and watching television." I don't know, maybe I was a problem child. (I am sure as you read this you will probably think, yes, he was a problem. Do you think maybe I was trying to rebel, trying to reach out for help? As I relive my life through writing this book, I can't help but feel that's what I was trying to do.)

Chapter 8

By this time in my life I started noticing girls. Jim's sister Linda was a very attractive blonde and about the same age as I was. It seemed as though every time I was at Jim's house she managed to get me alone and we would mess around a little bit, just some petting. She was always the aggressive one, but I didn't mind that. I wasn't really interested in her because I just could not mess around with my best buddy's sister, even though Jim did encourage it.

I was seeing another girl that lived off of Western Boulevard. At this time I don't recall her name because I didn't see her that often. I do recall going over to her house one night, around nine o'clock at night, and knocking on the door. Her father answered the door and said that she couldn't come out. She was standing inside, a short distance from the door. She kind of indicated she would sneak out to meet me. I walked down the street about two houses and sat down on the curb waiting for her. I must've been there for a good half hour when I noticed a car coming around the corner. The car stopped right across the street from me. It was the police. They came over to me and asked me what I was doing. I explained to them that I was hoping my girlfriend was going to meet me, that she just lived a couple of houses up the street. When the policemen and I walked over to her house, her father explained that he had talked to me and told me that she wasn't going to come out.

The police put me in their cruiser and took me home. It just so happened that my aunt was having a large party that night, and when the police got to the house, it was loaded with people. They were close friends, some family and people that she and Harold worked with. I must say, when I walked in there with the police, I was quite the center of everybody's attention and a great embarrassment to Aunt Inez. She had them take me to jail overnight and then she picked me up in the morning. I didn't think this mishap would ever end. We even had to go to juvenile court for a curfew violation and me being incorrigible. Incorrigible meant that I was an unruly child. It also meant Aunt Inez had to miss work and another day's pay. I was placed on probation for sixty days, and I was also told that if I messed up again I could go to jail. I promised I would be on my best behavior.

Needless to say, I stayed pretty close to home for about two weeks. My pals would stop by once in a while but wouldn't stay very long. They just wanted to say hello and asked when I would be coming out again. For the most part, I was more than likely in the yard doing yard work. I did go to my cousin Joyce's house two or three times with Aunt Inez.

While I was staying home there was another bad incident with Harold. Inez and Harold would go to work in the morning and I would stay at home by myself. Earlier I mentioned that I'd started smoking. Harold came home from work early one afternoon. I was in the living room smoking and watching television when I saw Harold park his car in front of the house. I went into the bathroom and threw my cigarette into the toilet and flushed it. I then went back into the living room and sat down on the couch. When Harold came into the house I said hello to him. He stopped in his tracks, looked at me and said, "You've been smoking."

I stood up and lied saying "No, that's not true." Harold said he could smell it in the air. I was thinking that both Harold and my aunt smoked, so how could they smell it? I thought for certain he was trying to bluff me. Again I lied and said it wasn't true. I threw up my arms, turned and started to walk away to avoid another confrontation. Harold, wearing a pair of pointed Stetson shoes, kicked me in the butt, at the base of my spine. For an instant I could not move and my whole body was tingling. Frightened, I started to cry. I told Harold that I couldn't move. He came over to me and pushed me and told me to go to my room. I was alright as soon as he made me move. He must have kicked me just right to have that type of effect on me. The next day, when I looked in the mirror, the lower part of my back was sore and slightly bruised, and my hips were also sore, but I was okay. The sad part is I couldn't tell anyone. If I did I would feel Harold's wrath once again. Besides, no one would believe me because to everyone else my aunt's son had no faults at all.

Every now and again I would see Pete, Rich or Bob drive past the house in a car. That would make me wonder what was going on with them. It seemed rather odd because I never saw the three of them drive past the house before. I thought I knew what was going on but I wasn't really certain. If what I thought was true, that made it a lot easier for me to stay home.

One day as I was walking down the street going to the store next to Alta Loma School, it happened. Jim and Richard pulled up in a car and told me to get in. When I asked them what was going on they said they were going to pick up the other guys and then go to the beach. They asked me if I was off of house arrest and if I was ready to have some fun. I replied with a yes and got into the car.

We picked up the other guys and off to the beach we went. Jim bought me a new bathing suit and a beach towel. While we were laying on the beach, I brought up the subject of the car. I was right, it was stolen. They had taken it from a car lot on Washington Boulevard the day before. They also informed me that we would not be taking the car back and we would steal another before we left the beach. Upon learning this, I could feel the fear start to rise within me. Jim looked at me and asked, "Do you have the balls?"

"Hell yeah, that's fine with me." I replied. When it was time to leave they asked me to go and find a car with the keys left in the ignition. I looked around the parking lot for a while and finally I found one that did indeed have the keys left in it. I reached inside the car and grabbed the keys, put them in my pocket, walked back to the beach and gave the keys to Pete. Pete and I walked back to the car and got inside of it. He put the key in the ignition and turned it. The car started right up and we took off. What a rush! I couldn't keep from laughing. We picked up the other three guys and took off for home. Everyone was laughing and having a good time as they checked out our new car. Was that ever easy! I couldn't believe what just happened. I helped steal a car! It really felt good stealing it even though I was very frightened at first. I think I was addicted even though I was frightened that maybe the owner would catch us and beat us up or call the cops. Now here we were driving down the road having a great time listening to music and laughing about it. I just knew this would happen again, and soon.

However, after being involved with my first stealing, I didn't hang around with the guys as much. I wasn't looking to get into trouble again. I didn't want to go to court again and I didn't really care for the thought of being locked up. Maybe I just had a premonition of things to come.

Besides that, I was having too much fun with girls. I liked girls my age or even a few years older. At thirteen I looked advanced for my years. I could and did pass for seventeen years of age or older. There was one girl, Lisa, who was about a year younger than I. She was a very pretty girl and we did go out to the theater and see a few movies. I would visit her at her home and listen to her play the piano. I must've thought I found my soul mate, for one afternoon I went out and bought some black India ink. I took a needle from home and wrapped some thread around the pointed end of the needle. Then I went to the park and tattooed her name on my upper left arm, where it still is today.

The older girls that I took out I only went out with a few times. Although they were fun to date and I learned a lot about sex and life, I really didn't want to get too involved with anyone.

Every now and then I would see Pete, Bob and the boys and we would go to the beach or to Hollywood Boulevard and go to the movies. There was one time that the three of us went to the movies and afterwards we took the bus down La Brea Boulevard to get to Washington Boulevard. At the Beverly Boulevard bus stop, Bella Lagosi got on the bus. The real Dracula himself! There were only the three of us on the bus when he climbed aboard. Of course we started yelling, howling and laughing when we saw him. He gave us that old Dracula look and then hissed at us, which made us laugh even longer. He was only on the bus for two more stops before he got off. Naturally we applauded when he got off of the bus. It was so neat that he played with us. What a very memorable moment that is!

When the bus reached Washington Boulevard we got off and started walking towards Rampart Street, which led to Jim's house. When we got to Rampart Street instead of turning left we turned right and crossed Washington Boulevard and went a short distance down the opposite side of Rampart Street. Parked there on the street, as always, was a large truck with a big bed full of fresh fruit. One of us climbed into the truck and threw fruit down for the rest of us to catch. When we thought we had enough, we went to Jim's house, eating fruit all the way there and then we shared the watermelon once we got inside the house.

There were times I really missed hanging around with the guys and eventually I started spending more time with them. Of course we started stealing cars again. It was to the point that we were stealing at least one car a week. We would just joy ride and then we would park the car someplace and leave it. It had gone on so long we didn't think we'd ever get caught, but every now and then we'd get snapped back to reality. With me, every time we were out riding around and I saw a cop I could feel a little fear creep into me. I didn't want to return to jail.

One day Bob and I were talking and he told me that the guys got into something a little too crazy and scary for him and he had no part of it. He said it had happened while I was on house arrest. According to Bob they were beating up drunks, or anyone else too weak to resist them, and taking their money. When he told me that I said, "That's not for me, I won't be doing it." I told Jim the same thing the following day when I ran into him. The subject never came up again.

There was another time we were all just riding around with nothing to do. Bob had his driver's license and was driving. We looked into the glove compartment and found a map of California. Looking at the map, we found there was a little river running through Bakersfield, California, so we decided to drive to Bakersfield and check it out. We were hoping it was something we could wade or walk around in or even catch some tadpoles or fish. It seemed to take forever to get there, but then again, we did get lost once or twice. When we finally got to Bakersfield we couldn't find this river or stream. What we did find was an old dried-up creek bed. Being a little disappointed, we turned the car around and headed for home. It couldn't have been more than fifteen minutes after leaving the creek bed that Bob said, "Hold on boys, the police are pulling us over."

When the officer walked over to the car, Bob asked him what the problem was as he produced his license. The officer said there seemed to be a lot of activity in the car and he wanted to see what was going on. Bob told him the car belonged to his uncle and he let us use it for the day, and we were returning from Bakersfield after looking for that creek. Bob even took out the map and showed him the creek we had been looking for. The officer explained to Bob that due to the drought the creek dried up earlier in the year. He said, "You boys be careful with your uncle's car. You can go now." Wow! Was that close!

Once on the road we all felt a little relieved and laughed and joked about it. You would think that episode would have made us a little smarter, but it didn't. We didn't take any more cars for a while, so I guess maybe that did frighten us a little.

About two weeks later Pete was picked up in a stolen car and taken to jail. He told the police what all of us had been doing and he gave them all of our names. Two days later the police were at my door to pick me up and take me to jail. When I was questioned they told me that the other guys caved in on me and they knew what really happened, so I might as well just confess. I tried not to tell them anything, but they told me all the evidence they had against us and it was all true. In time I did confess. The police officer told me that they had been looking for us for a few months and they knew it was kids that were taking the cars.

I was sent to the juvenile detention center just outside of Los Angeles. I ran into my buddies there, but we really didn't have time to talk. You could see in their faces that they were all scared. Life in the detention center was really bad and it made you apprehensive of everything. You didn't know if someone you didn't even know was going to jump your ass and punch you out or shank (stab) you.

After about ten days I was handcuffed and taken to court. Aunt Inez and Harold were present. She told the judge that I was totally out of control and that she tried to reprimand me and control me, but it was useless. The court decided that I should no longer reside in California. Inez and I had talked about this before going to court, and I told her I no longer wanted to live with her and Harold. She didn't tell me that she had already talked to my father about sending me back to Ohio to live with him, but that was okay. Anything was better than living with her while Harold was still around.

The court ordered that I be housed at the detention center until arrangements could be made to put me on a bus and send me to Ashtabula, Ohio, to live with my father. When the day came that I was to leave, I was escorted from the detention center to the Greyhound bus station. I was wearing handcuffs that were removed when I got on the bus. I was thirteen years old, alone and very frightened, and no one was there to tell me goodbye. I never had the chance to tell my aunt that she wasn't part of the problem, or maybe I just never took the time to tell her. Neither did I have the chance to tell her that I loved her.

The officer that took me aboard the bus handed me an envelop from Aunt Inez. It contained some money so I could eat on the trip and a message saying how sad she was knowing that I was leaving today and

119

she felt it would be best if she stayed away. She said that when I was older I could return and we could have a relationship again. At the time I wondered if that was true, or if she just wasn't interested in me. Oh! How I hated to leave her, the only mother I've ever known. What would life be for me now? As the bus left the station I vowed to return and make it all up to her. Someday I would be the man she wanted me to be.

As the bus twisted and turned along the rundown streets of downtown Los Angeles, I sat there looking out the window, watching people as they hurried along the streets to or from their jobs, occasionally seeing a drunk sitting in a doorway with a bottle in his hand. I wondered if someday I would be in one of those doorways. Only negative thoughts about me occupied my mind. I wondered what is it that makes me the way I am? Who am I? If only I could be someone else! Why am I making life so hard on me? If there is a God, where is He now? My sadness and bewilderment soon gave way to sleep, that deep dark hole I needed to occupy this time.

I awakened to find we had stopped to take on more passengers. When the bus left Los Angeles there may have been half a dozen people on it, including myself. Perhaps another half dozen got on board at this stop. A half a dozen is a good thing, I thought. I had a seat to myself and I was hoping to keep it that way. As I watched the people get on the bus, there was a woman, perhaps in her early to mid thirties, that sat in the seat across the aisle from me. She also had a whole seat to herself. We acknowledged each other and exchanged a few pleasantries.

My mind wasn't on conversation. I just wanted to be left alone, alone in my thoughts. I thought about my father and living in his home. I didn't know him very well, he never had much to do with me as I was growing up. I don't think he neglected me, he was just too busy with other things. After my mother passed away my father remarried and started another family. He now had three more sons and a daughter by his second wife. I never had any real siblings. I wondered what it would be like having younger brothers and a sister. Would I become part of the family? Could I be someone that my younger brothers would look up to, or will this just be someplace to stay until I'm old enough to be on my own? My God, my self-esteem is too low to even think about that. Perhaps time will change the way I feel about myself.

My father owned a fruit farm in Ashtabula County, Ohio. A small township by the name of Saybrook is where the farm was located. Ashtabula County is the farthest northeast county in Ohio. It borders with Pennsylvania to the east and Lake Erie to the north. It was only about thirty miles from where I lived to the Pennsylvania state line.

I had also found out that Ashtabula was a shipping port. I have to admit, I really didn't know what that meant. I wondered, did they ship in meat and fresh fruits and vegetables, or perhaps, textiles or building materials? I was somewhat interested, and I knew I would be finding out before long.

I was told that Dad had bought the farm in 1950, and their main crop was peaches. They had a cow for fresh milk, and they also put in a vegetable garden every year. I know it sounds really nice, but remember, I was coming from Los Angeles, California, to live on a farm. I didn't know anything about fruits, vegetables or cows. Most of all, I didn't care to learn about growing or raising any of these things. I was hoping they were not having me there just to become another farmhand. The more I thought about living with my father, the more I disliked the idea. Soon sleep overtook me again. I felt very safe while I was sleeping.

I was awakened by the woman across the aisle. She was pulling on my shirtsleeve and asking me if I was awake. "Yes, yes, I'm awake. What's wrong? What's happening? Are we okay?" I asked. She replied by saying she was awake and needed someone to talk to and I was the closest person. She informed me that she was on her way to Houston, Texas, to meet her husband. He was in the Air Force and they had been separated for quite some time. She talked and talked and talked. I didn't think she would ever shut up. She told me all about her parents and her childhood and about growing up. She talked about her wedding and married life and their plans to have children. She must have talked to me about herself for at least an hour or so.

I was so happy when she finally asked about me. She wanted to know where I was going, what I was doing traveling by myself and why I was leaving my home. She seemed very nice and sincere so I told her what had happened to me. She said her heart ached for me and she felt very bad about my circumstances.

She had been wearing gloves ever since she got on the bus. I thought that was rather strange. After hearing my story she proceeded to take off the gloves and show me her hands. Her hands looked like raw meat, the skin was peeling off in various places and they were dark red and white with blotches all over them. She never did say what was wrong with her hands, only that she was going to see some specialist when she got to Houston. In my lifetime I have only met one other person whose hands were in that condition.

We talked for hours and before long nighttime was upon us. My problems left me with our conversation. The bus had stopped earlier that evening so that everyone could get some dinner. When we got back on the bus, she suggested that we sit in the back seat so as not to disturb other passengers with our conversation. By the time we got to Texas and she got off the bus, we were really good friends. Not good enough to stay in touch, but good friends. As she hugged me I wished her well and hoped that she would have a good reunion with her husband and that the medical specialist could help her with her hands.

The balance of the trip was pretty mundane. It didn't take long until I was tired of riding on the bus. The closer the bus got to Cleveland the more concerned I became about my relocation. I really wanted to make a life with my father and his family. I thought that for the first time in my life, perhaps I would find a home where people really cared about each other. Without the influence of my old buddies, life should be just fine. I did know the difference between right and wrong. Something else in the back of my mind kept creeping up and disturbing me. If my father really cared about me and was concerned about my happiness, why is it he never was around me? How would things be any different now?

When the bus got to Cleveland, I got off of it with all my belongings. After much thought, I didn't follow the plan of traveling to Ashtabula and living with my father because I had so many doubts. I decided that somehow I would make it on my own.

I jumped on a Cleveland Transit bus and eventually wound up at Peter Dale's house. I told Pete what happened and what my concerns were. He told me I could stay there until I decided to go to my father's in Ashtabula. Pete told me I should go to my father's because he would be worried about me. I thought to myself, why would he be worried about me now, after all these years? I promised Pete that I would telephone someone in the morning. It was difficult for me to sleep that night, and I woke up just as tired in the morning as I was before I went to bed.

That evening when I had dinner with Pete and his family, he informed them that I would be staying there for a few days. Mrs. Dale thought that was just wonderful and said she would be looking forward to the next few days. Mr. Dale, however, frowned and made a grumbling noise. It was his usual displeasure noise. Pete must have said something to his mother about what happened to me in California and the journey back to Cleveland. She tried to make me feel very comfortable and hugged me every now and then. Mrs. Dale was such a nice woman.

The following morning I called my sister Jean. Sounding half panicked, she said I should come to her house as soon as possible. I tried my damnedest to explain to her that I was afraid to go live with my father. I explained to her that I had heard so many bad stories from her and my brothers about Dad, his wife and children that I needed some time to think about it. My brothers and sisters didn't care for my dad's wife. Jean wanted to know where I was at and where I was staying. Not responding to her questions, I told her I would call her in a couple of days.

After two nights of staying at Pete's house his father said that I would have to leave. He was concerned about the police finding out I was staying with them, as I was a runaway. I couldn't blame Mr. Dale. He left Germany to get away from Hitler's oppression and tyranny. I'm certain he was afraid of being caught doing something he shouldn't and then being sent back to Germany. It's kind of funny how things happen.

Something in the back of my head told me that I made it for a couple of days on my own. If I really had to, I could make it by myself. It may be difficult, but I could do it.

The next morning I took a bus to Jean's house. After a bath and a multitude of questions, my brother-in-law, Carl, and Jean drove me to my father's house. I guess maybe I felt a little braver with them along. My father and stepmother, her nickname was Chick, said they were concerned about me not being on the bus when it arrived in Ashtabula. Chick stated that the first thing they did when I failed to arrive in Ashtabula was to call Jean and ask if she knew of my whereabouts.

Dad didn't say much to me about not taking the bus to Ashtabula. He did say that he could understand me being nervous and upset because we really didn't know each other. First impressions are very important. You could tell he was really pissed off and was just holding it back. We made the best of that bad situation and moved on. They did offer me food, shelter and a chance for an education.

Living on a farm was really a lifestyle change for me. I think I adapted to being a farmer and I learned to live the farm life quite well. I had a great amount of fun with my siblings. They taught me a lot about the farm life and we got along just great.

My stepmother and I got along fairly well. She made a conscious effort towards liking me and I did the same towards her. She made it quite clear though that I was not one of her children, and I believe I made it quite obvious that she was not my mother. Most of the time I could tolerate her actions towards me and the remarks she would make to hurt me. I really don't know for sure if she knew that she was hurting me. As I look back now maybe some of the things I said to her, or things I did, I did them to spite her and hurt her as well.

My father and I had no relationship. He very seldom even talked to me. He wasn't mean or abrupt, he just didn't seem to have anything to say to me. It was as though he wanted no relationship with me at all. It wasn't what you would think a father and son relationship should be, and being a good child doing everything I was told to do didn't seem to matter.

Whenever I would visit other family members or when they would come to the farm to visit us, and I had a chance to talk to them about my father, I would tell them what the relationship between Dad and I was

126

like. They would tell me that my father loved my mother very much and that he was still grieving for her. As a young boy that didn't make much sense to me. They also said that perhaps he blamed me for her death and to just give it time. That would remind me about Harold telling me my father didn't want me. It weighed very heavy on my mind. I really needed someone to want me. It was looking like maybe I wouldn't be a part of this family either.

Chick and her children were Catholic, just like Pete and his mother. Man, I really liked that. At first I didn't go to church with them and they didn't ask me to go. At some point I told Chick I was very interested in the Catholic faith and we had a few discussions about it. She was very kind to discuss all my questions and inquiries. After a period of time I informed her that I would like to become a Catholic. She took me to church and we made arrangements for me to start taking lessons to become Catholic. I knew that becoming Catholic would fill a void in my heart, and only then would I feel like I really belonged. I made it quite clear to her I wasn't becoming Catholic because the family was Catholic. It was something I wanted to do ever since I went to church with Pete and his mother. However, I also hoped this would put my step mother and I on equal ground and we would be able to get along better. As things turned out, I was wrong.

Chapter 9

The church I was to take instructions at was named Assumption Church. It was located in Geneva, Ohio, approximately three miles west of the farm. I was to go once or twice a week after school for instructions. Dad and Chick never seemed to have the time to drive me to church, so I walked and hitchhiked to church for instructions and then walked or hitchhiked home afterwards. Sometimes it was late when I got home. I did this for six months regardless of weather conditions. I did become a Catholic. I was baptized, confirmed and made my first communion within ten days. I was a proud, God-loving young man, and I did it without anyone's help!

Approximately two months after my first communion my relationship with Dad and Chick seemed to deteriorate even more. Perhaps it was because whatever they did or said to me I didn't let it bother me. I was very happy and I showed it. Besides working outside doing farm work for my dad, Chick had me doing housework as well, such as cleaning the table after dinner, doing dishes and mopping the kitchen and bathroom floors. Every two to three weeks she would have me scrub the baseboards throughout the house. Come on now, how often do baseboards need to be cleaned? What do they do to get dirty? I tried talking to them and I was told everyone had a job and everybody had to work, that is what farm life

128

is. When I asked why my siblings didn't have chores to do, Chick said it was because they were too young. What angered me most was the smile on their faces as they told me this. I thought to myself that I am going to find a way to help myself get out of this mess.

I decided to find a job and go to work. Dad and Chick agreed to it as long as it didn't interfere with my work at home. Just west of the farm, on Route 20, was a restaurant called Tom-Thumb's. While coming home from school on the bus one day, I noticed a help wanted sign in the window. After finishing my work on the farm that evening I walked to the restaurant and applied for the job. I was hired on the spot and told to come in for training the following evening. The restaurant was close enough that I could walk to work, but most of the time I hitchhiked. I was trained to run the soft serve ice cream machine. I made ice cream cones, sundaes and milkshakes. The owner, Mr. Beutler, would even let me work cooking on the grill once in awhile if we were not too busy. The pay wasn't that great, but still Chick made me pay rent each payday. She said I was helping out the household and she would help me save my money, but there was never any money when I would ask her for it. What little bit of money I did get I saved.

One evening before I left for work, I counted my money and I had something like $74. I took it to work with me that night. Later that night I talked with Mr. Beutler and I told him that things at home were not so good, that my parents were talking about making me quit my job, and I didn't know if I would be in to work the next night. This part was true. When Dad and Chick told me that I would have to quit my job I was heartbroken. Working got me out of the house and it put a few dollars in my pocket. They explained to me that the farm and housework wasn't being done and that it had top priority.

Earlier that day when I had arrived home from school, I packed a small suitcase and hid it near Tommy Carrier's house. The Carriers were our nextdoor neighbors. I left work one hour early that night, picked up my suitcase and started hitchhiking towards Cleveland. My goal was California. I had no plans on how to get to California or what I would do once I got there. All I knew was that I had to leave. If I had to, I would hitchhike all the way. I thought about my siblings and how I would miss them, as we had grown close in the short time I lived in their home. What would they think of me leaving? Would they ever understand?

It was always very difficult to get a ride on Route 20, but later that night I arrived at the Greyhound station and bought a ticket for St. Louis. As I got on the bus, fear crept into my mind. What would happen to me if I didn't make it to Los Angeles? What if someone tries to hurt me? I had hitchhiked a lot in Los Angeles, and I never had a problem with anyone there. I reasoned that I was just getting over excited. I wasn't really certain what I would do from St. Louis to LA. I didn't have much money, but I just knew I would be all right.

As the bus headed for St. Louis I decided that I would wait around the bus station and see if any opportunities would come along. I will just wait and see what happens once I get there. St. Louis is a big city, and I thought that hitchhiking out of it might be a problem. I was worried about the police picking me up and hauling me off to jail before the first leg of the trip was over with. I worried all the time.

The Greyhound station in St. Louis is really large and it was very crowded. There were numerous people walking around or sitting on benches waiting to catch buses for various parts of the United States. I was hoping someone would come in that was driving west in their own car and was looking for someone to ride with them. Maybe I would meet and make friends with a family member that was waiting to pick up someone getting off of a bus. Ideally, they would be driving west, out of the city and they would offer me a ride. I knew the chance of that was pretty darned slim.

I walked around for a while and then sat on a bench for some time reading the newspapers and magazines. I also did a lot of people watching. At last I decided to get a cup of coffee and perhaps find something to eat. As I entered the restaurant I noticed a young lady sitting by herself in a booth across from the counter. I sat down at the counter across from the booth. While eating my hamburger and pie and drinking my coffee, she and I started talking. I found out she was seventeen and was returning home to St. Louis after visiting with her grandparents in Michigan. I told her I was eighteen and trying to get to Los Angeles to see the aunt that raised me. I told her that my aunt was very sick and they didn't know if she was going to live or die. I felt that being with her may help her return to good health. This young lady and I talked for quite some time. It seemed as though we must've talked about every subject there is.

Finally, she started to become concerned because her parents hadn't arrived to pick her up yet. I offered to walk her around the bus station to see if they were waiting for her in another area. She agreed and we left the restaurant. Once outside the restaurant we took no more than half a dozen steps and her parents were there looking for her. She introduced me to them and we said our goodbyes. I sat down on one of the benches and started reading again, watching as they left the building. She seemed to be a really nice girl.

I planned on hanging around the Greyhound station for a while longer, maybe for the next twelve hours, just to see if I could get a ride out of the city. I didn't want to hang around there too long because I was afraid I'd get picked up for loitering. That would likely get me sent back to Ohio.

I had just dozed off when I felt someone tap me on the shoulder. I looked up, fearing it might be the police, and found the girl's father standing in front of me. He thanked me for watching over his daughter while she was waiting for them to pick her up. She told him I was trying to get to California to see my aunt and I didn't want to hitchhike in the city. For some reason I felt a little embarrassed, probably because I had lied about my reason for going back to California. He told me that they lived west of the city and they would be more than happy to give me a ride. That would be their way of repaying me for watching over their daughter.

As we walked to the car he and I talked about my trip and how long I thought it would take to get there. He then suggested we go to his house and we could look at the map and see exactly how to get to Los Angeles. So that's what we did, and then he asked me to spend the night in their house and get a fresh start in the morning. I had breakfast with them the next morning and then he drove me to Route 40 and dropped me off so that I could start hitchhiking.

I found that hitchhiking was really crazy. Sometimes I would walk with my thumb out for what seemed to be hours. When I did get a ride, it would only last anywhere from fifteen minutes to half an hour. I started to wonder if maybe people just didn't hitchhike in Missouri. Then there were other times I would stick out my thumb and get a ride immediately that would last all day.

I was always very careful about what little money I had. I couldn't stay in motels because of the cost. After eight or eight-thirty at night I wouldn't hitchhike. I was always hopeful that I would get a ride that would last through the night, but it seldom worked out that way. What I did do before dark was try to find a place to spend the night. Sometimes it was under a bridge or in an abandoned building. Other times I would stay in wooded areas, sleeping on and covering up with cardboard and newspapers. I was always very careful about where I stayed because I didn't want to be picked up by the police.

For a while I tried finding an unlocked car to sleep in. That seemed to be the best way until one time things didn't turn out the way I expected them to. It was early morning and I was asleep in the back seat of a car, covered up with a plaid blanket I found laying inside. I was awakened by a man getting into the car, starting the engine and pulling away. He drove for approximately ten to fifteen minutes and then stopped at a restaurant. I was afraid to move! After he went into the restaurant I opened the door and slowly got out. To this day I don't think he knew I was even in the car. That was the last time I slept in cars.

A number of times I slept in people's homes. Times were very different then and people were, too. If a married couple or a family were to pick me up, I would tell them about my aunt being sick and my plight to reach LA. They would invite me to spend the night at their home where I could take a hot shower and have a good warm dinner. Most of the time after dinner I would fall right to sleep, and they would even wash my clothes for me. Before sending me on my way in the morning they would fix me a nice brown bag lunch. Once I stayed with an older married couple for two days. I will never forget their names, Bill and Irma. They had no children and they wanted me to stay in Missouri with them as long as I wanted to. Neither one of them worked, they were both retired. They owned a small farm and had some goats and chickens and Bill said they planted a large garden every year. They were both a lot of fun to be around and we shared many a laugh. After two days I decided it was time for me to move on. Before leaving, Bill gave me five or ten dollars to help me along the way and made me promise to come back someday.

When I think of all the people that gave me rides, women were the kindest and most critical of what I was doing. Needless to say, my appearance wasn't always the neatest and my hygiene wasn't always the best. I'm confident that after I entered the car they must have asked themselves, "Why in the hell did I pick him up?" However, most of them always turned a kind ear towards me and wanted to know my story. Many would ask what is a young man like you doing out here hitchhiking by yourself? How old are you? Do your parents know where you are? I would tell them I was nineteen years old and my mother died giving me life and there was no place in my father's life for me. I believed this part was true except for my age. I knew that I had lied to some people, but I felt it was for self-preservation. I was not panhandling or asking them for money, but quite often women would give me a couple of dollars and tell me it was for "just in case." There were times I would refuse the money, but they would insist, telling me I would need money when I arrived in Los Angeles.

Upon arriving in Los Angeles, my last ride dropped me off downtown. I took a couple of buses to get to Aunt Inez's house in West LA. She was surprised and shocked to see me, although she did say that my father had phoned her to let her know I was missing. I have to honestly say it wasn't a happy reunion. She was rude to me and told me what a stupid thing I had done returning to California. She didn't even invite me into the house. She informed me that I wasn't welcome to spend the night and I could not live with them. Then she asked me how much money I had. When I told her, she went in the house and came back with sixty dollars and gave it to me. She told me of a motel on Washington

Boulevard west of where she lived and said that I could stay at the motel and use the money to pay for my rent and have a little something left over so that I might eat. I left my aunt's house feeling pretty well rejected, but I had some money in my pocket, and I knew the place where I was going to spend the night. After being on the road for some nine days I was really tired and needed a good meal. The thought of a hot shower or bath and a real bed to sleep in seemed to invigorate me. The next big obstacle would be to find a job the following day.

I gave very little thought to my old friends and classmates, but I did sometimes wonder what had happened to them. I was in Ohio by the time they had to go to court. It would be nice to see them and have someone to pal around with, but I really didn't need any more trouble, and I'm sure it would have led to that. I had learned my lesson and had made up my mind before I left Ohio that I wouldn't be in contact with them.

The owner of the motel looked at me a little oddly when I checked in, but I really didn't care. I knew they had rented to stranger looking people than me. The bottom line was cash. I paid him and he gave me the key to my room.

The room itself was rather dark when I first walked in, and I really couldn't see what it was like. When I opened the drapes and let some sunlight in I noticed there were a lot of flying insects in the room. That was important to me because I really wasn't fond of bugs. In time I would kill them with a newspaper or something. The room itself didn't look very large and certainly not plush, but it would do until I could find a job and relocate to a better rental.

It was about two o'clock in the afternoon and I was really tired, so I showered and went to bed. If I should wake up in the early evening I would go out and find a place to eat. I woke up about ten o'clock and went to this little place that I knew of on Western Boulevard and Vermont. They served Mexican food and really large burgers. I had to take two busses to get there. Once I got there I had a bowl of my favorite Mexican soup that has tripe and hominy in it, and then I had one of their giant hamburgers. I went back to my room, watched TV for a while and then went back to sleep.

The next morning after awakening I took another nice long hot shower. After drying off, just before I started to get dressed, I noticed I was having a lot of itching in my groin area. Upon looking closely into the mirror, I could see I had body lice. I walked over to Aunt Inez's house and told her of my new dilemma. I never saw anyone laugh that hard. She said that I had crabs. She went back into the house and came out with a small tin can of talcum that she said would kill them. She instructed me to dust my body with the talcum and then take the sheets off of the bed and dust the mattress with it as well.

When I got back to the motel I informed the owners of what had happened to me and asked them for clean sheets. They told me that someone would be coming around that afternoon to spray the rooms with insecticide. I stayed in my room most of the day trying to kill or cripple anything that was flying, walking or crawling. That evening I went out to eat and came right back to my room and went to bed.

The next morning I went out looking for work and filled out several applications. I felt that I should be self-supporting before trying to go back to school. That afternoon I took a short nap. I woke up feeling pretty good about the way my day had gone. At least I had a few job prospects. My money was starting to run a little short and I couldn't go back to my aunt for anymore.

I ate a late dinner that night, it was about seven o'clock in the evening, and then decided I wanted to walk or hitchhike to Hollywood. I wanted to relax and have a little fun, and I guess I was pretty proud of myself for completing my trip. I was still keyed up and a little restless from my journey across the states. I thought that maybe walking around Hollywood Boulevard might help me. I used to have a lot of fun on Hollywood Boulevard and Vine and also on Sunset and Vine. It has to be the best place in the world to watch people. You could see some really weird and strange looking folks.

There was a music and record store on the northwest corner of Sunset and Vine. A person could just walk in, pick out the records they wanted to hear and then go into these little booths and listen to them before making a purchase. I used to enjoy going in and playing music just for the fun of it until one time I passed out in the booth. A number of people came to my aid, but I was okay. I guess maybe I had forgotten to eat for a few days.

Another great thing to see were the customized cars that ran the

138

streets of Hollywood. Almost all of them were chopped, channel and decked and had electric doors with hidden switches to open them. I can recall seeing a Model T with a porthole for a rear window. The paint jobs were just unimaginable and hard to describe other than to say they were absolutely beautiful.

As I was leaving the motel to go to Hollywood I noted that it was on the south side of Washington Boulevard and just west of La Brea Boulevard. I decided to walk east on Washington to La Brea and then start hitchhiking north to Hollywood Boulevard. While walking east I cut through a closed gas station. On one of the gas pump islands there was a table and on the table was an orange. As I walked through I picked up the orange and started peeling it, but before I got to the sidewalk a police cruiser pulled up beside me. The officers asked me where I got the orange, what was I doing, where was I going and where was I coming from. After answering all of their questions I was loaded into the cruiser and transported to Georgia Street Receiving in Los Angeles. (It is a hospital, police station and jail combined.) While being transported I talked with one of the officers. He told me that they knew who I was and that they had been looking for me. Someone had reported seeing me in West LA. That started me thinking. I had only been in the motel for two nights and Aunt Inez only gave me enough money for two nights, and she was the only one that knew I was in town. I'll bet she turned me in. I vowed that she'd never get a chance to do that again.

Once again, my father sent money and I was loaded onto a bus heading east toward Cleveland. This time when I arrived in Cleveland I grabbed my belongings and didn't even bother to go inside. I was afraid Dad would be waiting for me and I wasn't sure of his frame of mind. Someone had retrieved all of my belongings from the motel in West LA and they were stashed away in a compartment in the bottom of the bus. I waited while they unloaded the luggage from the bus, watching everyone who came into the arrival area, and then I grabbed my belongings and started walking towards the nearest Cleveland Transit bus stop.

I stepped inside the shadowy doorway of a business and waited for the bus to arrive. I was still being careful, hoping no one would find me. The bus was soon there and I climbed aboard and was headed for my old neighborhood. On the bus, I sighed a deep sigh of relief and kind of smiled to myself because I got away from the bus station without being caught. I planned on staying in the Cultural Gardens near Doan Creek, but first I wanted to call Jean and let her know what was going on. I was sure she was worried about me. Of course she was upset and scolded me. She informed me that Dad and Chick were at the bus station waiting for me and he was really pissed when they couldn't find me. Dad told Jean that they went to the bus station just to make sure I got off the bus and returned to Ashtabula.

Jean said she would send Carl to pick me up and I could come to her house and stay with them for a while. She also said that she would call my brothers and we could get together and have a family meeting to decide what to do. I reminded her of what life was like for me living with

140

my father and stepmother. I also reminded her of what it was like when my brothers lived with them. Although opposed to me living on the street by myself, she did understand my feelings. I asked her to give me two or three days to think about it and I would be back in touch with her. She was very opposed to this and asked me to please come stay with her and Carl and I could think about it for a couple of days at her home. She wanted to know why I didn't want to be at her house. I told her that I thought my father would be there. Through her hesitation we managed to say goodbye to each other. I could feel her concern over the telephone and it gave me reason to worry. Again fear entered my thoughts. What if something did happen to me?

Being alone and on my own, at times, was very frightening, especially when I was hitchhiking. I just didn't know what type of person was going to pick me up. Back in those days you didn't hear much about people taking advantage and hurting other people that were traveling, but still I was apprehensive.

I suppose living with Aunt Inez and Harold gave me reason not to trust people, especially men. I did get along with women just fine. Up to that time in my life I had no role model, and unbeknownst to me, that would be the story of my life. I learned to depend on me and only me.

The next day after arriving in Cleveland once again, I stayed pretty close to the Cultural Gardens with the exception of finding someplace to eat. I didn't know just what to do. I knew that I couldn't survive living in the gardens. What did my future hold in store for me? Nothing if I stayed here.

That evening I called Jean and told her where to have Carl pick me up. He was by himself when he picked me up and we talked about my circumstances all the way home. Although Carl was a gentle person, he was very upset about this whole thing. It wasn't just about me. He was also very concerned about Jean's health and her heart problem.

When we arrived at their house both of my brothers were waiting on us as well as Jean. We talked and I cried, and we talked some more and they cried. They became very angry with me and I became very angry with them, only this time I didn't run away to keep from arguing. I knew we were trying to find a solution that would work. I knew the only way we could do this was by talking.

I got extremely angry when they told me that they had phoned my father and he was on his way to Jean's house to pick me up. They had broken the trust I had in them. I told myself that the same situation would never repeat itself again and it would take years for me to ever trust them again. I told them that they had tricked me and I was going to leave. My brothers suggested that I didn't even try to do that. They said they wouldn't let me leave until I spoke with Dad and we tried to work things out.

When our father did arrived he was like a raging bull. He picked me up off the chair and slammed me against the wall and then slammed me onto the floor. By the time I knew what was going on, my brother Gay and Dad were into a fistfight. Once they were separated and tempers cooled off we all sat down and talked. Well, I don't know if you could say we talked, for Dad only listened. He really didn't have anything to add to the conversation. I did apologize to him for the problems I had caused him and his family. He did not respond. I told him that I just wanted to fit in. It was decided it would be best for me to go back and live with Dad and his family. During the return trip to Ashtabula we didn't talk. I really needed him to say something to me, something not in anger.

I mentioned earlier about how my father never or very seldom talked to me unless it was about some work that I should be doing or didn't do. So, he was true to form as we drove back to Ashtabula. Please don't get me wrong. Dad was a very good, hard-working man and he had many friends that thought the world of him. I love my father and I did respect him. I just wish I could have had a closer relationship with him.

Later in my life family members, my mother's side of the family, would tell me how much my dad loved my mother and how happy they were together, and that he still carried her photograph in his wallet. When my mother died, my father's world died and perhaps he blamed me for that. He really never recognized me as his son.

I assumed life could start anew once back on the farm. I was even looking forward to starting over. My grades in school actually came up a little bit, and I started playing basketball for the school team. I guess you I no longer had a negative outlook.

That summer I got a job working weekends and nights at Pete's Grille in Geneva-on-the-Lake. I was fifteen by this time, so working nights legally was no problem. I was flipping hamburgers and hot dogs and making French fries for Pete, and a few dollars for me. I really enjoyed working for Pete. He was more than a boss, he was a very good friend. He only hired kids and we all worked together really well. Even after work we would all hang out together for a while.

There were a lot of nights that I got home really late. I had no means of transportation so I would have to hitchhike or walk to work and back. It was about three and a half miles one way. It would have been so much easier if Dad and Chick would have helped me even a little bit. Having this job did create a lot of problems at home, but I didn't want to have to quit. I didn't cause any problems at home, and I did get the farm work and the housework finished.

After I started working at Pete's Grill, things at home started changing again, as you may have guessed. I felt as though they begrudged me working. For what reason I don't know. Pete paid his employees in cash and I still had to give a percentage of my pay at home. Chick always accused me of holding out and not being honest about giving her what she expected. I wouldn't hold out. I had no reason to do that. I was still making more money than I had made previously at Tom Thumb's. They always wanted to know how much money I was keeping from my check for myself. If they thought it was too much they demanded more money from me. Then they started complaining about the work around the house and the farm not being done. This was not true. I learned from my mistakes while working at Tom Thumb's. So I did start holding out and stashing money away again. When I thought I had enough money to last me for a while, I left again. This time I was much smarter and wiser.

When I got to Cleveland I looked in the newspaper and found a sleeping room that was near a Cleveland Transit bus line. I rented the room for $15 a week with kitchen privileges and then I went out and bought an alarm clock. The next thing I did was buy a newspaper and start looking for a job. Within the next few days I did find a job at the May Company warehouse in Cleveland. I made much more money than I did cooking and I could take the bus to and from work. The best part was, I got to keep the money I earned. I had to pay rent, but it was far less than I was paying at home.

While I was locked up in California I learned that if you change or transpose one or two numbers on your Social Security number it would take up to six months for someone to locate you. I did that at every job I had for the next three years. It's amazing what you can learn while being locked up. As a young adult in lockup, the idea of making money without working for it is very impressive.

As best I can remember, I worked for the May Company for maybe eight to ten weeks. By that time I thought I had enough money to last me a while. I recall having less than $200 when I left Cleveland. At the bus station I bought a ticket for Joplin, Missouri. It was from this location that I started hitchhiking to the west.

I never had any luck getting rides with truck drivers. I always dreamed of catching a ride with a truck driver that was going all the way out west and it would only take three or four days to get there. As I look back, hitchhiking was a lot of fun. Every day was a new adventure, and I did meet a lot of nice people that really treated me well. I will always be thankful and grateful for the life lessons they taught me. Then, on the other hand, of course there were a dozen or so real freaks. It seemed as though the more time I spent on the road the easier it became to spot the freaks and to avoid them.

It may have taken as long as a week to reach LA this time. I arrived early in the morning and the first thing I did was buy a newspaper. I was most familiar with West LA and that's where I wanted to live. Looking in the paper, I found two sleeping rooms that were available and they weren't very far from each other. I telephoned them and made arrangements to look at the sleeping rooms. The first house I went to wasn't very clean and it smelled like a wet dog. The rent was cheap, but I decided to see the other sleeping room before I made a decision. The other house was clean and the sleeping room was very nice. It also had a private entrance and kitchen privileges. This would be their first time renting the room and I would be the first person to rent it. The rent was a little more money than I wanted to pay, but I would be getting so much more for the money.

The house was owned by an older couple, Mr. and Mrs. Fox, and they said I could work off some of the rent by doing yard work if I cared to. They agreed to let me pay the rent weekly. I was hoping that they didn't think I was too young to rent a room. I told them I was new in town and I just graduated from high school and was looking for a job. I explained

146

that I only had enough money to rent a room for two weeks, and if I didn't have a job by then I would move on or perhaps go back to Pennsylvania. They must have liked me for they did rent me the room, and I moved right in.

The next morning I started looking for work. It took me about three days, but I finally landed a job. I went to work for the L. H. Mullen Company in West LA. They manufactured mechanical eyebrow pencils for Maybelline. My primary job was to ream out the hole on the tip of the pencil, but I also did a variety of other jobs.

I didn't have much of a social life, mostly because I really didn't want one. I tried to find happiness in all the things I did and in the things that surrounded me. I was trying to save up enough money to return to school. If I could work on weekends and earn overtime, that's what I would do. On the weekends when I didn't work, I would go to Santa Monica or Muscle Beach and lay in the sun and just hang out. On some other weekends I would go to a theater and see a movie. This didn't happen very often.

I had been working for about six weeks when I decided I wanted to go out somewhere. A movie was playing at the Egyptian Theatre on Hollywood Boulevard that I had been waiting to see. I decided to take a bus to Hollywood and see the movie. This turned out to be a bad decision.

I was early for the movie so I decided to stop in a coffeehouse called Coffee Dan's and have a cup of coffee. It was located just a few doors up from the theater. While having my coffee, a disturbance started in front of the theater. A few adults and some teenagers appeared to be arguing. I stepped outside to see what was going on and a policeman came up to me and started questioning me. Again, I was arrested and put into a police car and driven to Georgia Street Receiving. After a few days I was placed on a bus to be returned to Ohio.

When the bus arrived in St. Louis and they changed drivers, in the confusion of people departing and retrieving their belongings from beneath the bus, I decided to get off. I was certain the bus driver was instructed to watch over me and I'm sure that message was passed on from driver to driver. I telephoned Mr. and Mrs. Fox and told them I would be back within a week's time and not to rent my room to anyone else. I started hitchhiking in St. Louis, and within a week I was back in California.

My sleeping room was as I had left it and I moved back in. Mr. and Mrs. Fox had saved all of my belongings for me and anticipated my return. My job with the L. H. Mullen Company was still waiting for me as well. Of course I had a lot of explaining to do without making myself look too bad. No one ever really found out what happened to me within those two weeks. It was almost as though they didn't want to know. After a few weeks I told myself that this would be the end of my father looking for me. I told myself this every day, and I no longer looked over my shoulder. I felt like a free person.

When I decided it was time to go back to school I started spending the money that I had saved from working on clothing. Each week I would

148

buy a new article of clothing. One week it would be underwear and socks. The next week I would buy a pair of pants and a shirt and then shoes and tennis shoes. It took me a little time but I eventually had all of the clothing I thought I would need. I was very frightened that when I applied to go to school my records would show that I was a runaway from Ashtabula, Ohio, and my father would try to get me back there. In the past two years I must've missed a year and a half of school, so I really didn't know what grade I would be placed in.

Finally the day came, my nerve was up, and I walked into George Washington Junior High School and up to the front desk. I explained to them that I wanted to come back to school, and that I had gone to school there before and then moved to Ohio. I was asked many questions, and I answered them as best I could. When they told me to come back with a parent or legal guardian, I felt crushed. How could I do that? Who could I get to be a parent or guardian? Who do I know that would take that chance? I was very unhappy and depressed. Beside myself, I decided to spend more time working and saving my money. Maybe at some point in my life I could go back to school.

I found that between keeping myself in food and clothing, my money was leaving my hands almost before I got it. I started working the night shift at L. H. Mullen Company, and through the day and weekends I was doing landscaping for a Japanese landscaper. Working the two jobs left little time for anything else, but that was fine with me. Right now I just wanted to keep a low profile and avoid running into old friends. The only other outside activity I had was going to Muscle Beach and learning how to box through P.A.L. (Police Athletic League.) This was only on the weekends that I didn't work and when the weather permitted.

After several years I decided I wanted to move back to Ashtabula, Ohio. I guess maybe I felt the need for family. All of the years I spent working in California I didn't bother to contact Aunt Inez or any other family. I felt there was a little animosity between myself, Aunt Inez and the others. I know I had a lot of resentment towards them. My aunt was a real good southern cook, and I really did miss her cooking. I will have to admit there were times I thought I was doing the wrong thing by not staying in touch, and that I should contact her. Whenever I felt that way, I would start thinking of something else and continue on doing what I was doing. The time I did live in Ohio, she never once tried to phone me. There were things that would come to my mind about California and these things would upset me.

Chapter 10

It is November 30th, around noon, at the Bethlehem Steel office in Cleveland, Ohio. The three employees that are working, Glen Evans, Roy Dobson and Andy Sikora, are wondering why the *Morrell* has failed to report in for over thirty hours. Bewildered and anxious to find out the status of the *Morrell,* a phone call was made to a ship-to-shore radio station the night before by one of three men. The employee they talked to at the radio station told them that it was possible that the UHF antenna may have been blown over in the storm. As true as that may have been, the *Morrell* is now long overdue at Sault Ste. Marie, Michigan. This still didn't bring any clarity to the mystery as to the whereabouts of the *Morrell* and her crew. As the conversation in the office lingers on about the *Morrell*, the phone begins to ring. Andy Sikora, fleet dispatcher for Bethlehem Steel, answers the phone only to be informed that the freighter *S.S. G. G. Post* has found debris and bodies

B.F. Jones in storm- Capt Metz photo

wearing life jackets bearing the name of the *Daniel J.* Morrell. They were found floating in Lake Huron east of Grindstone City. Sadness, despair and disbelief overtake all three men in the office, like a dark cloud over their heads.

Back on the raft, looking at John again, I can still feel that same rage and that same love inside of me. However, the rage is tempered by the empathy I have for John. I start picking the ice off of his hands. I guess it is an act of love, compassion, and envy. In my mind I thought maybe, in some way, this action would bring him back.

I close my eyes and I start praying. Once again sleep overtakes me. Upon waking up I'm very thirsty. I look for the flare gun and the lanyard that's on it so I can put it in the water then suck the water out of it to keep myself hydrated. I can't find it. Oh, man, it's gone! The space between John and I can't be more than a foot. That's where I kept it and now it's not there. I'm so thirsty.

Lifting myself up on my left elbow again, I can see ice and snow all over my chest, shoulders, arms and legs. With my left hand I grab my right collar and start eating the ice and snow off of it. Wow, it really gets quiet, very quiet! I listen......It feels like someone's watching me...... I can feel their eyes...... I feel some type of presence. I start eating ice again, but I can still feel the presence. Looking up, I see a man standing at the edge of the raft. I don't question who he is or where he came from or anything. He looks down at me and says, "Stop eating the ice off your coat."

He is a very, very strange looking fellow. His hair is white, almost as white as snow, and it is very wavy, almost to the point of being curly. I'm not certain how he talks to me, but it is very thunderous. Yes, thunderous. His eyes are very deep set and they look strong. I guess that's the way to put it. When he talks to me, I don't know if it is verbal or if he speaks to my mind. I don't know. His eyebrows are equally as white as the hair on his head and they are very bushy. He has a very neatly trimmed white mustache that ends at the corners of his mouth. It is full and thick. His skin is white and it looks extremely smooth. It has a blue tinge to it, like skim milk used to have. He is dressed in some kind of a wrap-around blue sarong or perhaps a robe. All I can see is his head and torso. I am uncertain as to whether he has legs. After telling me not to eat the ice off my coat, he disappears.

I return to the laying down position and immediately find myself hovering above the raft. I am face down and slowly spinning around. I'm surrounded by dark, ominous clouds. They are all around me. Looking down, I see the raft. It is below the clouds, and all four of our bodies are lying on it. The raft, the bodies and the surrounding water are in a very brilliant bright light, almost as though the sun is shining directly on them. I become very frightened because I don't understand what is happening. Oh, what's going on? Wow! Wow! Maybe I'm dead, finally dead. Then, very slowly, I am being pulled backwards into the cloud, which now seems more like a tunnel. I feel like I'm on a clothes hanger, and I'm being pulled backwards. My arms and legs are extended in front of me. My speed seems to increase as I get further away from the raft, and the clouds are becoming whiter and brighter.

My fear vanishes and my disposition changes from frightened to happy and laughing. I turn around, looking in the direction I am being pulled, and laugh at the speed at which I am traveling. I guess I'm going to be okay, as I begin to feel secure, so I just relax. It is such a light-hearted feeling and I laugh even more. I feel very loved. I feel love all around me. I have forgotten about everything on earth and my pain and discomfort has disappeared. I don't know if I feel cold or warm. I'm happy and carefree. As I look at the end of the tunnel, I see a very bright white light coming from it. I am still laughing when I finally start slowing down. It seems like I am going a million miles an hour, and now a foot away from the end of the tunnel, my speed slows down.

Finally I stop and I feel something very solid under my feet. I take one step backwards, and I turn around. Wow! Oh, wow! The colors are so beautiful and so vivid. The grass is so very green. The sky, the flowers and trees are just so beautiful. I'm really taken back by the colors. Even more than that is this feeling of love that surrounds me. The feeling of love I have within me is like a fire inside of me. It's very exciting! I want to share it with everyone.

As I look around to my right there is a knee-high golden fence that radiates gold. Inside the fence are four to six people dressed in what appears to be white sarongs accented with gold belts and necklaces. Three of them are women and three are men. There are two golden steps that go up to a golden platform with two golden chairs that have white cushions on them. Almost everything radiates with gold except what isn't gold is pure white. The white even seems to radiate. At times the radiation is so bright it almost hurts my eyes when I look at it. All six of these people stop what they are doing and look at me. Their faces are stern and nondescript. It looks like they are searching my soul and questioning what they see. It's almost as though they are talking to a part of me I don't know. Five of them turn around and continue doing what they had been doing. They are no longer paying any attention to me. The one man that is still looking at me has a crown of gold upon his head and has a very intense look on his face. After a short while his face relaxes. He doesn't smile, but he has a look of approval on his face and he nods to me.

Somewhat confused, I start walking forward, passing the golden fenced-in area. Ahead of me is a man I have to describe as the Friar Tuck type. He is a short heavyset man, and the top of his head is bald with hair around the sides. He motions for me to come over to him. He acts almost impatient for me to get to him. He seems a little angry because I am taking so long to get there. I think perhaps that's just his nature. I'm about five or six steps from him when I notice to my left there is a deep dip in the terrain. There is a small white footbridge that crosses the dip in the terrain and could give me access to the other side.

On the other side of the bridge I see family members that have passed away. I know they are waiting for me, and they are very happy to see me. Upon reaching the man that had beckoned to me, he takes my hands in his, palms up, and says, "Let us see what you've learned. Let's see what you have learned."

I think it is a little odd that he makes this comment. I always thought it was about being good and bad. As he says this, pictures of my life appear in my hands. The pictures fly by in rapid succession as I stand there looking into my hands. The first picture is the day my aunt told me that my mother died when I was born. The man says to me, "You did the right thing." There are other pictures of my childhood, and things I did as a young man. Whenever I see a picture of something I think is bad, hurtful or not the correct thing to do, he reassures me, "On that day you were a teacher. As a very young person you seem to be aware of adverse situations and how to deal with them the very best way. Your whole life has been that way. Whenever someone did you wrong or deliberately tried to hurt you, you turned the other cheek and held your head up and moved on. You were always there for other people. Now, Dennis, you may cross over."

When I cross over the bridge, my mom grabs me right away and we hug each other and hold each other close for a long time. I feel a little awkward. I am happy to see her, but she is kind of a stranger to me. She says she has waited so long to finally meet me. My Uncle Gaynor is there and says, "I'm glad to see you, Butch. The other people standing here are relatives you knew briefly or never met. Most of them passed on before you were born or when you were a small child." As happy as I am to see family members, my thoughts are with my shipmates. I ask about my shipmates and the *Daniel J. Morrell*. I am told they are at the bottom of

156

the hill that we are standing on. I explain to everyone that I have to see them, and I excuse myself.

I'm not sure I have legs. I'm not sure anybody has legs, but it really doesn't matter. All I have to do is think about where I want to be and somehow I go there. When I arrive at the bottom of the hill, the forward end of the *Morrell* is there and I go on board. Most of my shipmates from the forward end are there to greet me. John Cleary is the first one I see, and he hugs me and I hug him back. We are all rather childlike and totally innocent. It is beautiful! The feeling of love is beyond comprehension. Before long everybody from the forward end of the ship has joined us. Everyone looks much younger, but I can still recognize them. We're all laughing and crying and hugging each other. It's as if I am empty inside, and they are filling me with their love. There is no conversation. Nothing is said about the shipwreck.

As we're standing there, I see the stern, or the rear of the ship, still afloat and coming towards us. It slowly abuts to the bow section, just like the two sections had never been parted. Someone's voice, it sounds like Stu Campbell, says, "Let's go back to the engine room and see the rest of the crew."

We all head back to the stern of the ship and into the engine room. The entire engine crew is in here, even the coal passers. No, I don't think it is the engine room. It looks more like the firehold. They are all just standing around. I guess standing, or whatever it is you do without legs. As soon as we come down the ladder into the firehold, everyone starts yelling and laughing and hugging each other. It is just so beautiful! We talk about where we are and about how happy we are being here. All my thoughts of life on earth are gone. There are no thoughts of my life, my family, my wife or anyone I know on earth. We don't talk about anything other than how much we missed each other and how good it is to be together. They are my family.

I see someone coming down one of the ladders, and it is the third engineer, George Dahl. His feet are probably even with my head when he looks down at me and says, "Dennis, what are you doing here? How did you get here? It's not your time yet. You have to go back."

Just briefly I look at my shipmates and they are all sad. I can see it in their eyes. I don't want to go back, I don't want to go back! I want to stay here with my friends where it feels so good.

All of a sudden I'm being sucked out of the room, back through the cloud and onto the raft. It is like the life raft breathes life into me when I land on it. Immediately I feel this terrible thirst. Looking around on the raft I can't find the lanyard. I lay there for a while just trying to get my wits about me and try to remember what has just happened to me. I look for the lanyard and the flare gun and I still can't locate them. I call out to the man that came to me the first time. I call him "Doc" for some reason. I guess maybe I feel that he administered to me during our first encounter. I call out several times and wait for him to reappear. Thirst overcomes me. I can't wait any longer. Lifting myself up on my left elbow, I grab the collar of my peacoat and start eating the ice once again. At once Doc is here. He is shaking the index finger of his left hand at me. I'm saying to myself, "You have to remember all of this, Denny. Nobody's going to believe you anyhow, but remember all of this."

I'm looking at his hand as he is shaking his finger at me. His fingernails are very rounded and very smooth. His hands are very clean and there aren't any calluses on them. He appears to be ageless, he could be eighty-five years or one hundred eighty-five years old. Whew! I figure nobody is going to believe this, so I'm going to have to remember as much as I can. He's telling me, "Don't eat the ice on your coat. It will lower your body temperature and you'll die." He stops shaking his finger at me and I lay back down.

Almost immediately, ahhhh, I'm on top of a hill. Ahhhh! I think I'm in Virginia. The sun is beating down on me, and I can feel the heat from it. It's just enough to make me break a little sweat. There's a gentle breeze that makes it comfortable. I'm wearing a pair of cutoffs, no shirt and some kind of shoes. I think they are flip-flops. I must be in colonial Virginia. To my right is a big white house, kind of a colonial looking place with really big pillars in front. There are women in front of the house dressed in bonnets and long flowing gowns. The gowns are pink, white and yellow with ribbons on them, something a lady might wear to a cotillion. The men are wearing Confederate uniforms and military caps. Other men have on bowlers or straw hats. Their conversation is about how will the Confederacy survive and live. They talk about people they know that had been killed in the war or friends and children still fighting in the war. Some of their children went to war when they were very young. I'm not concerned in the least about their conversation.

Behind me and over my left shoulder is a big oak tree that has a swing on it with a board to sit on. Children are laughing and playing on it. I'm lowering myself to the ground and sit on my butt with my knees under my chin and look down the hill. I stretch out my legs, lie back and put my head on the grass. The grass is really, really green and warm. Above my head I can see the green leaves from the oak tree. I hear the kids playing around the tree. It's like no one knows I'm here. This feels so good! Ahhhh! The sun is warming me up. I hear insects as they buzz around me and noises coming from the ground. It must be bugs. Oh, God, it's so good to be alive and be here right now!

I'm back, I'm back on the raft, but I can't feel the cold at first. Oh, now the cold is creeping in again. I'm getting tired, too. I'm very tired. There are seagulls above me. I can hear them as they fly above me. What do they have to squawk about? I'm wondering, wow, have I something to worry about here? I'm kind of laughing. I'm wondering if the seagulls are going to come down and scavenge on me once I'm gone?

When is the Coast Guard going to pick me up? When are they going to find me? How much longer can I wait? Do they know the *Morrell* is missing? How I wish I knew the answers to these questions! I wonder what kind of shape I will be in when they find me, and what will the long-term effects be on me? Ahhh...I'm cold now. I'm very cold. Whew! So cold. What happened to God? He must not be listening to my prayers. Why does he want me to suffer before I die?

Once again my thoughts return to my life before the shipwreck. I can't help but wonder if there's something in my past that caused God to punish me this way.

Morrell voyage- Steve Witucki

Chapter 11

I was around the age of seventeen when I made up my mind to go back to Ashtabula, so I bought a ticket on a Greyhound and headed east. Elvis was very popular at this time with his big hit, "Blue Suede Shoes." Everyone wanted to be like Elvis, except for me. I just felt the need to be around some family.

When I arrived in Ashtabula I went right to the YMCA and rented a sleeping room. It just didn't seem right to go to my father's house. I was uncertain what type of reception I would get or if I would even be welcome. The following evening I called Dad at home and we talked for a while. I thought I could hear and feel some anger and hostility towards me in his words, but we did talk. He invited me to dinner the following evening and said he would pick me up after he finished work. As we drove to the farm together there wasn't much conversation between us. He never even asked me where I'd been, what I had been doing or how I made it on my own. When we got to the farm everyone was happy to see me. We had a nice dinner and made idle conversation afterwards. After a period of time Dad drove me back to the YMCA. It was after this encounter that I decided to join the Army.

I took basic training at Fort Knox, Kentucky, and afterwards I was sent to Fort Gordon, Georgia, and trained to become a military policeman. Once I finished my training, I was sent to Troyes Fontaine Ammunition Depot in Bar Le Duc, France. I was then assigned to a security unit at the depot. I enjoyed France very much. The things I liked best were the food, of course, the wine, the cheese and the farming people. They were so laid back. What kind, sweet people they were. I learned to speak a little French and that enabled me to hold some primitive conversation with them. However, most of the French people did speak broken English. I very much enjoyed traveling and did quite a bit of it while I was in France.

Hale in France

I was at a dance one night in Bar Le Duc when I met this beautiful young lady. She and her family had moved to France from Russia. She lived in a small town with her mother. As things turned out, I spent three days and nights with her, absent without leave from the Army. I was court-martialed and spent thirty days in the stockade, but as luck would have it, once each week she would bring me a quart jar of canned cherries. These were not ordinary cherries. In France they called this type of cherry concoction "Kirsch." The juice that covered the cherries was made from distilled cherry seeds and it was about 180 proof. In the evening my cellmate and I would eat the cherries and drink the juice and all of us would get a good buzz going. It didn't take much. Apparently the guards were not aware of what she was giving me or they would have never let me have it. The thirty days went by fast.

I thought I was really in love with this young lady. She seemed to do everything just right. After I was released from the stockade we started seeing each other again. Man, she was very pretty! Her name was Eliane Schmidt.

Dennis and sister Jean

I had many different experiences in France and the other countries I visited. Most of the experiences were good, but of course there's got to be one or two bad ones. The best ones were of a spiritual nature. Then there are the ones I really don't want to think about.

In 1959 I had served my two years in the military and was discharged. I returned to Ashtabula and moved back into the YMCA. I wasn't really certain which direction my life was going to take me. Perhaps it was time to reflect. All of my life it was as though I was on the run, going someplace or no place in particular. Maybe now it was time for me to settle down and plant roots.

I went back to work at Pete's Grille in Geneva-on-the-Lake. I needed something to hold me over until I could find a real job. As soon as the season ended at Geneva-on-the-Lake I was offered a job at the Hotel Ashtabula. Some friends of mine talked to Chef Benny Vacca about taking

164

me on as second cook. I really did know how to cook. It was at a very early age that I decided this was one life skill I was going to have to learn if I wanted to survive through life. Chef Vacca did hire me as second cook. It was a good job and seemed to be the right fit for me.

While working at the hotel I met a woman named Bertha that I had dated a few times earlier that year. She was divorced and had two small children. Soon we started talking about seeing each other again and then we started dating. I was looking for more responsibility in life, hoping that it would help settle me down. I also needed a family and some type of home life. I could see where all of this was possible with her. A few months after we started seeing each other, we were married and started sharing our life together.

It was great for a while and then I started getting bored, or was there more responsibility than I was ready for? My wife was pregnant and prone to mood swings all of the time. I didn't know that women went through mood swings when they were pregnant, and I took all of her complaints personal. I thought she was striking out at me without reason. It seemed like I was going through the same situations I went through all of my life. It was a very complex time of my life and I started to become restless once again.

As soon as my daughter Cindy was born, things somewhat got back to being normal. With the loss of my wife's income, she had to stay home with the baby, our finances became really tight. With me working a split shift at the Hotel Ashtabula it was impossible for me to find a part-time job to help bring in more income. Of course, lack of money made our marriage more complicated as well. When things were good they were really good, and when things were bad they were really bad. Often, when things were bad, I would do things to make them even worse. I would become very contrary and argumentative and spend time away from home, mostly out of desperation and anger. I really wanted a good strong family life and the chance of this seemed to be slipping away. I blamed myself for most of the problems we were having. I had a very low self-esteem and sometimes I felt really useless and unneeded. Because of the way I felt I started running around on my wife. I wanted to be around people that had a better opinion of me than I had of myself. I wanted to be around people that enjoyed my company and didn't complain to me all the time.

I started hanging around with my old buddy Norm Balcomb. Norm was someone I ran around with while going to the Saybrook school. We would spend our free time hanging around West 32nd. Street in Ashtabula. At that time it was a pretty rundown area with a few scroungie bars within a one-block area. You could always find us in a bar called Molly's Lounge. Molly's, by today's standards, would have been considered a biker bar. It was always rough and tumble and there had been a few shootings and stabbings that took place there.

Norm and I would sit around and have a few rounds of beer and talk to some of the ladies and a few old friends as they came in. Norm was a little hot headed, but we were not out looking for trouble or to make problems for anyone. We just wanted to get away from home for awhile.

Needless to say, this always caused problems for my wife and me.

After three years of marriage we had our second daughter, Kathy. That made a grand total of four children in the house. Financially we were making it, but things were always really tight. I can remember one Christmas all I wanted was a Chapstick for my chapped lips. I promised myself that this would be the last Christmas we would have to live like this.

I had a chance to get into the painter's union and do some steeplejack work. Steeplejacks are men that paint in areas high above the ground. I thought this was a good opportunity for me to make some really good money. Being in the painter's union would assure me of other painting jobs in the future, so I quit my job at the Hotel Ashtabula.

A new bridge was being built across the Ashtabula Gulf. Actually it was two bridges, two lanes going north and two lanes going south. It was about ninety feet from the bridge to the ground below. As painters we would have to walk out on twelve-inch steel I-beams to our work areas. We would paint the bottom of the I-beam, the inside and the top of the beam. To paint the bottom of the beam, I would have to hook the heel of my left foot over the top flange of the opposing side of the beam (left side) while holding onto the same opposing side with my left hand. My right knee would be resting on the top of the inside flange on the right side. Then I could lean over and look at the bottom of the beam and paint it. When finished in one spot I would have to move backwards towards land, painting as I went. The bad part about all of this is I was painting above a river and if I looked down at the river, I would get the sensation of movement. That would make me a little dizzy, and with no safety equipment that also made it quite dangerous. Thank God that job didn't last very long! Soon I was on the street looking for work again. The more experienced painters were also looking for work. With all the experience they had I knew I would have a hard time finding a job.

After a long period of unemployment I finally landed a job as a head chef at Mark Little's Restaurant and Lounge. The restaurant was located on Route 20 in the Saybrook Plaza in Saybrook. The owners, Mark Little and his wife, lived almost right across the street from the plaza. They were an older couple, perhaps in their late 50s or early 60s. During working hours they were always at the restaurant.

We had a pretty good lunch crowd and the dinner crowd was great on the weekends. I enjoyed preparing meals and always tried to give them a good selection of food. I also had lunch and dinner specials. My second cook was an older Polish woman that had been cooking for many years. She was a great asset to me.

I thought Mark needed a lot more business than he was getting. There were weeks I didn't know how he made payroll. The liquor part of the business was probably what kept them alive, but just barely. As hard as Mark and his wife worked it was sad to see the business at a standstill. Not very long after I started working for them his wife died. I didn't continue working for him after that. I could see my job at Mark's wasn't going to last very long anyhow. The business just wasn't there.

168

I started thinking about sailing on the Great Lakes and I wondered if I could get a job as a cook on one of the boats. I knew that if I had a job like that, it would be my last great adventure. I understood that the pay was really good, too. I didn't think about sailing very often because I had to have a job now, I had to go to work immediately.

I found another job in Geneva, Ohio at the Townhouse Restaurant. I was working for a man named Bill Banks. Again I was head chef. Bill and his wife had a very nice business and I enjoyed working for them very much.

One night, after I finished work, I was driving home to Ashtabula by way of Route 20. As I approached the Saybrook Plaza I could see flashing lights just beyond the plaza. As I grew closer to the police car's flashing lights, I could see that Mark Little's house was on fire. I pulled my car onto the side of the road and got out. I wanted to see if there was something I could do to help. As I walked across Route 20, it was then that I saw Mark sitting on the curb of the road. Some of his clothing was burned or charred and he smelled of smoke and burned skin. When I asked him if he was all right all he could do was mumble to me that he tried to put out the fire. If my memory serves me well, Mark had fallen asleep with a cigarette in his hand. I stayed with Mark until the ambulance arrived and took him to the hospital. Several days later Mark passed away. For the longest time after his death, every time I went past the Saybrook Plaza, I would think of him and his struggle to find peace and happiness in the world.

In the fall I talked to my wife about me going sailing on the Great Lakes. We both agreed that perhaps it would be best for us and the children. Recalling the saying "absence makes the heart grow fonder", I was hoping that being away from home would put me on a different path in life. Hoping that maybe in some way this would bring us closer together, even though we were far apart. I didn't want to hurt her anymore.

In the fall of 1964 I decided to go to Cleveland to the Coast Guard station and find out what I had to do to go sailing on the Great Lakes. I was told that I would need a letter from one of the shipping companies located in the Terminal Tower Building on Public Square in downtown Cleveland. I went to the Bethlehem Steel office where I was given a letter promising me a job once I was cleared through the Coast Guard. I was also told that I would have to have passport photos taken and where I could go to get them. I did all of this in one day.

After turning the required paperwork into the Coast Guard, I was told that they would be sending me my sailing papers through the mail. All winter long I was anxious and couldn't wait until spring to get my sailing papers. Once they finally came I still had to wait for a phone call from Bethlehem Steel telling me where to go to catch a boat. My sailing certificate said I could be a coal passer, deckhand, a porter or in the galley. The galley is where I wanted to be.

At last it happened! I was told to go to Erie, Pennsylvania, and fit out the *Daniel J. Morrell*. I was given an address and a date and time to report. Due to a slowdown in steel production for the last several years, the *Morrell* had lain idle in Erie Bay. I could recall seeing her in the bay several times when I was in Erie prior to crewing her. She was towed in and docked at the foot of Cherry Street when I climbed aboard her. She was waiting for the crew to fit out so she could sail. Once I climbed aboard I found out that I knew some of the crew from Ashtabula. Vince Grippi's uncle, Sam, was going to work in the engine room as a coal passer. Vince and I went to school together. Just like me, this was Sam's first time on an ore freighter. The chief engineer was Joe Perrine. His son was in the same class as my half sister. "This is just like family.... I'll stay aboard and give it a try!"

Chapter 12

I think I'm better off talking to the seagulls. God doesn't seem to be listening to me today. "Hey, why don't you guys fly off and get me some help, bring somebody back?"

What's that noise I hear? Is that the seagulls? No, they are gone. Damn, it's a helicopter! Are my eyes deceiving me? Is my eyesight starting to go perhaps? Yes, it's a helicopter and they are right above me! I can feel my eyes well up as tears run down my cheeks. I will wave to them and let them know I'm here and still alive. I hope they see me wave. Yes, they're landing the helicopter in the water close to the beach. God was listening to me! Two of the Coast Guardsmen are getting out of the helicopter and walking towards me. I can see their feet in the water. Hurry, I don't want to die now that I'm so close to being saved! They're picking me up and laying me on my back on top of one of my shipmate's bodies. I look at them and say, "I love you guys. I love you guys! What took you so long?"

One of them says, "We thought the wind was blowing your arm

Dennis is rescued by the Coast Guard.
Port Huron Times photo by Ralph Polovich

around. We didn't expect to find anyone alive."

I'm being asked if I have any injuries and if I'm all right. I tell them I think I have some broken ribs. This is not true, I just don't want to explain to them about all the pain in my armpit and knee from the steel bar I was lying on. All I want is to get on that helicopter! Another Coast Guardsman gets out of the helicopter and walks over to where we are. Then the three of them pick me up and carry me over to the helicopter and lay me inside on the deck. Soon we are in the air. Immediately, as the helicopter lifts off from my point of recovery, a Coast Guardsman is there attending to me and making sure I am all right.

Liferaft location offshore

Lying there, I look up and see a Thermos on one of the bulkheads. I ask him if I can have a drink from the Thermos. I just knew it contained some good warm coffee and I was so damn cold. He responded with,

"No, we are not permitted to give you anything until we get you to the hospital."

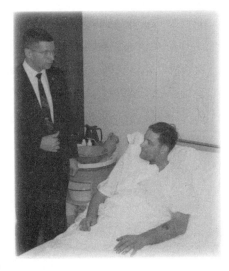

Dr. Oakes and Dennis

The flight might have last all of five minutes. The helicopter lands on one of the docks at Harbor Beach, Michigan. It was then that I notice what a dark gloomy day it is. Everything around me looks black or white or gray. An ambulance from Ramsey's Funeral Home is waiting to take me to the Harbor Beach Hospital. A small crowd has gathered on the dock to watch them put me in the ambulance. As they are taking me out of the helicopter, I am a little embarrassed, because I don't have clothing on. Before long I am on my way to the hospital. The doctors and nurses are waiting for me when I arrive in the emergency room. Attending to me is Dr. Robert Oakes and Dr. Robert Oakes, Jr., better known as Dr. Bob. The first thing he asks me is about my broken ribs. "I have no broken ribs," I say, and explain to them about the pain in my armpit and my knee. Nothing more is said about my ribs. Before they cut my clothes off of me, they ask me many questions about how I feel. They want to know if I have any pain or numbness and where the numbness is located. "No, I have no pain. Yes, I have places that are numb and places where I have no feeling and my left hand doesn't seem to want to work," I tell them. I'm very surprised to find out that I have a cut under my chin that requires stitches

174

and that I also have skin torn from two fingers on my left hand. They want to know which church I am affiliated with and what denomination.

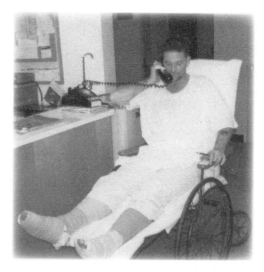

Dennis at Harbor Beach

Once they have my peacoat and life jacket off of me, they slip me out of my shorts and cover me with a sheet and blanket. They continue to work on me, stitching up my chin and bandaging my fingers. I believe these injuries occurred while I was sitting on the raft, while still on the boat. I was tightly holding onto that steel bar I was sitting on, with both hands around it. When we were swept overboard, I must have been holding too tight and it just pulled the skin off of my two fingers. My chin was cut from maybe hitting some of the rigging or perhaps my knee hit my chin. I really don't know.

Ace bandages are wrapped around both of my feet and my legs. Dr. Oakes then explains to me that I have one small broken frostbite blister on my left foot between my big toe and my second toe. While the doctors are still attending to me, I see the Huron County Sheriff and I called him over to where I am lying. His name is Robert Swackhammer. I ask him to call my wife in Ashtabula and let her know I am alright. He says that he will do that. I then give him my phone number. As he turns to leave and maybe takes a couple steps, I call him back and give him my area code.

Meanwhile, the doctors are talking amongst themselves as they continue to work on me. Soon they have me in a hospital bed, wrapped in several blankets.

(At a later date, Head Nurse Ruth Winterhalter told me that when they brought me in my color was blue and they put anything that would hold warm water in bed with me to help warm me up. I don't remember any of this. I understand after talking to Dr. Oakes, Jr. many years later that my body temperature was between ninety-two and ninety-four

degrees. He had called the Henry Ford Hospital near Detroit and talked to them about my condition. Harbor Beach Hospital was only a twenty-eight bed hospital at that time, and they never had a case of cold water survival until mine. The Henry Ford Hospital instructed them to warm me up very slowly and to be very cognizant of blood

Fr. McEachin

clots. Dr. Bob asked them at what temperature my heart would stop. Whoever he talked to told him that my heart would stop between ninety-four and ninety-five degrees. Dr. Bob informed them that my body temperature was down below that and I was still talking.)

I am Catholic, so after they have me settled in bed, I am visited by Father Cornelius McEachin. He is the pastor for the Harbor Beach area

176

parish. We talk for a short while and then he does something that really surprises me. He gives me the last rites of the church. I believe this really put death in the right perspective for me. Maybe I'm not out of the woods yet. I had thought that death was behind me now. I figured that now that they had found me I was safe and death was not even an option. I'm so concerned about having the last rites that I have confession several times that night before sleep finally finds me.

The nurses awaken me several times during the night so they can check my vitals. They wake me again early in the morning so I can prepare for the day. I have no pain at all, anywhere. I have numbness or no feeling at all in different parts of my body. Other places I can feel pressure, but I can't tell if it is a sharp object or someone just pushing on my skin.

After sleeping all night I still feel very tired and weary. I didn't

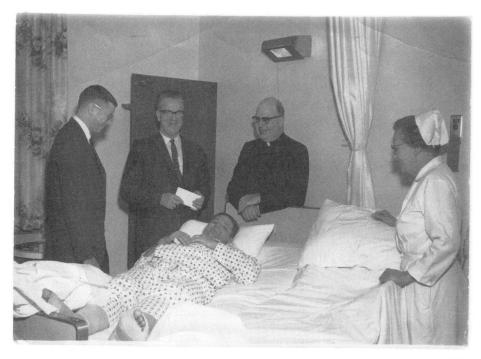

get much sleep on the raft, so I'm not really concerned about being tired. Sooner or later I will get all caught up on my sleep.

Doctor Oakes, Sr. is the first one to visit me in the morning. My very first question to Dr. Oaks is, "Have they found any more survivors?"

He replied with, "I haven't received any word of this yet today."

He proceeds to check my vitals then he unwraps my legs and takes a look at them very closely. Then he rewraps them and says nothing about their condition to me. With no pain I just assume they are fine. It also makes sense to me that by wrapping them, the doctor may be trying to eliminate that swelling feeling that I get when I put my legs over the edge of the bed. I am certain I am getting the best treatment money could pay for.

Doctor Oaks asks, "Do you feel ill or uncomfortable, or is anything hurting you?" I reply, "No, with one exception. I have a problem with my left hand. It is a little numb in some areas and no feeling in other areas. I have no strength and my whole hand is very difficult to move."

"Laying on that raft with your armpit on a steel bar caused some nerve damage," he explains to me. He then moistens a washcloth

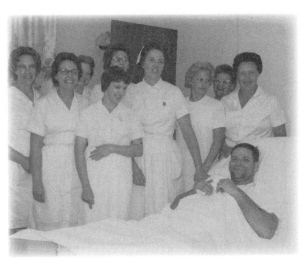

Dennis and his nursing staff

178

and tells me, "Squeeze this as hard as you can periodically. It will increase the circulation and help to strengthen your hand."

I feel starved to death and want so desperately to eat. I have been warned by Dr. Oakes that I would have difficulty eating for some time due to the exposure. While on the raft all I could think about was a glass of orange juice or a cup of hot consommé. I think that while asleep on the raft I had dreams about a glass of orange juice or a cup of hot consommé, even though I never liked consommé. I would go hungry rather than have a cup of it. I asked Dr. Oaks to at least let me have a glass of orange juice. He agrees to this.

When the nurse brings it to me I take a drink, but I can't keep it down. I can't even get it down. What a strange feeling that is! It's like I don't know how to swallow. By the following day I can drink the juice as long as I drink it very slowly. I later found out that Karo syrup had been added to my orange juice. It is supposed to strengthen me and help me recover from exposure quicker.

While I am trying to drink the juice, I consider it breakfast, one of the nurses comes in and brings in several newspapers for me to look at. She says that the sinking of the *Daniel J. Morrell* is on the front cover of all the newspapers. She also says it was on the television morning news programs as well. I don't know why, but I am overwhelmed. In all of the articles the emphasis seems to be on the only survivor. No one else had been picked up so far. At this time I don't feel I have done anything special other than to survive adverse conditions. I also feel that the attention should be on the people that haven't been recovered yet. All of this attention is exciting, but it is also a little depressing. I ask the nurse if any other survivors had been picked up. I keep hoping and waiting to hear some news about other survivors. I made it through the cold and the storm. I know there must be others out there just waiting to be picked up.

Soon the nurse is at my door again and I am given a bath. It feels really refreshing. A half hour to forty-five minutes later I notice how profusely I am sweating in different areas of my body. I can wipe the sweat off of my feet with the bed sheet, watch the sweat form on them again and then roll down my feet to the bed. At the most, it takes only about a minute to a minute and a half for this process to repeat itself. I have to admit, it is pretty interesting to watch. Other areas of my body the nurses have to wipe down because I am sweating so profusely.

My hands and fingers are still numb and I can't manipulate them very well. It is almost useless to try to use them for most tasks. However, I am squeezing the wet washcloth several times daily and I can see some improvement in my hands. Every day more feeling returns, and I use them a little better as each hour passes.

After my bath, I'm told I have company. Some people are here to see me. I am hoping it is my wife and some of my family. As it turns out, it is Mr. Dobson from Bethlehem Steel Co. and two officers from the Coast Guard. They are here to question me about the sinking of the *Morrell*. After we have our introductions, one of the Coast Guardsmen asks me if I had taken my sailing papers with me before I got off the boat. I ask him,

"Do you know what I was wearing when they found me?"

He says, "Yes, I am aware."

"Then where do you think I shoved them?" is my response. I am almost angered by his question, but I am alive and in love with everyone I talk to. My anger is short-lived and then we move on to the sinking of the *Morrell*. We talk for least an hour and a half. They want to know everything about the sinking and the weather conditions at the time. I have to tell them about being on the raft and the order in which my shipmates had died. I tell them of everything I saw and all of the conversation that I could remember. I answer all of the questions they ask of me. I am glad to see them leave, for I am growing tired of their questions. It is like reliving everything all over again.

Head Nurse Winterhalter spends quite a bit of time with me, more so than the other nurses. She is a tough nurse. She can find conjecture in almost everything I say. I tell her, with pride, how I was very conscious about my body heat and didn't urinate for over twenty-four hours because I didn't want to lose any body heat. Without blinking an eye or even looking at me she said, "And just what would you have done if it would have frozen?"

I just can't win with her. I do have to laugh at her comment. The entire nursing staff takes very, very good care of me. Later that day Nurse Winterhalter comes into my room again and we talk for a while. I ask her several times if they have located any more of my shipmates. Finally she looks at me and says, "I don't think they'll be finding any more of your shipmates alive, it's been too long." Silently I am thinking she is wrong. It was too long for me, but I still made it!

The first day in the hospital things are going very well, but by evening things are starting to change. The first thing to change is a phone call from the Joe Pine television show in Los Angeles, California. He wants to interview me live on the phone for his show. The doctors and nursing staff advise me not to take the phone call. They feel that he may be insensitive towards the ordeal that I just went through. I am surprised that California even knows about my ordeal. It is then that I find out the news media is trying to see me. I'm told about a female newspaper reporter that vowed she would interview me even if she had to break into the hospital to do so. I have a really hard time trying to understand why the news media is after me, and I am almost frightened of them. I did not make a personal effort to accomplish the impossible. I was a victim of circumstance, and I made the best of a bad situation. My faith in God and good luck brought me through it. To hide me from the media, the hospital staff puts me in the maternity ward.

The following morning Father McEachin comes in to visit with me. It is at this meeting that I confide in him about the things that I saw while on the raft. I am so filled with love and happiness. The happiness that I feel just bubbles out from me for all to see. I thought for sure people could see it. After telling him, he looks at me and says, "Oh, Dennis, I don't think you should talk about that."

I don't let him see how really crushed I am by his statement.

Something very beautiful has happened to me and the first person I share it with told me not to talk about it. I feel misunderstood and I have to wonder if maybe he feels I am deranged. After he leaves I decide not to talk about any of the things I saw or anywhere I was taken to. I vowed to be silent the remainder of my life. (All of my life a day hasn't passed that my thoughts don't return to the raft and everything that happened to me and the things I saw. I ask myself, over and over, if everything I saw was a delusion or a folly of the mind. The decision I made is on my mind for many years afterward and I'm always very careful about what I say around people. However, I feel by not talking about it, I am depriving people of something very special and beautiful that I'm certain happened to me, without any doubt.)

Lunchtime! I can hardly wait to eat. My experience the first time with orange juice was on my mind and I told myself to eat very slowly. I was absolutely ravenous. They serve me a soft diet, but that's okay, it's food. I'm eating slowly because I don't want to get sick again. Lunch, as meager as it is, seems to satisfy my appetite. However, I can't wait for dinner.

I am informed I will have to meet with the news media at some point today. They tell me that there are a couple dozen newspapers waiting to interview me as well as TV cameramen. That's really frightening to me because I don't know why they are here. I am not an outgoing person. I just want to be left alone.

Before the news media interview, my family arrives. I am

surprised that they arrived so soon. It's my wife, my stepmother and my half-brother Louie. After we share tears of happiness and talk about my health, I ask them how they got here so soon. They weave me a story about leaving home and driving in a bad snowstorm. They were almost to Cleveland when my other brother caught up to them in his car and said that an attorney had phoned the house and wanted to fly them to Michigan. Tickets would be waiting at Cleveland Hopkins Airport, and that was how they arrived so soon.

The interview with the news media is really scary. I'm not real certain when they arrived at the hospital. I am told that some of the reporters have been waiting since the night before. It is late afternoon or early evening before I speak with them. After talking with Father McEachin, I'm afraid I will say something wrong. I don't want people to think I am crazy or deranged. Too soon I am taken, lying in my bed, into a hallway which is loaded with newspaper reporters and TV cameras. As soon as I see them I become very frightened. I didn't expect to see that many. I'm unaware how long the interview lasts. They ask me every question they can think of, even some I can't answer and some that are heart wrenching and too difficult to answer.

The questions go on and on about the weather conditions, why wasn't there an SOS given and how did I make it through such adverse conditions. They also ask me about my injuries and my health. They want to know what happened to the rest of my shipmates, the ones that didn't make it to the raft, and did I see anyone else in the water. I am even asked

184

the sequence in which they died and if I knew what caused their deaths. Did we have any conversation and what was it about? I soon become disenchanted with their loss of respect and the lack of empathy. I ask to be taken back to my room.

Upon returning to my room, I have dinner. It is some solid food and some liquid. I have hot beef consommé, a chicken sandwich with lettuce and mayonnaise, and of course, some Jell-O. I'll never forget this meal.

Somehow answering the questions for the news media stirs something within me and once alone in my room I weep for my shipmates and pray that they are safe and they will be found alive. I am certain that some of them are still alive! Oh, how I want Sam Grippi, my best friend from Ashtabula, to be alive. I have a very difficult time sleeping throughout the night because my mind just won't leave me alone. I have too many questions that I don't know the answers to.

By morning I've resigned myself to there not being any other survivors. In my own mind, I know that I could have made it a little longer on the raft, but not very much longer. I think that now I should deal with the reality of the ordeal and not keep hoping and praying that more of my shipmates would have survived, only to be disappointed and heartbroken when I find out there are no others.

It is a very difficult day for me. I keep wondering why me... why me? Often I start weeping and I wonder why. I spend a large part of the day in prayer. I don't know why, but I can't pray for myself anymore. I think many years will go by before I can talk to God and ask for something for me. Today I am praying for my shipmates and their families. I thank God for sparing my life and ask Him what He has next for me. I guess he must have a plan for me or I wouldn't be alive today.

It is difficult for me to talk to Bertha about the spiritual experiences that I had on the raft. Faith was never an important thing to her. We had talked about her beliefs long before the shipwreck happened. Telling her about everything that happened to me would be like pouring water into a bucket with a hole in it.

My injuries don't seem to bother me too much. Everything is basically pain free except that I do have a cramp in the arch of my left foot that doesn't want to stop. That is the foot with the frostbite. I find that, while in bed, if I pull my foot close to my groin the pain will diminish. The only other discomfort I have is when I put my feet and legs over the edge of the bed. I can feel the blood rushing to enter them and they feel like they are going to swell up and pop like a balloon. That does take a little getting used to. My armpit and just above my knee are a little sore, nothing that really bothers me. There is an indentation on my left leg just above the knee from laying on the steel bar. To the best of my knowledge there are no marks or indentations in the area of my armpit.

There is one thing that does bother me that I wish I could be spared from. Every time a body is recovered I hear about it. I know that the people relating this to me mean well because they know I am concerned about my shipmates. The news on the television and in the newspapers give the gruesome details of how the bodies were found and in some cases, the condition of the bodies. It is impossible to keep these impressions off of my mind.

Later in the day I find myself in a wheelchair running the halls of the hospital. In the lobby, strangers are coming up to me and talking and wishing me well. I meet one couple, she had come in to have their baby, and they say if the baby is a boy they will name it after me. I feel so proud and honored that they would even consider my name.

The following day after the news media interviews, Louis and Chick return to Ashtabula. Bertha is staying with some people by the name of Nichols from Harbor Beach. They own a restaurant in

Bertha and Dennis

town, and my wife is content staying with them and they watch over her. They come to the hospital with her every now and then when she visits me. By this time I can eat and they bring me some of my favorite foods and ask what they can bring the next day. I think they are very nice people and I can't thank them enough for taking care of Bertha and giving me special attention.

When my wife and I find time alone I tell her that I am a changed man and that our life together will be much better. I explain to her how much stronger my faith in God is and that I know God will take care of us. I will try my best to be a better husband.

After about five days it is determined that I'm well enough to go home. Well, not really home, but to the Ashtabula General Hospital. Needless to say I'm very pleased to hear about this. They tell me that the Ramsey Funeral Home will be driving me there in one of their ambulances, and my wife could accompany me. I am hoping it will be a nice long trip back to Ashtabula. We leave Harbor Beach at about seven-thirty in the morning.

As we drive south on Michigan Route 25, I was looking out of the window at Lake Huron and a foreboding fear begins to rise in me. I really don't want to look at the lake, but it seems as though I'm compelled to stare. As I look out over that dark cloudy lake it appears to be looking back at me. I can almost hear the lake talking to me and telling me that it missed me this time... but there will be another time.

Soon we are on Interstate 75 heading south and I can no longer see the lake. Several different times this morning, people drive up next to the ambulance, look in and wave to us or toot their car's horn. That really makes me feel good and it brings a smile to my face. At noontime Mr. Ramsey pulls off the freeway at a rest area restaurant and asks us what we want to eat. He goes inside and comes back out with a large load of food. We have a nice lunch and good conversation before we get back on the freeway.

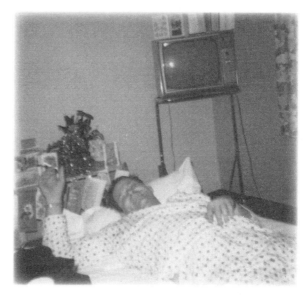

Dennis at Ashtabula

I can hardly wait to see my children again. They came to my mind so often while lying on that raft. I feel really bad that I hadn't spent more time with them as they were growing up. I know I have been a bad father, but then again, I had no role model to learn from. Before I was rescued I would pray for my children and wonder what they would do without me. I would remember the good fun times we had together.

We arrive in Ashtabula late in the afternoon. I am taken to a private room and removed from the gurney and put in bed. As soon as I get comfortable in bed the phone rings. It was my buddy Harvey Hayes calling from Erie, Pennsylvania. He tells me how happy he is to hear that I made it, and he knew that if anyone could make it, it would be me. When I ask him how he knew, he says he just knew. He tells me that within the next few days he will be up to see me.

Over the next several days it's like everybody I ever knew stops in to see me and wish me well. I also receive a call from another sailing buddy, Jack Lamb. I met Jack the first year I sailed. He was a wheelsman on the *Morrell* and we hit it off from the first day. He was a little crazy just like me. He said that he told his wife that if anyone could make it, it would be me. When I ask him how he knew that, he says, "There's just something about you." (I still wonder to this day what my friends saw in me to make them think I would make it.)

After being rescued off of the raft, my faith in God continues to grow. I know what is going to happen to me once I pass away, and I am no longer afraid of death. Every day I pray to God and thank Him for saving my life and ask Him to take good care of my shipmates and to tell them that they will always be in my prayers. Time will pass quickly and we will be together again.

My doctor in Ashtabula was Harman Tidd. He has been our family doctor for a number of years. When I arrive in Ashtabula I am still wearing Ace bandages around my legs and he continues to have me wear them. After being back for three or four days Dr. Tidd informs me that he doesn't think that gangrene is going to be a problem. Gangrene! I never gave gangrene a thought, but I did start worrying about it after he mentioned it. From what he tells me, frostbite starts out with a blister and then the blister breaks. Gangrene is the next stage. (I'm sure there's more to this process but this is a simple explanation of what was explained to me.)

After the scare about gangrene, Dr. Tidd starts sending me to therapy and whirlpool treatments. He explains to me that I have capillary vein problems that results in poor circulation and some nerve damage.

190

Some of the small veins have closed down and blood isn't reaching the nerves. I really like the whirlpool treatments and I'm certain they must be helping. Every now and then I can feel a little pop and a small pinprick in my feet, lasting for maybe one or two seconds. (The popping and pinpricking has lasted periodically for many years, at least until I was in my 40s.)

Shortly after arriving at the hospital I am informed that the Coast Guard will soon have a board of inquiry into the sinking of the *Daniel J. Morrell*. It is to be held at the hospital so that I can testify. I feel a little uneasy about this because I don't know what they want from me. (I didn't know at this time that this is a normal procedure.) There is a crazy rumor going around that I am responsible for the *Morrell* sinking.

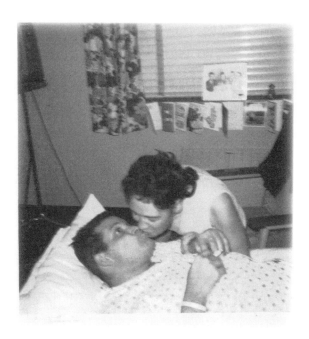

Chapter 13

When the day finally arrives for the inquiry, I am surprised at the amount of people that are in attendance for the hearing. Of course the Coast Guard is here as well as representatives of the National Transportation Safety Board and attorneys representing families of loved ones that perished in the shipwreck. My attorney is here along with members of the press from a variety of newspapers. My wife is also present.

It takes a little while for everyone to introduce themselves and tell who they are representing, but before too long we get down to the sinking of the *Morrell*. The Coast Guard has a dictionary full of questions for me as do some of the attorneys representing other victims. We talk about the time frame of the sinking as well as any conversation that took place before we went into the water. Diagrams are drawn showing the positioning of the raft on the boat and they want to know where people were seated or standing on or around the raft. Other diagrams are also drawn, one showing the two sections after they broke apart and what I saw from my vantage point on the raft before it went into the water. Then

192

there's another on the raft while it was in the water. One of their many questions is how long it took from the time the general alarm sounded until I found myself in the water. It is then determined that it only took eight minutes.

I have to explain to them some of the conversation we had before we found ourselves in the water, and how we were told that no SOS was given because they didn't have time to send it when the ship broke apart so fast. The Captain and First Mate had told everyone that there were other ships in the area and if we fired off our flares properly our rescue would be imminent. I also tell them about it being difficult for me to hear most of the conversation because of the wind and the noise around me. They basically ask, and I answer, all questions that they feel are relevant to the sinking of the *Morrell*. I too inject subject matter pertaining to the sinking that they don't think to ask. The board of inquiry lasts for approximately a day and a half. I am really relieved when they complete their investigation and the questions stop. Now, my only hope is that they will come up with a reason for the sinking.

Around the same time that the hearing was going on, I start hearing stories about the storm that the *Morrell* was in. Captain Connelly was the master of the *Townsend* and Captain Crawley was the master of the *Morrell*. At five minutes after midnight, Captain Connelly called Captain Crawley and reported that the *Townsend* was blown off course, almost broaching and falling off twenty-two degrees before she could be brought around with full left rudder and the engine full ahead. Captain Connelly reported the winds at sixty-five miles an hour with tremendous seas.

Other vessels were having their own problems that night. The *S.S. Benson Ford* was down bound and reported whole gale winds north by northeast at sixty knots and seas ranging twenty-five feet. She was also taking water over the stern. The *S.S. Kinsman Independent* was up bound on Lake Huron and estimated the waves at twenty-eight feet with winds at fifty-five knots. She was blown around and caught in a trough for four minutes. A Canadian steamer, *Howard Shaw,* was blown around and the *S.S Fred A. Mansky* reported they were almost blown around several times. The master of the *Henry Steinbrenner* turned to flee. It took eight terrifying minutes to get her out of the trough.

It was one hell of a storm that night, and how I survived it I will never know, but I am certain that God was watching over me.

Sam Grippi's body has not been recovered yet and it is mid December. I suppose I purposely avoid calling his wife only because I want his body to be recovered before I speak with her. I know his loss will be very difficult for her because they cared and relied on each other, plus Sarah has a bad case of sugar diabetes that has caused her many problems.

Much to my surprise Sarah and her sister come to visit me in the hospital. Sarah's sister came from New York to stay with her when she found out about the sinking. It makes me feel good to know that someone is staying with her. She talks about Sam and how lonely she will be without him. We talk about the night of the sinking and she wants to know when the last time was that I saw Sam. I explain to her that Sam worked in the stern of the ship in the engine room, and that night I only saw one person, Don Worchester, as I looked towards the rear. I can see she is starting to get upset. She wants to know where Sam is and why they haven't found his body yet. She's sobbing and crying as she and her sister leave me. Sam is constantly on my mind for the rest of the day.

Within several days I find out that Sam's body is finally recovered. It was located on the Canadian side of Lake Huron, north of Goderich and just south of Kincardine, Ontario. His brother had to identify his body was when it was returned to Ashtabula. The water and the elements had taken a toll on his body. Still, I want to go to the funeral. I let everyone know that I am going to go. Dr. Tidd thinks it will be detrimental to my recovery if I attend. He won't let me go, so I have another bad day.

Dr. Tidd lets me go home for Christmas Eve and Christmas Day. It feels good to be at 536 West 36th Street in Ashtabula. It wasn't very long ago that I thought I'd never see this place again and I have a new appreciation for it. We open gifts and have a nice dinner. Much too soon it is time for me to return to the hospital.

Upon returning to the hospital I start to walk again with the aid of a walker. I have to be careful because whenever I put my legs or feet over the edge of the bed or stand on them, they feel like they are swelling and going to pop. This doesn't make my legs or feet hurt, but it does make them very uncomfortable. Dr. Tidd says that in time I will get used to that feeling and will no longer notice it. He is hopeful that all feeling will return in time. I just have to be patient.

I get discharged from the hospital around January 6th. I have no feeling in my feet and different parts of my lower legs. Even after the discharge, I notice I am starting to have another slight problem. My toes are now turning downward. Dr. Tidd calls it hammer toes. While still in the hospital he had me pull my toes out straight with my fingers and stretch them. He said to do this as often as I could. Now that I am home I find that I can only do this once or twice a day and some days not at all. The only time I really think about my toes is when they hurt, and being numb, that is very rare.

One afternoon, it is still winter, my family and I go for a ride in the car. I am driving and the roads are a little snow covered with some icy spots. They are perhaps a little hazardous, so I take my time. Before going home we have to stop at a Convenient Mart to pick up a few things. Bertha goes in to pick up what we need while I stay with the car. I get out and see ice behind the front wheels and kick a little bit of it off before getting back into the car. On the way home we stop at my friend Norm's. I go in the side door and talk to him from the landing and then I leave to go home. Upon arriving at home I take off my hat, coat and snow boots and walk into the bedroom. As I take off my shoes I notice my left sock and shoe are full of blood. I carefully remove my sock. Apparently when I kicked the snow off of the car, I also kicked the nail off of my big toe on my foot. I had no idea that this had even happened, for there is no pain.

It is my understanding that after I recover and am well enough to work, Bethlehem Steel will guarantee me a lifetime job. Once my health improves considerably, the Ohio Department of Rehabilitation sends me to school to become a machinist. Upon completing the machinist class, I telephone Bethlehem Steel in Lackawanna, New York, about going to work for them. I am told they have no job for me. The school that trained me to be a machinist places me in a shop in the Cleveland area. That's okay with me because in Cleveland people don't know who I am, and they won't be staring at me.

I was placed on a job at the Rotor Tool Company in Euclid, Ohio. In the thirteen years I work there, I set-up and run a variety of machines, such as turret lathes, chuckers, automatic screw machines, automatic lathes and a wide variety of computerized numerical control machines. For at least five years I am one of two set-up men in the CNC Department.

By this time the problem with my hand has repaired itself and I have full use of my it. However, the problem with my feet continues. They are still numb, but if I walk across asphalt I can feel high and low spots in it from the pressure. My toes continue to hammer and walking is becoming quite painful. My toes have hammered so much I am actually walking on the tips of them, and they have large calluses and corns on them. Now I have pain so bad at times that I turn my left foot to the outside so I have to bend it at the ankle to take the pressure off of my toes. This causes another problem. I notice that I'm losing the range of motion in my big toe. I talk to my attorneys about this and they suggest that I see a specialist in Cleveland, which I do.

Dr. White says that my big toe only has 5 degrees of movement.

I will need surgery to improve it. The joint has calcified from lack of movement. He will have to go in and grind out the calcification and also insert a silicon disc between the bones. He is also going to remove one joint in each of the two toes that are giving me additional problems. Stainless steel pins will then be inserted into the toes to keep them straight. The pins will be removed after six weeks. When the pins are pulled out the toes should be straight and no longer painful. Dr. White scheduled the surgery and within a week I was in the hospital and having surgery. I am given a spinal for anesthesia, and I am awake throughout the surgery. It isn't bad, however I don't like to hear the cracking of bones when they are cutting them. After six weeks the pins are removed and I return to work.

My attorneys decide to send me to see a frostbite specialist at the University of Texas in Galveston. Frostbite specialists are very few. We have two other choices, a doctor that resides in London, England or a famous heart specialist who is also a frostbite specialist, but he has a tremendous waiting list.

The doctor in Galveston is someone I can really relate to. He explains to me how frostbite damages the nerves and veins and in most cases leads to gangrene and the loss of fingers, toes and ears. He even asks me something that really surprises me. He wants to know if I suffered from loss of faith syndrome while I was on the raft. At once I know what he is talking about, I just didn't know there was a name for it. I told him that I do know what loss of faith means, and that I prayed to God to take my life because I didn't want to suffer any more. I tell him about my

198

attempt to take my own life, but to no avail and about my arguments with God. He is the first person I have talked to that understands everything. He explains to me that people go through this loss of faith syndrome when they're in a situation they have no control over and may lead to their death.

After our talk he sends me to have a multitude of x-rays of my feet and legs. When I return to the examination room, he also returns and takes dozens of photographs of my feet and legs in different positions. Before leaving he tells me to be prepared for more surgeries and with any luck most of the feeling will return to my feet and legs.

I am having emotional problems because I really miss my shipmates. I can't get their loss off of my mind. I wonder how I made it and is it fair that I am the only one to survive? I was having these problems before I got out of the hospital as well, but then I was somewhat able to suppress them. It isn't on my mind all the time. However, it gets to the point that if I see the back of some man's head or his profile, I have to see his face. The back of a head or a profile reminds me of someone on the boat, and I just have to make sure that it isn't one of them. I can't and don't talk to my family about this problem. I don't think they will understand. I suppose time will heal all my problems. Now that I am able to walk better, I decide to visit with Sarah Grippi. Since I was not able to attend Sam's funeral I figure it is the right thing to do. The visit starts really nice, but somehow it turns very ugly and bitter. She seems to resent the fact that I survived the shipwreck and Sam didn't. There is nothing I can say or do to ease her mind. I have to leave her house. A while later her sister calls me and apologizes for her. Sarah's sister thought it would be best if I don't come around again for a while.

After this incident I just want to hide. Is this what people really think of me? It makes me feel dirty, unclean and ashamed. How I wish I hadn't survived! Even when I am out in public with my family I feel people staring at me. I'm not certain why they are staring. All I can think about is the incident with Sarah Grippi. I have no one to turn to, no one to understand.

I start going to church on a regular basis, four or five times a week. Most of the time I go with Norm Balcomb. On Sundays I go to mass and another night of the week. Norm and I drive to Bedford, Ohio, to the Church of the Nazarene for services. I also go to the local Lutheran church as well as a Pentecostal church. In addition to all this I occasionally meet with people from the Baha'i faith. My faith in God is unshakable and obviously obsessive.

I also start taking my daughters to different churches on Sunday. My wife refuses to go. I feel that my daughters need some type of foundation to believe in and to live by. I take them to a variety of churches only because I want them to be free to choose the faith they want to believe in, just like I did. Besides, we have a lot of fun together.

My mind really bothers me. I can't get the *Morrell* and my shipmates off of my mind. I often think about how much I miss them and want to be with them. Often now, suicide enters my thoughts, and when alone I cry a lot. I also have this nagging fear within me that makes my insides shake. I can't explain why this happens or figure out how to overcome it. I try to hold these feelings inside and away from my wife. I don't want her to worry about me. I know she would feel helpless, and there is nothing she can do for me.

Finally it gets to the point where I think I should see a professional about my mental health. I tell my attorneys and they make an appointment for me to see a doctor in Cleveland. My appointments with the doctor are really a joke. I sit there for an hour and we don't have any conversation, other than to say hello to each other. The doctor sits at his desk doing paperwork for the entire hour. When I complain to my attorneys they advise me to keep going to see him. I think they want proof that I need psychiatric help for legal purposes only. I go to see him once a week for two months.

Two months is completed, and I feel as though there is no one out there who understands enough to help me. I see no need for a psychiatrist if that's what psychiatric treatment is like. I guess if I am going to get any help, I am going to have to do it on my own and I don't know how. I know that I have to face my fears. How does a person go about doing that?

My wife and I start having problems again. Or better put, she is having problems with me. I've started drinking, smoking pot and running around on her again. It seems as though I am always running to or from something. This is part of the problem that I am having and why I wanted to see a psychiatrist. Bertha and I can never talk about things without arguing. After almost dying perhaps I just want to get the most out of life with what time I have remaining.

It is perhaps three years after my first surgery that I have to have another one. I was walking through the house one day and accidentally kicked the coffee table and broke one of the toes that had previously been operated on. I am also having problems with my little toe on my left foot. It is hammering and making it difficult to walk without pain. My job at Rotor Tool requires me to be on my feet all the time, so something has to be done with them.

It is while I am working at Rotor Tool that I start smoking dope. Marijuana helps to ease the pain in both my feet and my mind. Working in the shop makes it easy to get marijuana because it seems like everyone is smoking it. I light one up after work while driving home and then in the evening I smoke another one. Bertha and I decide it will be easier and much cheaper for us if I stay in Euclid through the week and just come home on weekends, so I rent a little place that I call home.

While working I try my damnedest to stay obscure. I keep a very low profile and I also have an unlisted telephone number. I never or very seldom ever talk about being a shipwreck survivor. If in conversation the subject comes up I answer one or two questions then change the subject. It is a grim reminder and something I am very ashamed of. I feel as though it is a demon on my back, something that is constantly there and I can't get rid of. I don't want to be Dennis Hale, the only survivor of a shipwreck. I just want to be Dennis Hale.

It is especially hard for me in Ashtabula. While sailing and being away from Ashtabula for at least three years, I find that I don't know too many people anymore, but the ones I do know I consider close friends. Everywhere I go in Ashtabula, with my wife or by myself, people stare at me. I don't understand their amazement and curiosity of me being the only survivor. It's just that when walking into a restaurant and every head in the place turns to look at me, it's embarrassing and makes me feel like some kind of freak.

Weather has also become a problem for me. If there is a thunderstorm coming with high winds I leave work, go home and usher my family into the basement to make sure they are safe. I even do this if there is a snowstorm. I am always very cognizant of the weather. I really feel it is out to get me.

This was all still very fresh in my mind when on November 10, 1975, the news of the sinking of the *Edmund Fitzgerald* is constantly on the television and radio. It took me back to the sinking of the *Morrell* and everything my shipmates and I endured during the sinking. I can feel the coldness of the air and the harshness of the wind and waves as I perceived the men of the *Edmund Fitzgerald* endured them. I shiver and shudder with the thought of their pain and suffering and tears swell up in my eyes. I try not to think of the *Edmund Fitzgerald* at all. I want to block it out of my mind. I don't want to remember. It takes quite some time before I learn to deal with her sinking.

I become an advocate for safety on the Great Lakes. I write a letter to President Gerald Ford and a variety of congressmen and senators pleading for more strict safety rules in governing the inland seas. I receive responses from some, and to the others I guess my voice was unheard.

In time, it becomes extremely difficult for me to walk. I made an appointment and go to see an orthopedic surgeon in Willoughby, Ohio. He determines that he will have to do a Ray amputation on my left foot and re-pin the broken toe. The Ray amputation will take off my little toe and a small amount of the side of my foot that contains the bone to my little toe. I have the surgery and I'm laid up for about six months while my foot heals. I don't think the scab is ever going to come off of my foot, as it is very slow to heal.

After being on sick leave for six months I return to work at Rotor Tool. The surgery did help, but honestly, I have never been without foot pain from the time of the sinking. I guess you could say every step that I take is a reminder of the night of the sinking and the friends I lost.

It is while I am working at Rotor Tool that Bertha and I separate, and in a short while I'm granted a divorce. Divorcing is a hard decision for me, but I think I have found someone else that will take better care of me. That other person and I marry eventually, but that marriage only lasts for three years.

Now my life is a real shambles. I have this fear within me that I can't explain. I feel as though I'm chasing after something unknown to me. I don't think that going to counseling will help me, not after my first experience with it. I have no one that I can talk to. I can't even pray

204

anymore. God has done so much for me I don't feel I have the right to ask Him for more.

I have also been smoking a lot of dope and taking a lot of different pills. Perhaps this is the only way I can cope. Now all of my good friends are either dopers or wives of dopers or heavy drinkers. When I drink, it is wine. Needless to say, my life is now out of control.

After thirteen years with Rotor Tool I quit my job to advance myself and go to work for TRW. I am hired in as a CNC operator and quickly advance to set-up man. I remain with them for approximately ten years before going into a smaller shop and learning the tool and die trade.

During this period of time and beyond I'm in and out of different hospitals for more surgeries on my feet. By this time I have had ten surgeries on my left foot, plus the amputation and one surgery on three toes on my right foot. The problem, as it is explained to me, is that the frostbite has damaged the small capillaries in my toes and restricts the blood flow to the nerves and muscles, therefore causing the toes to hammer. I also have something called halex rigidous in the great toe on my left foot. With this condition I can only flex my toe about five degrees. Walking any distance is very painful.

I am still having problems with my mind and thought patterns. My shipmates are often on my mind, but time and patience has taught me to deal with it. I'm not afraid of the weather as much as I used to be. I know there is nothing I can do to change the weather, so I've learned to live with it and have respect for it. If I could only talk to someone that will understand, perhaps that would make a difference.

It is while I am working at TRW that the Great Lakes Shipwreck Society in Sault St. Marie, Michigan, somehow manages to find me. Shirley Farnquist from the society calls all the Hales in the Ashtabula phonebook until she finds my brother Claytor. He refuses to give her my phone number but tells her that he will call me and let me know that she is trying to get in touch with me.

After talking to Claytor I do call Shirley. The Shipwreck Society is having their annual banquet at Lake Superior State College. A Great Lakes historian and shipwreck diver named David Trotter and a colleague by the name of Larry Copeland had dove on the *Morrell* and made a film that was to have it's premiere showing at the banquet. She says that she would like for me to be there. I tell her that I don't know, and I will have to get back to her.

Dennis with artist Bob McGreevy and Larry Coplin (Coplin collection)

At first the thought of attending the banquet frightens me. For so many years I have stayed out of sight and been obscure and now to be out in public worries me. I'm afraid of the people that know about me and want to meet me. I don't want to face their questions and I'm also afraid of my answers. I have nothing to hide, but I do have some tender caring feelings within me that I don't want to talk about. It would be hard to talk about watching my shipmates die and watching them freeze to death. I thought it would be very difficult to talk about any of the shipwreck.

Dennis signs some of his first autographs-

However, after a few weeks of facing the reality that I couldn't stay obscure all my life, I change my mind and decide to attend the banquet. By the time my wife and I leave for Sault Ste. Marie I even feel a little excitement within me and anticipate meeting new people.

We arrive in Sault Ste. Marie the evening before the banquet. We are being lodged at Lake Superior State College. Our accommodations are very nice and the room is extremely spacious. Throughout the college there are displays of shipwreck artifacts from a variety of ships that sank in Lake Superior. I am very fortunate to view the displays this evening before the crowds come the following day.

On Saturday, the day of the banquet, the college is jammed full of people, most of which are divers and historians and the balance of the group are boatnerds and the curious. I can't begin to tell you how many different people I meet, and to my amazement, no one asks me about the sinking of the *Daniel J. Morrell*. That takes a lot of pressure off of me.

That evening my wife and I change clothes in anticipation of the banquet dinner. Earlier that afternoon I had taken a couple of index cards and wrote down the names of some of the people I wanted to thank for inviting us to the banquet. I also wrote down some brief statements about the *Morrell*. I had been told earlier that I didn't have to talk about the *Morrell*, the sinking or my survival unless I felt like it. At that time I told them I definitely did not want to talk about the *Morrell* and the sinking, but after meeting these people, I've changed my mind and decide to say a few words.

Dennis at the banquet- Coplin photo

After being seated at the head table my wife points out in the program that the banquet is dedicated to the men of the *Daniel J. Morrell*. I know now that I will have to get up and speak, and I am very thankful that I had written on the index cards earlier in the day. I do feel troubled and ill at ease about speaking, and even with the index cards I don't know exactly what I am going to say.

After I am introduced and make my way to the podium, it is then that I notice the size of the crowd. The tables in the small room are placed very close together. The room is jam-packed. There are people leaning against the walls, sitting on the floor and taking every inch of space they can find. When I start talking, much to my amazement, I tell the entire story of the sinking. I become very emotional, choking back the tears while talking, and when I look at the crowd I can see other people crying as well.

We are to leave Sault Ste. Marie the following day, Sunday. However, due to bad weather and high winds, the Mackinac Bridge is closed, so we can't leave until Sunday evening.

We stay at the college most of the day and I load the car with our belongings in preparation for our return trip home. It's hard to believe how good I feel! It's like a great weight has lifted off of my shoulders. I attribute this to knowing I will be returning home and because I am leaving an uncomfortable situation. Strangers would no longer be watching me. It takes a year or so before it dawns on me that perhaps speaking was good for me. Could it be that speaking defused some of the anxiety that I felt inside?

Chapter 14

The following year I had two or three more speaking engagements and at last I decided to answer questions from the audience. There were still some things that were very hard to talk about and others that I never talked about, but I found that if someone asked me a question about one of these things, I would answer the question. Yes, talking about the sinking did help me. Not only was I facing my personal dragons, I was slaying them. Speaking at the Great Lakes Shipwreck Historical Society Banquet was my first step to recovering from the sinking. At the time I was speaking about it, I just wasn't aware that speaking was a kind of therapy for me.

As well as things appeared to be going for me I was still having plenty of problems. I had to go into the hospital every three to five years for more foot surgeries. I would have one or two toes operated on at the same time, then I would wait until my toes were really painfully sore before going to see the doctor again. I already knew what he was going to tell me.

Another thing that bothered me was the fact that I just couldn't be happy. I wouldn't show it outwardly, but inside I was very unhappy. It was like I was always running to something or away from something and I don't even know what it was. Now that I think about it, I've been running all of my life. I have been married and divorced four times. Not only did I ruin my life, I ruined everyone's life that was involved in my life. Why does it take this man so long to see what he has done to other people that have shared their lives with him?

I think my childhood did help form the man I am today, and it was also crucial to my survival on the raft. Maybe leaving the back door and the window to my bedroom open in the winter did toughen me up, as I would say to myself as a child, and prepared me for whatever life had in store for me. Sleeping on a piece of cardboard in the weeds along some road with newspaper stuffed in my clothing to help keep me warm and perhaps a piece of cardboard over my body may also have helped. I did spend many late autumn or early winter nights, while I was hitchhiking, in this type of situation.

Can anyone say with any certainty that life is predestined? Over the years I have said to myself, why me, why me? I had no more to live for than the other twenty-eight men who perished from the shipwreck. This question has plagued me for so many years, and I just can't find an answer to it. Several psychologists that I have had sessions with had a variety of reasons. I was told that I just didn't know how to die and that maybe my life was predestined. As valid as these responses may have been, I really don't know why I was chosen to survive.

Prayer, prayer was my lifeline. When I was alone and I had no one else to talk to and I didn't think anyone cared, I would talk to God. Then I knew someone was there for me. I prayed for all of my shipmates, not just the ones that were on the raft with me, but all of them. I would get a vision of their face in my mind and ask God to take care of them and to take care of their families as well.

I did more than pray to God. I would have conversation with Him. I would speak to Him about my life and tell Him all the faults I have and ask forgiveness. As I talked with Him I would tell Him that I forgave everyone that ever harmed me in any way. I would stress to Him my concern over my shipmates and to please keep them safe and alive.

In my mind I honestly believed that some of my shipmates had been rescued already. I could see them in a nice warm galley having a cup of coffee, a sweet roll and talking BS with other crewmembers. How I did envy them as I struggled to stay alive! I had faith in God and deep down inside of me I knew He was going to save me.

I do believe that one of the first things I did after hearing the general alarm that helped save my life was putting on my life jacket and having it next to my skin. The floatation area of the lifejacket consisted of sealed plastic bags filled with kapok and air. Kapok is a silky fiber obtained from the fruit of the silk-cotton tree. It's used in mattresses and pillows and it's good insulation. It is also used in life preservers. After I went out on deck to see what the emergency was, then returned to my room looking for more clothing only to find my peacoat, then putting the

212

peacoat over my life jacket was the best thing I could have done. I believe having the plastic bags filled with the kapok over my lungs kept them from freezing, and I understand that a peacoat is good insulation whether it is wet or dry. This action was just dumb luck.

You may find this hard to understand, but I also believe that not having clothing on was also a contributing factor to my survival. I noticed with my raft mates that their clothing was freezing and encapsulating them in ice. This had to drop their body temperatures really fast. Without clothing on my lower extremities I did manage to keep my feet and legs moving periodically for at least twelve hours. After twelve hours I only moved my feet occasionally to rub them together.

As badly as I wanted to die, I just never gave up hope. I would find some reason to keep going even if it was to play a game of solitaire, scan the water looking for a boat to come and rescue me or to count the number of times I blinked my eyes. I would find a reason no matter how trivial. I would say to myself that I've struggled all of my life to stay alive and I'm not going to let this kill me. This is just another stumbling block in my life.

It's been just over forty-four years since the sinking of the *Daniel J. Morrell*. For the first twenty-some years I just wanted to be Dennis Hale. I didn't want to be affiliated with any boat sinking or any type of survivor. I was afraid that being the only survivor had too many responsibilities, and there would be too many questions to answer from people I didn't even know. The question part really worried me. Just what type of questions would they ask me? Would I be able to stand in front of them and answer the questions without crying? Would I have to tell them about the things I told Father McEachin, and would they have the same reaction? I was concerned that people might think I was a little odd. I didn't realize how compassionate and how much empathy people felt for me. However, the first time I spoke at Lake Superior College I was astounded by the way people treated me. When I did cry, they cried with me.

For the second twenty-some years I have taken the responsibility of being Dennis Hale, the *Daniel J. Morrell's* only survivor. I somehow feel like I'm keeping the memory of the *Morrell* and my shipmates alive, and that's very important to me. A day doesn't pass without thinking of them and praying they are well.

I realize that throughout life we have friends that come and go. I guess you could say that's the nature of life. However, losing twenty-eight of them at one time is awfully hard to overcome. I don't know if I think of them because I want to or their faces just appear in my mind and I have to think about them. I'll tell you this much, it's nice to never be alone because they are always with me.

In the past twenty-some years I have also grown as a man. I have faced many of my personal challenges and have overcome them. Some were very difficult to accomplish while others happened quite naturally. By this time in my life I am doing quite a bit of public speaking and that has helped me overcome a lot of obstacles in my life from the shipwreck.

214

I found that a person cannot overcome tragedies in their life if they don't face up to them. It's taken me an awfully long time to learn that, but after the first few times of talking about the tragedy it became easier and easier. Today you can ask me anything about the sinking and I will answer your question. Sometimes the questions are hard to answer due to the feelings I have about that particular subject, but I answer them anyhow. I feel this is good therapy for me because after a while I become desensitized to the question.

After the sinking of the *Morrell* I vowed that I would never sail again. Just the thought of being on the water terrified me. Talking or thinking about it made my skin tingle and fear would overcome me. I would think about the cold and the wind and the loss of my friends. I just knew that fear would never let me sail again. Life can end very abruptly if you are accidentally caught in a storm. With all the time I spent on the raft thinking about the ship sinking and the loss of my friends, perhaps it just gave me a phobia. I just didn't want to take any more chances. However, time and patience changes a lot of things in one's life.

In 1999 I was offered a once-in-a-lifetime trip on the Motor Vessel *Roger Blough*. The *Blough* is a beautiful freighter, 835 feet long by a 105-foot beam. Her captain, Larry Dalghren, he's called Duke, was well seasoned with many years of sailing on the Great Lakes. When I received this news it was like a pleasantly painful shock of electricity that went through my body. At first I was very apprehensive. Wow! That was a pretty scary thought, but then the company told me I could bring seven of my friends with me. Well that changed my whole outlook on things and I decided to go. I thought that if my life is predestined, it's already been proven that I'm not going to die due to a sinking ship. I had to take this trip. It was one of the last fears I had to face. I had to do this for me.

I invited Jim and Pat Stayer and Tim and Joan Juhl. They helped me write my first book. I also invited Frank Mays who was one of two survivors off of the *Carl D. Bradley*, Great Lakes folk singer and songwriter Dan Hall, and my old *Morrell* sailing buddy Harvey Hayes. Ahead of

Dennis on the *Blough*

time Harvey and I made plans for him to drive from Erie, Pennsylvania, to my house and then we would drive together in my car to Sault Ste. Marie, Michigan. Finally the day arrived that we were to catch the *Blough*. Everyone was happy and in a great mood and ready to sail. As we climbed aboard at Sault Ste. Marie from the supply boat Ojibway, I kept asking myself if I knew what I was doing. However, once aboard the *Blough* I felt very comfortable. It felt like I was putting on a pair of old shoes.

The trip itself was just wonderful. From Sault Ste. Marie we went up Lake Superior, docked at Two Harbors, Minnesota, loaded iron ore

216

pellets and headed for Chicago. While in Two Harbors a box of smoked chubs were delivered to me. Kaye Struve, the daughter of Albert Whoeme who was lost on the Daniel J. Morrell, had sent the fish to me. She knew how much I like smoked fish. I was very delighted and excited to have that box of fish in my hands! My friends and I gobbled them right down. We were all very grateful to Kaye.

Frank Mays and Dennis Hale

Throughout the day we explored the ship, venturing into the engine room, the pilothouse, talking to the engineers and the mates, trying to find out all we could about the ship. At night we watched television, played cards, or sat out on the deck looking at the night sky with the multitude of stars in the heavens.

We did happen to notice that the boat's crew somewhat shied away from us. We really didn't know if they were told not to interfere with the passengers were if there was some type of superstition because Frank

217

Mays and I were aboard. I understand that sailors are funny people with many superstitions. Fortunately the Stayers brought enough copies of the first book, *Sole Survivor*, on board to give each of the crew a copy of it. So one afternoon we walked back to the crew's break room and started passing out the book and engaging them in conversation. To our surprise the crew finally warmed up to us.

One evening towards the end of our trip we were all tired of playing cards, watching the stars and television. Dan Hall thought it would be a good idea to write a song about our voyage. Most of us had been sitting around drinking beer and we agreed it would be a fun thing to do. It was a lot of fun doing it but of course we had to leave some of the lines out of the song. Thus was born the song *Sailing Down to Gary*. We met with the crew in the galley the following day and sang the song to them and they

Dennis and Capt. Duke Dalghren

really cracked up. I'm sure the crew left the galley humming that song. We took that to be a good sign.

I can't talk about the *Blough* without mentioning the sumptuous food we were served. Every meal was outstanding. Breakfast was at seven o'clock A.M., and a variety of meals were available. At nine-thirty or ten o'clock one of the stewards would bring us up sweet rolls or pastry. Then at noon we would go back to the galley for lunch. At three or four o'clock in the afternoon the steward would bring us hot hors d'oeuvres or freshly cut fruit. Then there was dinner if you would care to eat. If you got hungry through the night you could always go back to the galley and fix yourself something to eat. If you ever get the opportunity to sail on the *Blough*, don't pass it up. Traditionally, Saturday night is steak night. Our meal started with huge shrimp cocktails followed by a salad and the largest T-bones I've ever seen, cooked to order just the way you wanted it, plus all the trimmings and dessert. We were even offered a second T-bone.

The captain, Duke, was one extremely nice guy. He basically gave us the run of the ship except when he was docking the ship, and then we had to stay out of the pilothouse. Of course that makes a lot of sense because he needed to have an unobstructed view of the area and not have any type of confusion going on around him. We had dinner with him on several occasions, and he would visit with us in our living quarters.

Too soon our six-day trip came to an end, and I really disliked getting off of the boat. We could tell the crew even hated to see us depart. It felt very good being aboard the *Blough* and it brought back a lot of old pleasant memories. I knew then that my fear of sailing was still somewhat present, but that someday I would like to try sailing again, which I did.

The trip didn't end just then. I had to take my buddy Harvey back to my house to pick up his car. The trip back to my house was great. We talked about old times and how wonderful it was being on the *Blough*. Often, following our trip, my thoughts would go back to our adventure on the *Blough*. I would have to call Harvey and tell him of my thoughts, or he would call me and tell me of his thoughts.

It must have been the later part of 2002 that I became involved with a group in Columbus, Ohio. It is called the International Association on Near Death Studies or, as referred to by its members, IANDS. I had heard of them many years before, I just never made contact because I didn't know where they were located. I now know they are located throughout the United States and overseas. The majority of the people attending these meetings have had near death or after life experiences. The others are interested or curious or they have family members that profess to having had a near death or after life experience.

To me it was like finding the missing link. I always felt like what happened to me alone on the lake was something a person just didn't talk about in the company of others. Father McEachin gave me that opinion. Here I was now, amongst a group of people that I shared a common denominator with. I said to myself, "I guess I'm not such a weirdo after all!"

Nancy Clark started the IANDS Columbus group many years before I began attending the meetings. She is also the facilitator. We have our meetings the first Saturday of every month at the Columbus Mennonite Church. We have a speaker or a discussion group on afterlife or near-death experiences. As badly as I wanted to attend every meeting, there were months it was just impossible due to weather, or I had a prearranged speaking engagement. Going to the meetings was like going home to me. I was accepted and not judged for the things I had to say.

It was while I was attending these sessions, perhaps in 2004, that I made friends with Randy. He was the backup facilitator and a member of the Mennonite Church. Randy was also the psychologist that several of the members had sought solace from.

After attending the meetings for six or eight months and getting to know Randy a little better. I decided that now was the time to see if Randy could help me with my problems. I knew I was suffering from posttraumatic stress. Perhaps Randy could succeed with me were others had failed. Whenever I thought back, with disappointment, to my first encounter with a psychologist, I didn't know if anyone could help me. But I felt very comfortable with Randy and that's more than I could say about my first psychologist. I just knew things would be different this time.

Before starting any sessions, it was agreed that I could take voice recordings of every session. We would meet in his office twice a month and have a two hour session each time. This made for a long day for me. It was a four-hour drive to his office in Columbus then two hours with him followed by the return trip home.

Starting with the first session, I was hypnotized. The idea was to start with my childhood and step-by-step go through my life.

Starting with my childhood was somewhat traumatic. Somehow, throughout my life, I was able to disregard or hide in my mind all the bad things that happened to me. Through hypnosis all of the bad circumstances and incidents came rushing back at me and bothered or hurt me more than the first time. I recall becoming very

Hale family picnic

emotional at times. Yes, I was a bad child but not without reason. I did cause a lot of my own problems. If I had been treated differently or if I would have had my mother, I'm sure I could have been a different person. It took several sessions to get through this segment of my life.

222

After going through my childhood and adolescent years we arrived at the time and place in my life that I decided to go sailing and then ultimately the sinking of the *Daniel J. Morrell.*

Unaware of what might happen to me by reliving the sinking again, I was very apprehensive. After all, it had been thirty-eight years ago, and I didn't know if my heart could stand going through that once more in addition to other emotional issues I had. I did know that this was one thing I had to do at all cost.

Just as I had assumed, the sessions were bad at first. I did a lot of shivering and shaking and holding myself and crying. Randy put a stop to that by telling me I couldn't feel the cold. He also told me to place myself above the raft looking down upon it. Even doing it that way it was still hard to hold back the tears. Looking at myself lying there in the dark and cold, shivering and not knowing what to expect next, at times, it was just too much. Then I would see myself going through the waves and not knowing if I could make it through to the other side and a breath of air. I would remember the wind as we broke through the backside of the wave.

My tears were the product of fear, pain, grief and the sadness of having to see my shipmates and I having to experience the scenario I just described.

After that first session I explained to Randy that I didn't want to be above the raft looking down on it. That was too much like being a spectator. I wanted to be on the raft and experiencing everything all over again. As painful as it was to watch, I wanted to know what my thoughts and feelings were and if there was some hint as to why life wasn't drained from me as well. Randy didn't like that idea but he did agree to it, and I agreed, with his help, not to feel the cold.

After several sessions I began to feel better about myself in general. I always looked forward to the next session. I had a total of twenty sessions or ten months of driving twice a month to Columbus. To this day I feel that the time I spent with him was the best thing I ever did for myself.

He said I did some remote viewing. I really don't know how to explain remote viewing. It's kind of like sending your mind to different places. I do know that our Government teaches their spies how to use this to spy on other countries. Yes, I know this sounds crazy.

He also felt I had a premonition of my sister's death. In my mind, as I see it, he is probably right. There is just no other explanation to what I saw while I was on the raft, before her death. At her wake everything was so precise to what I saw while on the raft. The people, the food, even my half sister and her family were all the same.

The afterlife experience is something I have talked about for years. There is absolutely no doubt in my mind that it happened to me. It was a very beautiful experience that I will cherish to the end of my days, and yes, I will continue to talk about it.

I know that some of the things I speak about in this book may be considered odd or different or even hallucinations. However, every strange occurrence was instrumental in keeping my body temperature from getting

224

too cold. I didn't realize this until many years afterwards. Needless to say, after experiencing these strange occurrences, they stayed on my mind, and I often wondered if I was really seeing them or if I was just delirious. I now know that I wasn't delirious. I knew what was happening around me all the time. I knew when I was asleep and I knew when I was awake. When the Coast Guard picked me up off the raft I began talking to them and making sense. I even knew I was lying to them about my injuries.

I can't begin to tell you all the questions that have gone through my mind over the years. Questions I guess I'll never have the answers to.

About a year after finishing my sessions with Randy, a friend of mine, Brian Morgan, and I decided to go to Port Huron, Michigan, for a maritime artifacts sale. Brian is a big-time collector, and if I see something I like and it's in my price range, I buy it. While on our way to Port Huron we decided to stop in Detroit and see if we could get aboard the mail boat J.W. Wescott and take ourselves a little ride. That worked out really well. We took a ride while they delivered the mail, and we also had a good photo opportunity of the boats the Wescott was delivering mail to, then we were on our way to Port Huron again.

Brian also approached me a few years ago about doing an article for the American Steamships Historical Society magazine, *Steamboat Bill*. Brian is an over the road truck driver. I really didn't know how he was going to find time to write. Knowing Brian as I do, I knew he would do a great job. I told Brian I would be pleased if he did the article and to feel free to call me or stop when he was driving through Ashtabula. I could meet him and we could have coffee and talk about the article, and we did that several times. He would say to me, "I hope this is going to be all right. I've never done anything like this before."

I would say to him, "Don't worry. It will be all right. I'm sure you'll do a good job."

Dennis Hale, Andy Sykora, Brian Morgan

Brian's research was impeccable. He also contacted Great Lakes artist Robert McGreevy and received permission to use his painting of the Morrell coming onto Lake Huron for the cover of *Steamboat Bill*. Without a doubt, the cover was very impressive.

Due to the wonderful job Brian did on the article for the magazine, both he and I were invited by the American Steamship Historical Society to Baltimore, Maryland, to speak at their annual conference and dinner. They also invited us to take a day trip with them on the liberty ship John Brown.

The dinner started at six-thirty P.M., and the evening presentations followed the dinner. The president of the society gave a short talk on the future goals they would like to achieve and their current financial condition. Brian was the next speaker, and he talked about his involvement with the society and the number of years he had been a member. He also had kind words to say about me. He then spoke about the number of years we have been friends. Next I spoke about the sinking of the *Daniel J. Morrell* and took questions from the attendees. There were many questions for both Brian and I from a variety of people. It was a very enjoyable night. By the time everything was over it was almost midnight.

We got up early the next morning and waited for the buses to arrive to take us to the docking area for the *John Brown*. After boarding I would estimate that perhaps six hundred people were on board. When the *John Brown* was fully loaded and the lines were cast off, we headed out and onto the Chesapeake Bay. What a wonderful trip it was! We had both breakfast and lunch on the boat and then after lunch they had simulated Japanese fighter planes shooting blanks at the *John Brown* and the crew returned fire. All in all it made for a pretty exciting day. By the time we got back to the hotel we were all pretty well tired out. I felt relieved because once again I proved to myself that I can be on the water without dire results.

My next big challenge was at Atwood Lake, Ohio. Brian invited us down for the day to have a little picnic with his family and take a ride on their pontoon boat. After the pontoon boat we went on Brian's sailboat and then a small speedboat. It was all a lot of fun, and I'm sure we will do it again someday. My fear of being on the water is definitely gone due to these experiences.

In April of 2009 I was contacted by Yap Filming Company out of Canada. They were in the process of filming for National Geographic on the sinking of the *Edmund Fitzgerald*, and they wanted to include my story in their film. I told them that I would be interested in filming.

On June 9th, I drove up to Bad Axe, Michigan, and checked into the Holiday Inn Express where they had made reservations for me. After meeting everyone we had dinner together and talked about events of the following day. Needless to say my anticipation was growing and I could hardly wait for the next day.

On June 10th after having breakfast we left for Harbor Beach to make ready for our trip out to the Morrell. Whenever we arrived at Harbor Beach I was introduced to Captain Gary Vanet. After all the diving and filming equipment was loaded onto the dive boat, I climbed aboard the *Sylvia Anne* where I met the rest of Captain Vanet's crew, Tom Mehringer and an old friend of mine, Skip Kadar. Skip, as well as being a good friend, is an author of three or four Great Lakes books. Also on board the boat was the filming director, Victor Kushmaniuk, a very nice man I like to think of as a friend, a cameraman and the sound technician.

As soon as all the crew and divers were aboard, the lines were cast off and we were headed out onto Lake Huron. It took two hours of sailing time before we arrived at the map coordinates for the sinking site of the

Daniel J. Morrell.

During the two-hour trip we talked about the sinking and the location of the bow section. We had a little conversation about the stern section of the boat, which they were to dive on the following day. There were also questions about my survival and how I managed to stay alive. Videos were taken inside the pilot area and also on the fantail, or stern, of the boat. The trip seemed to fly by as everyone kept me in conversation so I wouldn't have time to think about what I was doing.

We had beautiful weather that day. The lake was as smooth as a piece of glass. Yes, I was a little fearful. I did recall leaving Harbor Beach some years ago by ambulance and looking out at a forbidding Lake Huron and feeling that it hadn't finished with me yet. I was very thankful that the weather was agreeable this day and after arriving at the wreck site, all my fears began to vanish.

After suiting up and getting their air tanks on, the two main divers, father and son Mike and Warren Fletcher, and a safety tech diver, Stuart French, wearing a rebreather, jumped into the water for their trip to the bottom and the

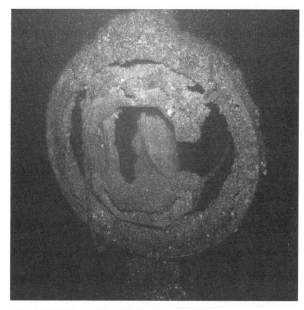

Mast of the Morrell (C for Cambria Iron & Steel Co.)
Tom Mehringer Photo

Daniel J. Morrell. The bow section lies at about one hundred eighty-five feet and the divers used SCUBA air with the exception of the tech diver. The stern section is about two hundred twenty feet deep, and they would use a mixture they called tri-mix. We had no plans on visiting the stern section on this day.

There was a happy feeling of excitement and anticipation in the air as the divers went into the water.

The air tanks only allowed the divers about twenty-two minutes on the bottom and then there was perhaps another hour and a half decompression time as they came up. I'm not absolutely certain about the decompression time. During this period of time I was being interviewed,

Inside Morrell pilothouse- Tom Mehringer Photo

most of which took place on the bow of the boat.

The *Morrell*, resting upright on the bottom, had a plastic line that was attached to the forward mast that went upward and was connected to a floating plastic bottle on the surface. Someone handed me this line and then everyone disappeared from the bow and left me alone. I really felt connected to the *Morrell*. I was flooded with all types of emotion that I held back, not wanting to be embarrassed. However, I'm sure if the others looked really close at me they may have seen a tear in my eye. As I sit here and write about it, my emotions start to become aroused. I take a deep breath, and it's like fresh clean air putting my thoughts aside.

Once the divers came to the surface and climbed aboard the dive boat, everyone wanted to know the condition of the *Morrell* sitting on the bottom

Rope from Morrell wreck mooring

and details about the dive itself. The divers were flooded with questions from everyone. At one point Mike, the lead diver, turned to look at me and said, "How in the hell did you manage to survive in that temperature? The bottom temperature of the lake is about 35°, approximately the same temperature it was for you on the raft. I'm so cold I can hardly stand it. I can barely move my fingers." Looking at Mike, I noticed that the color of his lips had a blue tinge to them. Slightly surprised and bewildered by his statement for a moment, I then once again realized how lucky I am to be alive.

The following morning I left Bad Axe to return to Ohio. I'm not certain when the film will be shown on the National Geographic Channel and I don't know if they will use the segment I was in. The program is to be a six-part series investigation into the sinking of the *Edmund Fitzgerald*. They would like to answer the question that's on everyone's mind. Why did the big *Fitz* sink? I wish them luck in solving the mystery.

Well I guess that brings us up to today. I'm well and doing fine. I just turned seventy in January and I feel great. Well, I did have an appendectomy last fall, and about a month after that I had to go into the hospital for a procedure on my heart, but that was just an overnight stay. I had what they called an oblation.

I still work for Arrow Glass Company out of Jefferson, Ohio. However I do work reduced hours, about twenty or twenty-five per week. I don't know how long my age or my health will let me continue work. I really like working there and it will be sad for me to have to leave. I know I can't work forever, so I'll probably retire completely soon.

You have just read my life, friends. It wasn't as bad as you may think. Life is kind of funny. It must have an automatic adjust button. A person has to just live out life's circumstances without question, and deal with whatever comes along.

Just like everyone else I don't know how much time I have left in life, but I will spend that time talking about the *Morrell* and the men that sailed with me on her. I know that when my last day is here, the same men will be there to greet me and take me to wherever I will be going.

If by chance you should come to hear me speak of my experience, or in a crowd you should see me look at you and a warm smile crosses my face, please don't feel offended. You may just resemble or remind me of many brothers and close friends I lost along the way.

Morrell bow after discovery- Drawing by Bob McGreevy

Al Jardine (Noronic survivor), Ed Brewster (Cedarville), Frank Mays (Bradley) with Dennis Hale (Cris Kohl photo)

Above- Dennis in 1996. Opposite page- various shots of the Daniel J. Morrell

A dramatic sequence of photos from the tug *Koral* as the steamer
Michipicoten sinks in a storm. The event is very similar to the loss of the
Morrell, which was built at the same shipyard only a year later (1906).

Images courtesy Algoma Central Corporation (1972)

Marine Board of Investigation

24 March 1967

SS DANIEL J. MORRELL, O.N. 203507, sinking of in Lake Huron on 29 November 1966, with loss of life.

FINDINGS OF FACT

At approximately 0200 (2:00 A.M.) EST 29 November 1966, while en route from Buffalo, N.Y. to Taconite, Minnesota, in ballast, the SS DANIEL J. MORRELL, broke into two sections during the height of a storm and sank in Lake Huron in the approximate position of latitude 44° 15.9'N and 82° 50'W. At the time of the sinking neither lifeboat was launched and no distress message was transmitted by that vessel. The first notification of alarm for her safety was received by the U.S. Coast Guard Rescue Coordination Center at Cleveland, Ohio, at 1215 (12:15 P.M.) EST 30 November 1966. Of the twenty-nine crewmembers on board at the time, twenty-two are known dead, six are still missing and one person survived. U.S. Lake Survey, Lake Huron Chart No. 5 encompasses the area.

The following crewmembers, who lost their lives as a result of this casualty, have been recovered and positively identified:

238

Arthur I. Crawley, age 47	Master
Phillip E. Kapets, age 51	1st Mate
Duncan R. MacLeod, age 61	2nd Mate
Charles H. Fosbender, age 42	Wheelsman
Henry Rischmiller, age 34	Wheelsman
Stuart A. Campbell, age 60	Wheelsman
Albert P. Wieme, age 51	Watchman
Norman M. Bragg, age 40	Watchman
Larry G. Davis, age 27	Ordinary Deckwatch
Arthur E. Stojek, age 41	Deckhand
John J. Cleary, Jr., age 20	Deckhand
John H. Schmidt, age 46	Chief Engineer
Valmour A. Marchildon, age 43	1st Asst. Engineer
Wilson E. Simpson, age 50	Oiler
Arthur S. Fargo, age 52	Fireman
Chester Konieczka, age 45	Fireman
Leon R. Truman, age 45	Coalpasser
Nicholas Homick, age 35	2nd Cook
Joseph A. Mahsem, age 59	Porter
Charles J. Sestakauskas, age 49	Porter
George A. Dahl, age 38	3rd Asst. Engineer
Saverio Grippi, age 53	Coalpasser

The following crewmembers aboard the DANIEL J. MORRELL at

the time of sinking are still missing:

Ernest G. Marcotte, age 62	3rd Mate
John M. Groh, age 21	Ordinary Deckwatch
Alfred G. Norkunas, age 39	2nd Asst. Engineer
Donald E. Worcester, age 38	Oiler
David L. Price, age 19	Coalpasser
Stanley J. Satlawa, age 39	Steward

The following crewmember of the DANIEL J. MORRELL is the only survivor of this casualty:

Dennis N. Hale, age 26	Watchman

All Merchant Mariner's Documents that have been recovered in this case have been forwarded under separate cover.

The weather in the general area of the casualty was: seas 20 to 25 feet, northerly to north northeast; visibility 4 miles; sea temperature 44° to 47°F; air temperature 33°F; barometer 29.10. A recording of the wind by the Harbor Beach Coast Guard station, was taken from the Weather Bureau Wind Recorder, indicating that the wind was variable from 2200 (10:00 P.M.) 20 November 1966 to 0500 (5:00 A.M.) 29 November 1966, ranging from 30 knots to 57 knots (35 MPH to 63 MPH) and gusty, shifting back and forth from northwest to east. At 0128 (1:28 A.M.) 29 November, the wind shifted from northeast over to east northeast and except for a period of five minutes when it shifted to the northwest, it

240

generally remained from that direction until 0207 (2:07 A.M.) At about 0200 (2:00 A.M.) the wind velocity was 35 to 40 knots (40 to 46 MPH), with gusts to 57 knots (63 MPH). Further information regarding weather conditions is indicated in succeeding paragraphs.

The weather forecast for Lake Huron as originated by the Weather Bureau, Chicago, Illinois, and broadcast to become effective at 1200 (12:00 P.M.) EST 28 November 1966 was:

a. Gale warnings. For the northern one-third, northeasterly winds 34 to 40 knots (40 to 46 MPH), occasionally northerly 41 to 47 knots (47 to 53 MPH) the following 12 hours and northwesterly winds 28 to 33 knots (30 to 37 MPH) the following six hours.

b. For the southern two-thirds, westerly winds 34 to 40 knots (39 to 46 MPH) the first six hours, northwesterly winds 41 to 47 knots (47 to 53 MPH) the following 12 hours, with winds diminishing northwesterly 28 to 33 knots (30 to 37 MPH) the following six hours. The weather for the entire period snow, or rain and snow the entire 24-hour period.

c. The forecast effective 1800 (6:00 P.M.) EST 28 November 1966, was: Gale warnings continued in effect. Northerly winds 28 to 33 knots (30 to 37 MPH) at the beginning of the period but increasing to 34 to 40 knots (39 to 46 MPH), occasionally gusty, or occasionally 41 to 47 knots (47 to 53 MPH) and snow, or rain and snow for the entire 24 hours.

d. The forecast effective 1200 (12:00 A.M.) EST 29 November 1966 was: Gale warnings continued in effect, with northerly wind 41 to 47 knots (47 to 53 MPH) for the entire 24 hours; snow, or rain and snow the entire 24-hour period.

The Daniel J. Morrell was a non-self unloading bulk freighter. The forepeak, or collation, and the after peak bulkhead were watertight. The blind hold bulkhead at the forward end of the number one cargo hold and the after bulkhead of number three cargo hold were watertight to the main deck. There were no doors in a watertight bulkhead below the main deck level. The main deck was at the level of the site tank tops. Two non-watertight screen bulkheads separated the three cargo holds. Openings were located at the port and starboard corners of the screen bulkheads at the tank top level for drainage purposes. Water was removed from the cargo spaces by means of suctions at the port and starboard after corners of number three cargo hold. Water could be pumped into the cargo hold through this same piping arrangement.

There were 14 combination side and double bottomed tanks, 7 on each side of the center vertical keel. The exact capacity of any of the ballast tanks is unknown; however, the capacity of each tank was approximately 8.5 short tons per foot of length. The feed water tank was located below the engine spaces. The hull was of riveted construction and the vessel was transversely framed. There were 18 hatches with sliding steel type hatch covers and Mulholland hatch securing clamps. The hatches were on 24-foot centers. The dimensions of the hatches were 12 feet by 36 feet. In 1942, new side tanks were installed. In 1945 the vessel was re-boilered, with boilers constructed by Babcock and Wilcox Company. In 1956 new plate tank tops were installed, at which time there was much removal of steel internals. In 1956 the vessel was re-powered with a Skinner Unaflow engine of 3200 H.P. Prior to being re-powered the old engine plant was triple expansion steam of 2000 H.P. The Skinner Unaflow engine was of lighter weight than the engine previously installed. The old shaft was 12 inches in diameter, the new shaft diameter was 14 inches, the old propeller was of 4 bladed cast-iron construction and the new propeller was 5 bladed. The maximum speed of the vessel increased approximately 2 ½ to 3 MPH, but there was a little more vibration noticeable subsequent to the new engine installation. A former chief engineer of the Daniel J. Morrell knew of no problems created by the installation of the new Skinner Unaflow engine.

The berthing quarters for the deck officers and personnel were located forward. Quarters for all other personnel were located aft.

The lifesaving equipment for the Daniel J. Morrell included two 21 person lifeboats aft and two 15 person liferafts; one raft located on the spar deck between number 3 and number 4 hatches and the other located on the boat deck aft. The boats were of steel construction, built by the Welin Davit and Boat Corporation. Davits were of the sheath screw type. Lifeboat releasing gear consisted of common hooks. Boat falls were wire rope. There were no electric boat winches aboard. The lifesaving equipment provided no means of protecting personnel from exposure. The liferafts were of wood and metal construction, built by Frank Morrison, Inc., and were the catamaran float free type.

The power for the general alarm system consisted of dry cell batteries located both forward and aft. The alarm switch was located in the pilothouse, and once the switch was engaged, the alarm would continue to ring forward and aft. In the event the wiring was severed aft of the forward superstructure, the alarm bells aft would not ring. The source of the electrical power for all other units on the vessel was to 60 KW Westinghouse generators which were adjacent to the main throttle. There was no emergency lighting system on the vessel, although there were battery powered battle lanterns aboard.

There was one AM and one FM radio installation located in the pilothouse, with remote stations for each located in the captain's cabin. There was no emergency radio aboard. The vessel was equipped with radio direction finder and radar. Steam piping and electrical cables were installed immediately below the spar deck on the starboard side. There was no public address system aboard. The vessel was equipped with sound powered phones and engine order telegraph for communication between the engine room and the pilothouse. Wires and cables for the systems were also located beneath the spar deck starboard side.

There was no cargo loading plan prepared by Bethlehem Steel Corporation, nor is one required by regulations. Vessel operating personnel, however, believe that the procedure generally used is one which produces the least strain on the hull structure. As the cargo is admitted into the holds the ballast is removed. The chief mate plans the loading of each cargo. His usual procedure is to put partial loads in hatch number 18 and then in even number hatches proceeding forward. Then partial cargoes are loaded in the odd numbered hatches starting with number 17. Additional cargo is distributed in the hatches until the completion of loading.

The Daniel J. Morrell departed Buffalo, New York for Taconite, Minnesota on November 26, 1966, and cleared the Buffalo breakwater at 2300 (11:00 P.M.) EST that date. She was on her 34th and last scheduled voyage of the 1966 operating season. The vessel was in ballasted condition at the time of the departure because of known rough weather existing in Lake Erie. There is no record of the exact distribution of ballast or drafts upon her departure. The lead fleet engineer for Bethlehem Steel Corporation observed the vessel at the time of her departure from Buffalo and was aware of no vessel structural defects at that time.

In accordance with company policy requiring all vessels of the Bethlehem fleet to communicate with the company dispatcher at Cleveland to make daily position reports during the early Spring and late Fall, at or about 0900 (9:00 A.M.) November 27, 1966, Captain Crawley called Mr. Dobson, the dispatcher, by radio telephone and reported that he was due at Detroit about 0630 to 2100 (6:30 to 9:00 P.M.) 27 November. On the evening of 27 November, 1966, Captain Crawley called to report that the Daniel J. Morrell had anchored below Detroit, Michigan, at 1800 (6:00 P.M.) due to adverse weather. At about 2100 (9:00 P.M.) 28 November 1966, Captain Crawley called Mr. Dobson again to report that he had heaved anchor at 0655 (6:55 A.M.) 28 November 1966, that he had passed Detroit that he was short two deck hands and one fireman. At the time of the sinking, the vessel was actually one fireman and one oiler short of the crew required by the Certificate of Inspection. It is noted, however, that the vessel was carrying more crew in number than was required. There were no further conversations or contact between the master of the Daniel J. Morrell and company officials in Cleveland, Ohio; and no report or notification from any source was received to indicate there might have been any problems on board the Daniel J. Morrell from the last radio contact at 0900 (9:00 A.M.) 28 November 1966, until the time of sinking.

Upon departing Buffalo, the Daniel J. Morrell had orders to stop for fuel (coal) at Consolidation Fuel Dock (Mullen Dock), Windsor, Ontario, Canada, in event fuel was required. The Daniel J. Morrell did arrived at the above dock at 0705 (7:05 A.M.) 28 November 1966 and, after taking on 221 tons of stoker fuel, departed at 0730 (7:30 A.M.). No draft reading of the vessel was taken by dock personnel. The ETA of the Daniel J. Morrell at Taconite was about 2100 (9:00 P.M.) 29 November 1966, bearing unexpected delays. The J. W. Wescott Company, Detroit, Michigan, an automatic reporting station for Bethlehem Fleet vessels passing Detroit, reported that the Daniel J. Morrell passed Detroit upbound at 0753 (7:53 A.M.) 28 November 1966.

The smooth log of the Daniel J. Morrell, covering previous trips in 1966, indicates its usual ballasted condition upon departure from Buffalo without cargo, as was the case on 26 November 1966, was approximately 8 to 10 feet forward and 16 to 17 feet aft, depending on weather conditions. Testimony from the Daniel J. Morrell's previous master, Captain Hull, indicated that this ballasting procedure as carried

246

out by Captain Crawley followed basically his own ballasting procedures while on that vessel. In good weather he normally carried about 6 feet of water in #1, #2 and #3 tanks and about 8 to 10 feet in the after tanks. Then as the weather increased in severity, he would fill all ballast tanks in an attempt to increase his draft forward and aft. All tanks were filled simultaneously while the vessel was at unloading ports. A draft of 14 feet 8 inches was sufficient to submerge subject vessel's propeller completely. Bethlehem Steel Corporation dispatchers designated the ports at which vessels are to load and unload bulk cargo and the cargoes to be carried. The determination as to whether or not a vessel will proceed in the face of a storm is in the province of the master. The cargoes carried by the Daniel J. Morrell were coal, rock (limestone), and Taconite.

The Edward Y. Townsend, also of the Bethlehem Fleet and the sister ship of the Daniel J. Morrell, was moored astern of the Daniel J. Morrell at the Bethlehem Steel Plant, Buffalo, New York, at the time of the later vessel's departure from Buffalo. The Edward Y. Townsend departed Buffalo for Taconite Harbor, Minnesota, at 0310 (3:10 A.M.) 27 November 1966 in ballast. Captain Thomas J. Connelly was master of that vessel. At approximately 2310 (11:10 P.M.) 27 November, the upbound Edward Y. Townsend passed the Morrell while it was anchored in the Detroit River below Detroit, Michigan. At that time, the masters of the two vessels engaged in radio conversation concerning the weather conditions in Lake Huron and the intention of the master of the Edward Y. Townsend to anchor in the upper St. Clair River to await more favorable weather. The

Edward Y. Townsend then continued upbound and anchored below Stag Island in the St. Clair River at 0400 (4:00 A.M.) 28 November 1966. The next communication with the Daniel J. Morrell was at about 1300 (1:00 P.M.) 28 November 1966 as it passed the anchored Edward Y. Townsend. The two masters discussed the noon weather report for Lake Huron and the weather that might be anticipated. The wind at Stag Island at the time was estimated as westerly and light (6 to 18 miles per hour).

Prior to heaving anchor at 1453 (2:53 P.M.) the master of the Edward Y. Townsend listened to radio conversation between unidentified vessels in Lake Huron and to shore station radio broadcasts, to get some indication of on-scene weather in the southern part of Lake Huron. The wind in the southern part of Lake Huron was westerly and light to fresh (6 to 28 miles per hour). Immediately prior to his heaving anchor, the masters of the Townsend and the Morrell again conferred by radio. At this time the Daniel J. Morrell was in the vicinity of the Lake Huron Lightship. The conversation generally concerned weather conditions. The next conversation between the two vessels was at about the time the Edward Y. Townsend was abeam of Harbor Beach. That vessel logged Harbor Beach Breakwater Light abeam at 2028 (8:28 P.M.) at a distance of 4.3 miles and the master was attempting to follow the recommended upbound track as indicated on Lake Survey Chart No. 5. The Daniel J. Morrell was ahead of the Edward Y. Townsend, proceeding upbound at this time but her exact position is unknown. Again, general weather conditions were discussed. At this time the wind was northerly, at about 35 miles per hour and increasing

248

rapidly. The sea was estimated to be northerly eight feet and building up. Distance between crests was approximately 250 to 300 feet. The next communication between the two vessels was at about 10:00 P.M. and concerned the deteriorating weather and sea conditions and courses of the two vessels. The wind was still northerly and had increased to about 50 miles per hour. The seas were then 12 feet and northerly. The Edward Y. Townsend, although riding fairly well to this point, had started to pound and roll. Captain Connelly restricted movement of personnel between the forward and after sections of the vessel from 2200 (10:00 P.M.) 28 November until 2200 (10:00 P.M.) 29 November 1966, because of the fear of broaching. Captain Crawley indicated that he was steering 347° T in order to make good 341° T, the recommended upbound course. There was further radiotelephone communication at about 2315 (11:15 P.M.) and at this time the wind had increased to an estimated 50 to 55 miles per hour and the seas were still building up. Until this time the Edward Y. Townsend had experienced no difficulty in steering or holding into the sea. While on Lake Huron the Edward Y. Townsend carried nine feet of water in #1 port and starboard tanks. All other ballast tanks were full except that the after peak tank was filled to within approximately one foot of the top. The master of that vessel had considered proceeding to Thunder Bay to anchor in protected waters and had discussed this possibility with Captain Crawley. An alternative which had been discussed by the two masters earlier was whether to return to Port Huron. Captain Connelly deemed it safer to head into the sea. He stated that there would be more twisting action of his vessel in a quartering sea and expressed the fear of broaching and not being able to get his light vessel out of the trough. At about 2350 (11:50 P.M.) 28 November 1966, Captain Crawley called the Edward Y. Townsend. The master of the latter vessel said, "I will call you back," and hung up the phone. At the time of the call the Edward Y. Townsend had just started to blow around or broach into the seas. The vessel fell off to starboard approximately 22° before it could be brought back on course with left full rudder. At approximately 0015 (12:15 A.M.) 29 November 1966, Captain Connelly called Captain Crawley. At this time Captain Crawley indicated that the Daniel J. Morrell had just had a similar experience to that of the Edward Y. Townsend, in that his vessel had also been blown off course. This conversation was brief because both masters were busy attempting to hold the two vessels into the sea. At no time did Captain Crawley indicate what his exact plans were concerning vessel operations or itinerary. This was the last known contact with the Daniel J. Morrell. From the time of the Daniel J. Morrell's departure from Buffalo, New York on 26 November 1966, through the last communication with the Edward Y. Townsend at 0015 (12:15 A.M.) 29 November 1966, the master of the Daniel J. Morrell had not reported any difficulty with his vessel, radios, equipment, structure, operations, machinery, or problems of any kind except weather conditions and the difficulty of holding the vessel into the sea.

Communications between the two vessels through the time of the last contact had been normal. Channel 16 (156.9 Mcs.) (FM) had been used as calling frequency and channels 6 and 8 (156.3 Mcs. and 156.4 Mcs.) (FM) were used in conducting radio conversation at all times between the two vessels. Channel 51, the calling and distress frequency (2182 kc.) or channel 52, (2003 kcs.), the working frequency for the AM radio, had not been used between the two vessels. The Edward Y. Townsend was maintaining a continuous listening watch on channel 51.

Captain Connelly estimated the wind to be northerly at 65 miles per hour at 0015 (12:15 A.M.) and described the seas as "tremendous." The height of the seas was 20 feet and the distance between crests was still 250 to 300 feet. By 0200 (2:00 A.M.) the wind was about 65 miles per hour and had shifted to the north-northeast. Seas had built up to about 25 feet. The Edward Y. Townsend was pitching, rolling and pounding at this time but even though there was difficulty experienced in holding her into the sea, she did not fall off more than approximately 25° and did not roll more than approximately 20°. During the height of the storm some solid water was taken over the bow. At approximately 0145 (1:45 A.M.) and again at about 0345 (3:45 A.M.), Captain Connelly attempted radio contact with the Daniel J. Morrell without success. He attributed this failure to make radio contact to radio problems on the Morrell. The radar on board the Edward Y. Townsend had been turned on at approximately 1800 (6:00 P.M.) 28 November 1966, but at no time was there known radar contact with the Daniel J. Morrell and she was not sighted visually. No attempt was actually made to establish radar contact with that vessel.

Captain Connelly could not give an accurate distance separating the two vessels subsequent to the heaving of the anchor by the Edward Y. Townsend at 1453 (2:53 P.M.) 28 November 1966. His best estimate was that 20 miles separated the two vessels at that time and that the distance probably had shortened by the time of the casualty because the Daniel J. Morrell had experienced adverse weather earlier.

The last estimated position of the Edward Y. Townsend prior to 0200 (2:00 A.M.) 29 November 1966, was 06 6° T and 7.7 miles from Point Aux Barques Light, at 2350 (11:50 P.M.) The master was attempting to follow the recommended charted trackline of 341° T. He indicated that at 0200 (2:00 A.M.) the vessel would have made good approximately three miles from the 2350 (11:50 P.M.) position.

From the time of passing the Lake Huron Lightship until 2028 (8:28 P.M.) 28 November the Edward Y. Townsend was able to make turns that would normally give her 13.9 miles per hour over the bottom and was making good approximately 13.3 miles per hour when it passed abeam of the Harbor Beach Breakwater Light. Due to weather conditions, Captain Connelly had to reduce speed to 90 revolutions per minute at 8:45 P.M. and 75 revolutions per minute at 2045 (8:50 P.M.), which would give him approximately 10 and 8 miles per hour over the bottom respectively under normal conditions. His vessel was making an estimated 5 to 6 miles per hour at 2050 (8:50 P.M.) By 2350 (11:50 P.M.) the vessel was making about two miles per hour over the bottom. After 2350 (11:50 P.M.) it was necessary occasionally to increase to full speed to keep the vessel's bow from falling off; and the engineers automatically reduced RPM when the propeller came out of the water. This occurred at approximately two-minute intervals. Thereafter the engineers attempted to maintain 80 RPM.

By 1130 (11:30 A.M.) 29 November 1966, the winds had diminished to approximately 50 to 55 miles per hour. At 1400 (2:00 P.M.) 29 November 1966, the Edward Y. Townsend, after gradually changing course to head into the wind and sea, was at an estimated position of 56.3 miles bearing 203° True from Cove Island Radio Beacon. The master of the Edward Y. Townsend found the wind and sea conditions in the area off Point Aux Barques more severe than anticipated as a result of weather forecasts and on-scene weather in the lower two-thirds of Lake Huron prior to his passing Lake Huron Lightship. He could not recall having experienced sea conditions of this magnitude on the Great Lakes. He expressed the opinion that he could not have lowered his boats safely had such action been necessary.

On 29 November, water was discovered in the cargo holds of the Townsend to a depth of approximately 45 inches at the after bulkhead. This water extended forward to the mid cargo hold length. The master was surprised to discover such a quantity of water because none had been pumped into the holds intentionally. This quantity of water was attributed to side tank leakage since the time of departing Buffalo. A former third mate of the Daniel J. Morrell stated that the only water normally found in the cargo hold was the result of leakage from the ballast tanks. The only times that he has seen a considerable tonnage of water in the cargo holds of Great Lakes bulk carriers was when water was placed in the holds

253

deliberately. He stated that carriage of such water in the holds as ballast was a normal Great Lakes practice. He expressed the belief that if too much water is carried in the cargo holds the hatches may be damaged by water impact as the vessel rolls.

A former master of the Daniel J. Morrell testified that he has pumped water into cargo holds when in heavy seas in order to keep the propeller submerged. He believed that this cargo hold ballast would make the ship more stable. He would, however, limit the depth of water to three feet at the after cargo hold bulkhead. The reason expressed for this form of ballasting was that the propeller must be kept submerged in order to prevent damage to propulsion machinery.

Tarpaulins were not installed over the sliding plate type hatch covers of the Edward Y. Townsend on 28 or 29 November 1966. The master stated that this type hatch cover leaks very little and that tarpaulins are normally used during Spring and Fall months when the vessel is loaded with cargo. The previous master of the Daniel J. Morrell stated that he does not require tarpaulins to be installed over the hatch covers when there is not cargo aboard, even in bad weather.

On 30 November 1966, the Edward Y. Townsend stopped for fuel at Lime Island in the Lower St. Mary's River. At this time the master received a report that there were some loose rivets in the deck plating, starboard side, weather deck (spardeck). Upon further inspection, it was found that there was a crack extending from the forward starboard corner of number 10 hatch to and running beneath the deck strap which is located

254

between the hatches and the sheer strake, starboard side. Prior to this time the master was not aware of any structural damages. Normal working and springing had been experienced but it was not considered excessive. The damages were reported to the company officials who in turn made the required report to the Coast Guard.

The M/V Benson Ford, having anchored at Bois Blanc Island, Straits of Mackinac, because of weather conditions, heaved anchor at 0850 (8:50 A.M.) EST, 28 November 1966, and proceeded downbound into Lake Huron. The loaded vessel was basically following the recommended downbound track line. At the time of heaving anchor there was a northerly gale. The log book for the Benson Ford indicated that she passed Presque Isle at 1509 (3:09 P.M.) EST at which time the wind was NNE whole gale. Log book entries from 1947 (7:47 P.M.) 28 November to 0702 (7:02 A.M.) 29 November 1966, the time of arrival of that vessel at Lake Huron Lightship, indicated northerly whole gale winds. The master of the Benson Ford estimated that the storm was at its greatest intensity between the hours of 2200 (10:00 P.M.) 28 November and 0600 (6:00 A.M.) 29 November. During this period the wind was "fairly constant" at an estimated 60 knots (69 MPH) and the seas were from the north northeast at 20 to 25 feet, 250 to 300 feet from crest to crest. The vessel did take some water over the stern and there was the normal difficulty in shiphandling to be expected with heavy following seas. After overhearing a conversation between the Edward Y. Townsend and the Daniel J. Morrell concerning the possibilities of proceeding to Thunder Bay for shelter, the master of the Benson Ford joined the discussion to give information concerning the status of anchored vessels at Thunder Bay. He reached the definite opinion that both Captain Crawley and Captain Connelly were planning to seek shelter at Thunder Bay. During this conversation both upbound vessels had indicated that their speeds had been reduced. Although the Benson Ford was experiencing difficulty with his AM radio due to "static electricity," he was maintaining a continuous listening watch on channel 51 and had overhead some communication on that channel. No actual distress communication was received on the 28 or 29th of November, however. At 0015 (12:15 A.M.) 29 November, the Benson Ford was at an estimated position of 055° T, 19.7 miles from Point Aux Barques Light. During the period 0100 to 0130 (1:00 to 1:30 A.M.) the Benson Ford picked up a radar contact off her starboard beam at a distance of about 5.8 miles. At this time the Benson Ford was on a heading of 180°. The target was not identified but was believed to be either the Daniel J. Morrell or the Edward Y. Townsend because he knew of no other vessels in that general area. The target was intermittent due to weather conditions and no other target on his starboard side was observed. The Benson Ford suffered no damages as a result of the storm. The master of the Benson Ford indicated that the weather conditions experienced were more severe than expected. He had anticipated winds from the NNW. He also expressed the opinion that he would not have been able to safely lower his lifeboats during this storm, had it been necessary.

The SS Kinsman Independent, a Great Lakes bulk freighter

constructed in 1907, proceeded upbound into Lake Huron and passed the Lake Huron Lightship with a cargo of coal at 1727 (5:27 P.M.) EST on 28 November. The master, Captain Zernie Newman, stated that at that time there were light winds from the west. As the vessel approached the Harbor Beach area the wind had moved to the north and was 45 knots (51.8 MPH). The engine was held at ¾ speed in order to maintain steerageway. This speed was 83 RPM, which would normally give the vessel a speed of approximately 10.6 MPH. At 2205 (10:05 P.M.) speed was reduced to 68 RPM. At 0145 (1:45 A.M.) 29 November 1966, when the Kinsman Independent was in position 010° T and 3.2 miles from Harbor Beach Light, it was blown off course and was caught in the trough of the sea for approximately four minutes before being able to reverse course to return to Port Huron. The vessel had been unable to retain its former heading. Until being blown around she had been able to hold into the sea without too much difficulty. The wind had increased to an estimated 47 to 55 knots (54 to 63.4 MPH). The draft of the Kinsman Independent on entering Lake Huron was 17 feet 2 inches forward and 18 feet 9 inches aft. The horsepower of this 592 foot vessel is 1800.

Captain Newman had expected the wind and seas to go to the northwest and that his vessel would be in the lee of the eastern shore of Michigan. At the height of the storm the estimated height of the sea was 15 to 17 feet and he observed two "rollers" with an estimated height of 25 to 28 feet. Until his return to Port Huron for refuge, Captain Newman had intended to continue through the storm to Superior, Wisconsin. Captain

Newman indicated that he had experienced one storm on the Great Lakes that was more severe than that experienced on 28 and 29 November. This was a 1952 storm in Lake Superior in which the winds were about 95 MPH and the seas 25 feet high.

Captain William L. Hull was Second Mate on the Daniel J. Morrell in November 1958 when that vessel was proceeding in a storm in Lake Superior. The winds at that time reached 100 miles per hour and the seas reached a height of 25 feet. The Daniel J. Morrell was then in ballast and additional water ballast was carried in the cargo hold.

The following upbound vessels were also in the general area off Point Aux Barques, during the storm on 28 and 29 November 1966:

a. SS Howard L. Shaw (Canadian)

This 451 foot 6 inch vessel of 4769 gross tons, built in 1900 at Wyandotte, Michigan, passed Lake Huron Lightship at 1545 (3:45 P.M.) 28 November 1966. At 2115 (9:15 P.M.) she was abeam of Harbor Beach, proceeding at three-fourths speed and making one to two knots (1 to 2 ½ MPH) over the bottom. At 2330 (11:30 P.M.) 29 November 1966 she was blown off course, and after making two unsuccessful attempts to regain her heading into the sea, proceeded to Port Huron for refuge. The Howard L. Shaw was light and in ballast. She had no radio contact with the Daniel J. Morrell while in Lake Huron on 28 or 29 November.

b. SS Fred A. Manske, O.N. 206695

This is a 504 foot self-unloading Great Lakes bulk freighter, built in 1909 of 2500 horsepower. Although the vessel was almost blown

258

around, she proceded upbound to her destination, through the area off Point Aux Barques, during the storm. The master was reluctant to come about because of the topside weight of the self-unloading boom.

c. SS Robert Hobson, O.N. 226175

This 586 foot Great Lakes bulk freighter, built in 1926 of 2200 horsepower, passed the Lake Huron Lightship at 1736 (5:36 P.M.) EST 28 November 1966. She was blown around at 0230 (2:30 A.M.) 29 November 1966, approximately three to four miles above Harbor Beach, and proceeded to the Port Huron area. The Robert Hobson, which was loaded with coal to the winter marks, sustained no known damages. The master of this vessel indicated that the winds experienced were not surprising but the seas were more than were anticipated under such wind conditions.

d. SS Harry Coulby, O.N. 226742

This 615 foot Great Lakes bulk freighter, built in 1927 of 5000 horsepower, passed the Lake Huron Lightship at 0126 (1:26 A.M.) EST 29 November 1966. When at a position 6 miles above Port Sanilac on the upbound track, it experienced one wave estimated to be 20 feet in height and took solid water over the bow. At this time the master was informed that conditions were more severe in the Point Aux Barques area and that other vessels were returning downbound in the snow storm. He then intentionally reversed course and proceeded to the Port Huron area. The master of the Harry Coulby said that the master of the Henry Steinbrenner reported that it took 8 minutes for that vessel to come about. The master of the Henry Steinbrenner intentionally turned his vessel around and returned to Port Huron.

e. Several other vessels were reported to have been blown around, turned around voluntarily or proceeded through Lake Huron at various times during 28 and 29 November 1966.

The U.S. Coast Guard Cutter Acacia (WLB-406), having departed Harbor Beach, Michigan, at 1650 (4:50 P.M.) 28 November 1966 with a deck load consisting of two Coast Guard craft, the CG-40507 and CG-36550, while en route to Sault Ste. Marie, Michigan, was diverted to assist personnel on the grounded M/V Nordmeer off Thunder Bay Island Light. At 2215 (10:15 P.M.) she was released from the Nordmeer assistance case. At 2330 (11:30 P.M.) CG-36550 broke loose due to heavy weather. At this time the vessel was at an estimated position of 44° 12' N, 82° 51' W and was attempting to reach shelter at Thunder Bay. At 0300 (3:00 A.M.) 29 November 1966 both the CG-40507 and the CG-36550 were loose on deck and were receiving damages. The seas were estimated to be 15 to 25 feet in height. The wind was reported as 40 to 50 knots (46 to 57 ½ MPH). The Acacia then came about at an estimated position of 44° 30' N, 82° 55' W to head for shelter. She was unable to enter Harbor Beach because of the heavy seas and accordingly proceeded to Port Huron, Michigan, for safe refuge.

While the Daniel J. Morrell was taking on fuel at Windsor, Ontario on the morning of 28 November 1966, Dennis N. Hale boarded the vessel and assumed his regular duties as watchman. Hale had a total of three years sea service, all of which was served on board the Daniel J. Morrell.

260

He had been serving as watchman for approximately a year.

Hale normally stood the 4-8 watch and commenced his last watch shortly after the vessel passed the Lake Huron Lightship at approximately 1530 (3:30 P.M.) 28 November 1966. Between 1600 and 1640 (4:00 and 4:30 P.M.) Hale, as directed, entered the cargo holds for the purpose of marking leaks and cargo bucket damages, which were incurred during normal unloading operations in way of side tank slopes. Damage to side tank slopes had been repaired several times during the 1966 operating season. The vessel's smooth log indicated that the last repairs in that area had been completed in Buffalo, N.Y. on 26 October 1966. He marked three leaks, one in the general area of number 6 hatch and two in the general area of number 8 hatch. He was unable to drive wedges into the holes because the cracks were not parted sufficiently to receive wedges. The largest of the cracks was described as "moon shaped" and 8 inches long. The three cracks were "spurting water." He was unable to enter the number three cargo hold because free surface water extended from the after bulkhead of number 3 cargo hold to midway into number 2. He estimated the depth of water to be 18 inches at the after bulkhead of number 3 cargo hold. Hale attributed the water to leaks from the side tanks and so informed the master of the amount of water in the cargo holds. The vessel's hatch covers were in place and tarpaulins were on deck, rolled up adjacent to the hatches. At 2000 (8:00 P.M.) 28 November, at the time of completing his watch, Hale indicated that it was snowing but the weather was not severe, and the vessel was riding "well." He was able to proceed aft to the galley for food after getting off watch. However, at the time of his going to bed at about 2130 (9:30 P.M.) the weather was worsening. Hale's quarters were located on the spar deck, starboard side forward, adjacent to the anchor windlass room. At the time of going to bed he could hear the anchor bumping against the bow. Other than the noise produced by the anchors, Hale was not aware of the actual weather and sea conditions from the time of going to bed until at or about 0200 (2:00 A.M.) 29 November 1966. At about that time he was awakened by what was described as a loud bang. A few minutes later he heard another bang. At this time, books from his bookshelf fell out into the deck. The bookshelf had no retaining bar and was installed in a fore and aft direction. He became alarmed and decided to get up. He then learned that his bunk light was inoperative. About this time the general alarm was sounded. He jumped up, grabbed his lifejacket and ran out into the starboard passageway. There were no lights on in the forward section of the vessel, but as he looked aft he could see lights on the after superstructure. He noticed that the center of the vessel was "higher" than the after part of the vessel; that is to say, it was in a hogging condition. He went back into his room to look for his pants, but in the darkness and excitement he could find only his peacoat. He then proceeded to the forward liferaft. There was melting snow on the deck. He had looked for the lifeboats but was convinced that they both had already been lowered. While still forward he could hear what he took to be metal cracking and working or rubbing together. When he reached the forward liferaft, there were several men standing around it. He thought the whole forward or deck crew was there at that time. No attempt was made to proceed to the lifeboat area because of the damage in the midship section. Someone said, "get on the raft and hold on tight." He indicated that virtually all deck force personnel, including the master, 1st mate and 2nd mate sat on the raft to await the sinking of the vessel. No attempt was made to throw the raft over the side and no instructions regarding the use of lifesaving equipment were given by any of the ship's officers in Hale's presence. One crewmember tried to get men off the raft in order to open the storage locker to reach the distress flares. The master decided to wait until the raft was in the water to use the flares. The crewmembers assembled at the raft were in various stages of dress, some with various items of clothing missing. For example, Hale was wearing only a pair of shorts, lifejacket and peacoat. They were all wearing lifejackets. Hale knew that there were two vessels following fairly close behind the Daniel J. Morrell earlier and Captain Crawley had indicated that there had been a vessel sighted off the port bow. Hale did not actually see any other vessels immediately prior to or at any time after the sinking. Two men had attempted to tie themselves to the raft with line. Hale saw only one person on the after end of the ship, but he could not be certain of his identity. Although there were no lights in the midship area, Hale indicated he did observe that the crack in the vessel started in the area of the gunwale bar, starboard side, in the general area of hatches 11 and 12, and proceeded across to the port side. The forward section's deck at the starboard side seemed to drop lower than the after section in a

263

twisting effect. Hale could see metal sparks as the two sections of the vessel rubbed together. He could also see steam coming from the parted steam line. Then the vessel broke into two sections and the stern section appeared to be pushing and ramming the forward section. This, together with sea and wind action, caused the bow section to work around to port, reaching a perpendicular angle in relation to the stern section. The stern section appeared to be still under power and continued to bump into the port side of the bow section. As the bow section swung to port and parted from the after section, it started settling and very shortly thereafter the forward liferaft and several members of the crew were washed over the starboard side. Time elapse from the sounding of the emergency alarm until the vessel parted was estimated to be eight minutes. The raft was thrown well clear of both sections of the vessel and no one remained on the raft as it entered the water. Hale came up within approximately 10 feet of the raft. By the time he reached the raft, two deckhands, Arthur E. Stojek and John J. Cleary, Jr., had already arrived. Then Charles Fosbender, wheelsman, reached the raft and they were all able to crawl onto the raft. Hale saw no one in the water prior to his going over the side. After his entry into the water, the only persons he saw were the other three on the raft and one person still on the forecastle of the vessel. He never saw a lifeboat or the after raft in the water. Hale was of the opinion when the forward raft entered the water that the after raft was still on the vessel. None of the four men on the raft were on watch at the time of the casualty. No one indicated to Hale any knowledge as to the cause of the casualty,

264

incidents leading up to the actual sinking or whether radio distress signals had been transmitted. Hale heard the master state on 28 November that channel 52 was inoperative. There were no other known radio problems on board the Daniel J. Morrell. The vessel's speed or heading, and the direction of the wind and sea in relation to the vessel at the time of the casualty is unknown. He did not know the vessel's location at the time of sinking. Approximately 15 minutes after Hale entered the water he observed the after portion of the bow section settle evenly beneath the water, followed by the stem. The raft was at a distance of approximately 200 yards from the bow section and an estimated one-half to one mile from the stern section when the bow sank. The stern still seemed to be under power and lights were still visible. The men on the raft did not see the stern section sink. Other than the actual breaking up of the vessel, no fires, explosions or any other material, machinery or equipment casualties were observed by Hale while on board or after going over the side. The liferaft was provided with the equipment required by Federal Regulations. Hale used several of the distress flares within a short period after sinking as there were other vessels known to be in the general area. Two flares were lost over the side. After having fired the signal pistol two or three times, the handle and barrel separated into two pieces. He was able to hold them together in order to fire off the remaining parachute flares. Hale knew of no other deficiencies with lifesaving equipment. All the parachute flares and hand held flares were used within the first 24 hours. The storage locker and other portions of the wood and metal raft structure sustained damages as it went over the side. However, it remained intact and offered adequate support for the four men. The men lay on the raft huddled together on one end, there being no other means of keeping warm. Hale testified that Cleary and Stojek died around 0600 (6:00 A.M.) 29 November 1966 and that Fosbender died around 1600 (4:00 P.M.) the same day. They were all believed to be conscious until shortly before death. The cause of death for these three men was listed on their Death Certificates as drowning. Exposure was listed as an antecedent cause. The liferaft supporting Hale and the three deceased men was located by the Coast Guard at 1600 (4:00 P.M.) 30 November 1966. Hale was semi-conscious when he was taken from the raft. He was able to give preliminary testimony to Coast Guard Investigating officers on 1 December 1966. He suffered from exposure, frost bite of his feet and right hand and sustained other minor injuries. As a result, he is still incapacitated.

Hale testified during the preliminary interrogation that prior to the sinking, the vessel was "sound" as far as he was concerned. However, he stated that there were some rivets marked for replacement by Frank Brian, wheelsman, throughout the cargo holds just before winter lay up in 1965. He could give no estimate as to the number of marked rivets. He indicated that he didn't know if any had been replaced but that he knew some still had not been replaced prior to the 1966 season. These rivets were alleged to be in the shell plating between the side tank tops and the spar deck. At initial questioning, he knew of no other structural

266

discrepancies. When questioned before the marine Board, he testified that over 1000 rivets were marked for replacement in the shell plating between the main and spar decks, port and starboard, and that these rivets had not been replaced at the time of the casualty. He related that about a week prior to the latter questioning, Harvey F. Hayes, deck watchman on board the Daniel J. Morrell in 1965, told him that one-fourth of the shell rivets in the side tanks were bad. Neither the company representatives, inspectors, surveyors, or previous vessel personnel who were questioned had ever seen or heard of defective or marked rivets in the shell plating between the main and spar decks.

Hayes testified that the 1st mate had given Frank Brian instructions in mid-November 1965, in his presence, for Brian and Hayes to enter No. 4 and 5 port tanks to mark leaky rivets with paint. He stated that Brian was in charge as he had 30 years experience. Hayes stated that he observed two leaking bead welds in the area of lapped butt plates. He indicated that the worst leak was approximately seven inches in a vertical direction. He also stated that there were 250 to 500 leaky shell rivets marked in these two tanks from above the turn of the bilge to within two feet of the side tank tips and that the vessel's side plating was partially wet when the leaky rivets were marked. He saw no sheared or missing rivets. The leaky rivets were allegedly grouped to the extent that the men painted circles around some areas up to 3 and 4 feet in diameter. A report of the condition of the rivets was reportedly made to the 1st mate by Brian. Hayes also entered the cargo holds to mark up bucket damage for repair during winter lay up.

Hayes stated that several of the vessel's side tanks were leaking during the 1965 season and that as a result of his personally sounding vessel tanks, he had observed the collection of up to 3 inches in a side tank within a 24 hour period. He personally observed up to 7 inches in side tanks and on one occasion up to 10 inches that he attributed to leakage. The port side tanks 4 and 5 were leaking more than the others.

Hayes testified that he had never discussed the structural condition of the Daniel J. Morrell with Dennis Hale. Hayes' total sea experience consists of service on the Daniel J. Morrell from 3 June to 21 December 1965, as deckhand and deck watch.

Mr. Frank Brian informed the Board that he has never entered side and double bottom tanks to mark leaky rivets. He considered this work to be the mate's responsibility. He did enter all the Daniel J. Morrell's port side and double bottom tanks in the spring of 1965 to remove debris left by shipyard personnel. On this occasion he saw no structural defects.

After being informed by an official of the Bethlehem Steel Corporation at 1215 (12:15 P.M.) EST 30 November 1966, that the Daniel J. Morrell was overdue, the U.S. Coast Guard Rescue Coordination Center, Cleveland, Ohio initiated an all ships broadcast, requesting that all vessels be on the lookout for that vessel. A fixed wing aircraft, CG-1266, en route from Alpena, Michigan, to Detroit, Michigan, was directed to offload cargo at Detroit and then commence a search for the Daniel J. Morrell. At 1312 (1:12 P.M.) 30 November 1966, the Coast Guard in Cleveland, Ohio, was informed that the

SS G.G. Post had sighted a body wearing a life jacket stenciled with the name, "Daniel J. Morrell", 8 miles, 005° true from the Harbor Beach Breakwater Light. The

CG-30386 had already been dispatched by the Harbor Beach Coast Guard Station and actually recovered the body at 1210 (12:10 P.M.) 30 November 1966. The Coast Guard aircraft, CG-1266, arrived in the general area of the disaster at 1335 (1:35 P.M.) and was designated as on scene commander. The following Coast Guard units participated in the search:

<u>Vessels and small craft</u>

USCGC Mackinaw (WAGB-83)

USCGC Bramble (WLB-392)

USCGC Acacia (WLB-406)

CG-30386 and Cg-36463 from Harbor Beach Coast Guard Station

CG-40560 from the Port Huron Coast Guard Station

CG-40558 from the Saginaw River Coast Guard Station

<u>Aircraft</u>

Helicopters CG-1395 and CG-1412 and fixed wing aircraft CG-1242 and CG-1266 from CG Air Station, Traverse City, Michigan

Helicopters CG-1401 and CG-1415 from CG Air Station, Detroit, Michigan

Upon arrival of the CGC Mackinaw in the area of the casualty, she was designated as the scene commander.

In addition to the first body recovered at 1210 (12:10 P.M.) 30 November 1966 by CG-30386, additional bodies, the survivor and debris were recovered as follows:

a. At or about 1600 (4:00 P.M.) 30 November 1966, seven bodies were recovered by CG-30386 and helicopters CG-1401 and CG-1415, within a five-mile radius of a position seven miles, 025° true from Harbor Beach Breakwater Light.

b. At about 1600 (4:00 P.M.) 30 November 1966, three bodies and one survivor were recovered from the Daniel J. Morrell's forward liferaft, on the beach, three miles below Huron City, Michigan, by helicopter CG-1395. The survivor, Dennis Hale, was transported by the helicopter to the Harbor Beach General Hospital.

c. At about 0930 (9:30 A.M). 1 December 1966, one body was recovered ten and one-half miles, 137° true from the Harbor Beach Breakwater Light by the CGC Mackinaw.

d. At about 0945 (9:45 A.M.) 1 December 1966, at a position of 43° 40'N, 82° 20.5'W, two bodies were recovered by the CGC Acacia.

e. At about 1355 (1:55 P.M.) on 1 December 1966, at a position of 43° 37'N, 82° 20'W, six bodies were recovered by the CGC Acacia.

f. At about 1445 (2:45 P.M.) 5 December 1966, one body was recovered under the Daniel J. Morrell's after liferaft at Point Aux Barques by a commercial salvager. The raft was generally in good condition, with only minor damages.

g. On the morning of 11 December 1966, one body was recovered by the Ontario Provincial Police on the beach eight miles north of Kincardine, Ontario.

The active search continued until 1905 (7:05 P.M.) EST 4 December 1966. Daily surveillance searches were conducted along the shoreline several days thereafter, as weather permitted, in attempts to locate the remaining bodies and vessel debris.

In addition to a number of Great Lakes vessels there were several Coast Guard units in the Lake Huron area that were maintaining continuous listening watches on channel 51 (2182 kc.) at the time of the casualty. No distress message was received from the Daniel J. Morrell by Coast Guard units or other vessels in the area. The material and debris from the Daniel J. Morrell recovered and collected during and after completion of the active search including two liferafts, several life jackets, life rings, boat oars, etc., as indicated in Exhibit 52, have been released to the vessel owners.

During November and December 1960, while the Daniel J. Morrell was on drydock in Ashtabula, Ohio, approximately 9500 shell rivets and 13 shell plates were replaced. Numerous replacements and repairs were completed to internals in way thereof. Various other repairs were also completed at this time. All the above repairs were allegedly required as result of the vessel surging against the dock at Taconite Harbor,

Minnesota, on 2 December 1959; heavy weather on 18 November 1958, in Lake Superior; rubbing of the bottom in Nicolet Lake on 3 August 1958; the vessel's striking of a dock prior to 26 June 1960, at an undetermined time and place; the vessel's striking of a wall at Lock 4, St. Mary's River, Sault Ste. Marie, Michigan, on 15 June 1960; and as a result of cargo loading and unloading "bucket" damages prior to the date of drydocking. It is noted that bucket damage repairs included cropping and renewing sections of auxiliary deck stringer plates at some hatches. One 9" by 24" section of the inboard edge of the auxiliary deck stringer at hatch number 11 starboard side was cropped and renewed by welding. All repairs during the drydocking of the Daniel J. Morrell in November and December 1960, were completed and tested satisfactorily.

The subject vessel was next drydocked in Toledo, Ohio, on 18 February 1966 and was given credit for drydocking by the U.S. Coast Guard on 25 February 1966. From drydocking in December 1960, to drydocking in February 1966, there were no reported major damages to the Daniel J. Morrell and no major repairs or alterations were completed to the vessel during that period. However, there were minor repairs completed during this period, such as routine "bucket damage" repairs in way of cargo holds.

Seven (7) inspectors and surveyors participated in the 1966 drydock inspection of subject vessel. This group included the Fleet Engineer of the Bethlehem Steel Corporation and his assistant, a representative of U.S. Salvage, a representative of the American Bureau

272

of Shipping and three Coast Guard inspectors including one boiler and two hull inspectors. During this inspection, the entire external body, all side and double bottom tanks, forepeak and afterpeak tanks and all other vessel compartments were inspected thoroughly. As a result of this inspection, three shell plates in the starboard "E" strake were removed and replaced by two longer plates. The plates removed were E-21-S, E-22-S and E-23-S, located between frames 107-127. The plates were installed with welded butts and riveted seams whereas the previous installation consisted of riveted butts and seams. In addition, eleven (11) bilge brackets and three (3) web floors in the area involved were cropped back and replaced or partially replaced because of buckling. These repairs were necessitated by damages sustained at an undetermined date and discovered during the 1966 drydock inspection. The three (3) plates were set in approximately two inches. The remainder of the hull plating appeared to be in good condition. There was no condition found during the drydock examination to indicate the necessity for drilling or gauging to determine the thickness of metal. While the vessel was on drydock, approximately 50 shell rivets were replaced as required by the inspection party. In eight (8) of the vessel's side and double bottom tanks, the Coast Guard inspector required numerous minor or routine type repairs, such as the refastening of stiffeners and brackets and repairing cracked welds in brackets, stiffeners, and angles. In the number 4 starboard double bottom tank the Coast Guard inspector required that a seven (7) foot by one and one-half (1.5) foot section of the after watertight bulkhead be cropped and replaced, necessitated by a fracture in the bulkhead plate adjacent to the bottom transverse standing angle. Numerous repairs were completed in cargo holds. These were necessitated by bucket damage. The senior Coast Guard hull inspector present during the drydock inspection made the following entry in the Drydock Examination Book for February 1966: "It was noted that approximately 80% of the bottom keelson shell rivets had been renewed recently, probably at the last credit drydocking. Deterioration seems to be affecting these rivets more than other bottom rivets. Although it does not present a problem at this time, they may well require renewal at the next drydock exam." He considered that the amount of deterioration was not sufficient to justify the issuing of a requirement to replace the rivets. This entry was made in the Drydock Examination Book for future reference only. Neither of the Coast Guard hull inspectors could determine the reason for the "unusual" deterioration, but did postulate that electrolytic action was involved. All repairs that were required by Coast Guard inspectors or other members of the inspection party were completed satisfactorily and were inspected by Coast Guard inspectors after completion. Upon completion of the drydock examination, all drydock inspection items were checked off in the Drydock Examination Book as having been completed and the senior hull inspector and the boiler inspector signed the entry; "In my opinion the vessel is fit for the service and route specified." There were no outstanding requirements upon completion of the drydock examination of the Daniel J. Morrell. All inspectors and surveyors interrogated indicated that at the conclusion of

274

the drydock inspection, this vessel was in good condition.

The last annual inspection was completed 15 April 1966, at the Lakefront Ore Dock, Toledo, Ohio. All items required to be inspected by Federal regulation were examined and were determined to be in satisfactory condition at the completion of the annual inspection. The Load Line Certificate was endorsed by an American Bureau of Shipping Surveyor, on 26 February 1966. Fire and boat drills were conducted at annual inspection and at the time of mid-season inspection at Buffalo, New York, 20 July 1966. During the annual inspection, all personnel except the master, the mate and the chief engineer were exercised in the starboard lifeboat. The port lifeboat was swung out. Crew performance during the boat drill was considered to be fair because crew members were slow in launching the boat. The first mate then instructed the crew as to their duties. The performance of the second and third boat crews was much improved. The fire and boat drills during the mid-season inspection were conducted satisfactorily. There were no requirements outstanding against the vessel or its equipment at the time of completion of the annual or mid-season inspections. Subsequent to the date of completion of annual inspection and prior to the date of the casualty there were no known hull or structural damages suffered by the vessel.

Prior to winter lay up of the Daniel J. Morrell in December 1965, a winter work list was prepared for that vessel and was signed by the master for deck items and by the chief engineer for engineering items. The deck section of the work list was prepared by the 1st mate. Of the 46 items on the winter work list all were completed except two, which were not of structural significance. The deck section of the work list contained the following item, "Leaks in the hull will be marked. Port tanks make water." No other item pertaining to midship structural strength of the vessel was contained on the list. The master and chief engineer serving on board subject vessel at the time of winter lay up in 1965 both testified that no other vessel deficiencies were reported by crew members prior to winter lay up. Captain Hull served as master of the Daniel J. Morrell from July 1964 until 3 August 1966, when he was relieved by Captain Crawley. Captain Hull stated that the side tanks and cargo holds of the Morrell were entered by vessel personnel for the purpose of marking leaky rivets in the shell plating and bucket damage in the cargo holds and to inspect for other damage in the Fall of 1965. He estimated that a maximum of twelve (12) leaking rivets were reported in the shell plating in way of side tanks, although he could not remember which side tanks were involved. He indicated that the reason the side tanks were entered for checking rivets was that some of the side tanks were "making water." He said that maximum leakage into any side tank was approximately 5 to 6 inches over a period of a 3 or 4 day trip. He did not report the leaks to the vessel owners nor did he direct personnel to enter the tanks until shortly prior to winter lay up because he did not consider the leakage to be significant or excessive.

Captain Hull considered that the leaking shell rivets had been corrected during drydocking. However, during the 1966 season there were

276

two or possibly three unidentified side tanks that leaked slightly. He did not inform the company of this condition.

The fire and sanitary piping to the forward part of the vessel was installed through the port side tanks. Leaking joints in this piping necessitated repairs during the 1966 season and the vessel operators had planned to relocate these pipes on the spar deck during winter lay up in 1966-1967. The fire line was also used for washdown. This same situation has existed in the past on other vessels of the Bethlehem Fleet and similar corrective measures have been taken. Upon departing the Daniel J. Morrell on 3 August 1966, Captain Hull knew of nothing that would cast doubt as to the soundness of that vessel. He had received no report or complaints from vessel personnel and made no report to company officials to indicate any outstanding vessel structural, equipment or mechanical deficiencies through that date.

A Coast Guard inspector boarded the Edward Y. Townsend at Sault Ste. Marie, Ontario on 2 December 1966, to conduct a heavy weather damage survey. The following conditions were found:

a. The visual part of the crack on the spar deck was approximately 13 inches in length with a maximum opening of approximately 1/8 inch. The crack was almost perpendicular to the axis of the vessel. There was a herringbone effect giving the indication that the crack commenced somewhere beneath the number 10 hatch coaming's forward supporting standing angle at the starboard corner.

b. At the forward starboard corner of number 10 and number 11 hatches, rivets in the deck strap showed signs of working. There were no signs of working on the spar deck, port side. Visual inspection of the shell plating, sheer strake and gunnel bars, port and starboard, revealed no apparent change in form resulting from stress.

c. In numbers 3, 4 and 5 double bottom and side tanks, starboard, there was minor distortion of metal adjacent to some side keelson lightening holes and there was evidence of previous minor stress corrosion. At some of the distortions there was evidence of working. It could not be determined whether the minor distortion was the result of recent working or was previously existing, but there was indication that rust and scale had recently been jarred or popped loose from some of the stress corrosion areas. There was only one crack noticed in way of the stress corrosion. This was a crack approximately six inches in length commencing diagonally from the edge of a lightening hole. This crack was not a new one as scale or rust had formed over the edges. There were several rivets in the center vertical keel that showed signs of recent working. There was an old crack of approximately 6 feet in length in the after bulkhead of number 4 starboard double bottom tank between the outboard side keelson and the turn of the bilge. This crack was in the same general location as one discovered on the Daniel J. Morrell in February 1966. Some of the shell rivets at the bulkhead standing angle in this area were loose, leaked slightly and showed signs of deterioration. It could not be determined whether the bulkhead had worked recently but there was no apparent distortion. The distortion, stress corrosion and evidence of working rivets were more pronounced in the number 4 side and double bottom tanks than in adjacent areas. The corresponding tanks on the port side showed some signs of minor distortion at the lightening holes of the side keelsons.

d. The metal in the midship area of the vessel, including deck, shell, internals and all structural members appeared to be in surprisingly good material condition. The weardown, or deterioration, was considered negligible.

e. Other than the normal stress corrosion, cracks and evidence of working rivets as indicated above, there was nothing found that would explain the reason for the crack in the spar deck. Excluding the crack in the spar deck, no evidence of major structural weakness was found.

f. The Edward Y. Townsend's Certificate of Inspection was withdrawn as a result of this inspection and requirement was issued directing the vessel to be drydocked for further internal and external inspection and necessary repairs. A Permit to Proceed to the location of a drydock was issued, authorizing the vessel to be towed unmanned.

g. The owners of the Edward Y. Townsend have agreed to provide samples of metal removed in way of the crack for analysis at such time as repair work is commenced. At present, the vessel is in a winter lay up status at Sault Ste. Marie, Ontario.

From initial construction through the date of subject casualty, the SS Daniel J. Morrell and the SS Edward Y. Townsend had no significant structural or propulsion unit changes or alterations that would alter their classification as sister ships. The latter vessel was reboilered in 1946 and repowered with a Skinner Unaflow engine in 1954.

The Bethlehem Steel Corporation contracted the McQueen Marine Company, Amhertsburg, Ontario, Canada to locate and positively identify the sunken Daniel J. Morrell. Due to adverse weather conditions experienced while attempting to locate the Morrell between 13 December 1966 and 20 December 1966, attempts to locate and identify that vessel were abandoned on the latter date.

The Commandant, U.S. Coast Guard contracted with Ocean Systems Incorporated, Alexandria, Virginia, through the cooperation of the Supervisor of Salvage, U.S. Navy, to locate, identify, take television pictures of vessel structure and retrieve metal sample from the Daniel J. Morrell. The U.S. Coast Guard Cutter Bramble (WLB-392) was used as a working platform for the entire survey operations. On 6 January 1967, after mooring over a target located by magnetic detection equipped aircraft from the U.S. Naval Air Station, Grosse Ile, Michigan, divers working from the Bramble were able to positively identify by television pictures the stern section of the Daniel J. Morrell. Further diving operations were then continued from 14 January 1967 to 2 February 1967.

As a result of the diving operations, the following facts were established:

a. The stern section of the vessel was resting on the bottom of Lake Huron in approximately 200 to 210 feet of water on a heading of about 320° true. It has settled appreciably in the mud, and has a slight port list. She has a slight trim by the forward end. There were piles of mud on the spar deck adjacent to the point of the crack and it appeared that the forward end had plowed into the bottom first. This area of the stern was buried in mud to within 6 feet to 7 feet of the spar deck.

b. The primary crack in the deck and sheerstrake on the starboard side occurred at web frame 107. This frame is located adjacent to and even with the forward coaming of number 11 hatch. The fracture line on the deck, starboard, ran through a transverse row of rivet holes to the hatch coaming. The forward portion of the number 11 hatch coaming was missing. The crack in the starboard sheerstrake was basically vertical and passed from rivet hole to rivet hole. The location of the break on the port side was between hatches 11 and 12 at about frame 113. The break in the deck stringer followed a transverse row of rivets. The crack in the sheerstrake, port side, was vertical and did not occur in the area of rivets. The port deck seam strap cracked through a line of rivets about six inches forward of the break in the deck stringer. All underdeck longitudinals in the area of the break were bent, twisted, torn loose and displaced from their normal positions. Remaining deck and side plating as well as longitudinals show evidence of severe distortions. Some longitudinals were doubled back upon themselves. Deck and side plating showed evidence of extreme bending. Some sections had been bent back upon themselves to approximately 180° from original. The deck stringer starboard side had been bent down to an angle of about 90°. A section of this plate was recovered for analysis. The surface of the crack in this plate contains chevrons pointing inboard. A large section of the sheerstrake starboard with a section of the seam strap and "L" strake attached was also recovered. Chevrons on the edge of fractured surface on either side of the 3rd rivet hole below the upper edge of the sheerstrake pointed toward that rivet hole. This section of side metal had been bent outboard and around upon itself to $180°$ from normal. The retrieved metal shows signs of little or no wear down or deterioration and the rivets contained therein were in very good condition. The edges of rivet holes showed no signs of wastage. The forward edges of the retrieved metal were shiny and flattened as if they had sustained severe pounding by other metal.

c. Cargo hatches and the coal bunker were found open. Hatch covers were strewn about the area of the hulk. Many hatch clamps had been broken.

d. The port and starboard lifeboat davits were found in the cranked-in position. The port lifeboat was missing and has not been recovered. The starboard lifeboat was hanging over the starboard side still attached to the after boat falls. Its boat cover was in place. The after mast had toppled and had fallen in the area of the missing port lifeboat.

e. None of the missing crew members of the Daniel J. Morrell were located as a result of the diving operations.

f. The forward section of the Daniel J. Morrell was not located.

g. Diving operations were hampered by silt, weather and sea conditions and the divers were not able to make an internal survey to determine distortions or weaknesses that might have contributed to the

282

casualty.

The report of the metallurgical study, dated 6 March 1967, of steel plate samples from the Daniel J. Morrell and completed by the Battelle Memorial Institute, Columbus Laboratories, Columbus, Ohio, supports the following facts:

a. A brittle fracture typical of many prior ship fractures in pre-1948 steel occurred in the spar deck and sheer strake on the starboard side at frame 107.

b. The source of the fracture in the deck plate was not contained in the sample recovered from the hulk. However, the chevron pattern in the fracture indicated that the fracture initiated inboard of the sample retrieved.

c. The fracture in the sheer strake at frame 107 initiated at the third rivet hole below the upper edge of the sheer strake.

d. The original weight of the deck and sheer strake was 40 pounds per square foot (assumed to be 39.98 pounds rather than 40.8 pounds). This corresponds to a thickness of .980 inches. The average thickness of the sample retrieved was .965 inches, which would indicate corrosion of less than 2 percent.

e. The chemical and physical properties and microstructure of the steel were typical of ship plate steel used prior to 1948. The nil ductility temperature as determined by "The Standard Method for Naval Research Laboratory Drop Weight Test" was 50° F. The 15-foot pound "V" notch Charpy transition temperature averaged 97° F.

Of the 22 persons recovered, 13 drowned and 9 died of exposure.

The Federal Bureau of investigation has given authority to include their reports showing positive identification of the persons recovered into the record.

CONCLUSIONS

Based on the foregoing Findings of Fact, it is concluded that:

The casualty was caused by a structural failure in the hull girder amidships which resulted in the break-up of the vessel, and subsequent sinking with loss of life.

The cause of the structural failure was a combination of factors which produced successive brittle fractures. These factors were:

a. High load due to extremely heavy weather conditions.

b. A notch sensitive steel.

c. A notch. Among others, some of the possible locations of the notch are:

A radial crack in a rivet hole.

A welded plate insert on the inboard edge of the auxiliary stringer at number 11 hatch, starboard side.

Recently incurred bucket damage to the inboard edge of the auxiliary stringer in the vicinity of frame 107, starboard side.

d. Temperature of 33° F, which was below the nil ductility temperature of the steel.

The exact location of the initiation of the fracture (whether bottom, deck or side shell) is unknown. However, the most probable location was on the spar deck starboard side at frame 107 in way of the number 11 hatch corner.

A number of other factors, including one or any combination of the following, might have contributed to this casualty:

a. The free surface water in cargo holds 2 and 3 might have caused an unusual strain to an already weakened area as a result of the dynamic forces of shifting weight due to pitching, rolling, pounding, and possible twisting of the vessel as its bow was blown around.

b. The vessel might have broached and sustained the crack while attempting to hold into the sea as she was broaching or while attempting to regain her heading into the sea. It is concluded that any ballasted vessel of a design similar to that of the Daniel J. Morrell would suffer severe stresses and strains in sea and wind conditions such as those present on 29 November should it remain in or at angles to the trough for any length of time. This evaluation is predicated upon the fact that a 600 foot vessel at an angle of approximately 30° to seas having crest of 250 to 300 feet apart will suffer severe hogging, sagging and twisting stresses.

c. The crack in the midship section occurred at Frame 107. The welded butt joining plates E-20 and E-21 was located on the starboard side also at Frame 107. Although there is no evidence to indicate any defect in this weld, the possibility exists that the butt weld contained an undetected defect at installation.

d. The crack in the after bulkhead of the number four starboard double bottom tank was very similar in dimension and location to the crack found on the Edward Y. Townsend during the heavy weather damage survey conducted on 2 December 1966. Although this may be coincidence, it may tend to indicate the existence of a pattern of structural weakness on the starboard side of these two practically identical sister vessels and possibly other vessels of approximately the same age and of similar design. This is supported by the facts that the crack commenced on the Edward Y. Townsend and the Daniel J. Morrell in the same general deck area, both vessels were headed into the wind and sea under the same weather and sea conditions, both vessels were light and in ballast and both probably had basically the same free surface water in their cargo holds.

The actual drafts, extent of ballasting, exact courses and speeds, and reaction to sea and wind conditions on board the Daniel J. Morrell from the time of entering Lake Huron until immediately prior to sinking, could not be determined. However, it is assumed that they were basically the same as those that existed on the Edward Y. Townsend during the same period.

Although the vessel sailed from Buffalo short of the crew required by the Certificate of Inspection, the shortages were in required ratings only. The actual number of persons aboard exceeded the number required. There was no evidence of violation of law on the part of the master or company officials in this regard. There is not evidence to indicate the crew shortage contributed to the cause of the casualty.

The lifesaving equipment on board met the requirements of the Federal Regulations and there is not evidence to indicate that any person lost his life due to faulty or improperly maintained lifesaving equipment. However, under the circumstances that existed at the time of sinking, the lifeboats and life rafts aboard could not be used properly to save lives. Under the existing sea conditions, the lifeboats could not have been lowered and launched successfully. Notice is taken of the fact that when Great Lakes freight vessels break in two, it is probable that approximately one-half of the crew would be at the forward end and unable to move to the after end where the larger percentage of lifesaving equipment is located. Had the boats been lowered safely, there would have been little hope for survival of persons aboard for an extended period since there was no means of protection from exposure. The common boat hooks in use are considered to be adequate only in calm water operation. The life rafts proved to be substantially constructed since one of the rafts showed signs of much abuse incident to the sinking and still provided adequate support. Even though these rafts were intended to float free, it could not be established why the forward raft was not thrown over the side prior to sinking. It may have been that the vessel broke up in less time than estimated by the survivor and that the master might have considered, in light of the slush on deck, the angle of the deck after the rupture, the time available, and the weight of the raft, that to wait for the vessel to sink was the safest, or only available procedure. Once in the water, the rafts offered no protection against the elements. It could not be established how and when the after raft went into the water. Had there been approved inflatable life rafts forward and aft, they probably could have been launched by vessel personnel and would have offered some protection from exposure.

The six persons listed as missing are presumed dead.

The electric cables leading forward from the source of power parted in the midships area as a result of the commencement of the crack in that area and prior to the sounding of the general alarm. The steam line, the general alarm cable and all other means of communication between the pilot house and the engine room were also parted at about the same time. After this, there was no source of power forward except batteries for the general alarm.

The radio installation on board the Daniel J. Morrell met the requirements of the applicable Federal Regulations. The system proved to be inadequate under the existing circumstances. Power was lost forward before bridge personnel were aware of the extreme condition that existed amidship. Great Lakes vessels are not required to carry emergency radios. Therefore no means for transmitting a distress signal was available after the cables were severed. More lives might have been saved if a distress signal had been transmitted. Although it was known that problems existed in the use of channel 52 prior to the sinking, a distress message probably could have been transmitted had there been a source of power forward. There was no evidence of any difficulty in reception on any other radio frequency on the Daniel J. Morrell.

The free surface water sighted by Hale in the cargo holds resulted from side tank slope damage. It is apparent that Hale would not have been directed to enter the holds for marking leaks in the side tank slopes and driving wedges into the cracks if ballast had previously been pumped in intentionally. It could not be determined whether this water was pumped from the cargo holds subsequent to its discovery by Hale in the afternoon. The tonnage of free surface water in the cargo holds could not be accurately determined since the vessel drafts are not known. In lieu of the estimated 18 inches there might have been nearer 45 inches of water at the after bulkhead of number No. 3 hold, as was the situation on the Edward Y. Townsend. It is noted that water extended to approximately the center of No. 2 hold on both vessels when discovered. It is estimated that the quantity of water in the cargo holds could have been from 300 to 800 tons. The effect of this quantity of water is not considered to have significantly changed the vessel's stability, which was more than adequate even with the reduction of the metacentric height cause by the free surface water. There was no evidence to indicate water was intentionally pumped into the vessel's cargo holds during this last trip.

The signal pistol came apart probably because the screw type hinge pin located forward of the trigger assembly and connecting the barrel of the pistol to the handle was either jarred loose or worked loose in use.

It is concluded that the inspections conducted by the Coast Guard during the 1966 drydocking, annual and midseason inspections were conducted in accordance with the Federal Regulations and in keeping with Coast Guard standards. There were no known deficiencies concerning the vessel's structure, equipment or machinery at the time of completion of these inspections.

The operators of the Daniel J. Morrell had not been informed of leaking rivets or any major structural, machinery or equipment deficiencies from the beginning of the 1966 season until the time of sinking. They were aware of minor items that had been repaired periodically, e.g., bucket damage to side tank slopes, radio deficiencies and leaking sanitary and fire main piping.

Other than the leaking shell rivets, which allowed leakage into the side tanks, leaking side tank slopes – which is common aboard Great Lakes bulk (non self-unloading) freighters-, and the non-use of tarpaulins or equivalent means for insuring tightness of the hatches there was no evidence to indicate that vessel watertight integrity was not being properly maintained.

There was evidence of violation of 46 CFR 97.15-20 in that although the hatch covers were in place, tarpaulins, gaskets or similar devices were not used to ensure watertightness of the hatches prior to entering Lake Huron on 28 November 1966, in the face of adverse weather. However, there is not evidence that this violation either caused or contributed to the cause of the casualty. There is evidence that other vessels are proceeding during Fall and Spring months while in a ballasted condition without ensuring watertightness of the cargo hatch covers. There is evidence that it is common practice to install tarpaulins over sliding steel type hatch covers only when the vessel is loaded, regardless of weather conditions. Other than the evidence of violation of 46 CFR 97.15-20, there was no evidence to indicate that there was any misconduct

290

inattention to duty, incompetency or willful violation of law or regulation regarding this casualty on the part of persons licensed or certificated by the Coast Guard.

No personnel of the Coast Guard, other agency of the Government or any other person either caused or contributed to the cause of the casualty or to the loss of life as a result thereof.

The evidence indicates that it is a practice for some Great Lakes ship masters to intentionally put water in their cargo holds in adverse weather in the belief that it will not only make their vessel ride better but will make it more stable. There is an apparent lack of knowledge of the reduction of stability caused by free surface effect.

It could not be determined whether the general alarm or other means of communications alerted all persons in the after section of the vessel. There was sufficient time before the sinking for all persons aft to be informed. It is unknown whether any persons were actually trapped inside the vessel at the time of sinking.

Although the requirements of the Federal Regulations were met, the general alarm system as installed is susceptible to improvement. There was no method for activating the system aft once the lines leading forward were parted.

Although the cause of death of the three persons on the raft with Hale was listed as drowning, they probably drowned from their own body fluids, or mucus, since they were still on the liferaft and all were believed to be conscious until immediately prior to death.

Although the lifeboat davits were not cranked out, the after crew might have removed the grips. It is also considered possible that the force of water might have broken them loose. It could not be determined what happened to the port lifeboat as it was never located. However, it could have sustained damages from the fallen after mast or the air tanks could have been crushed by water pressure.

All persons who are missing or known dead probably lost their lives before the Coast Guard was informed that the Daniel J. Morrell was overdue. A positive vessel reporting procedure is considered highly desirable.

There were leaking rivets in some of the Daniel J. Morrell's side tanks upon arrival in Toledo, Ohio, for winter lay up in 1965. The tanks causing most concern were the numbers 4 and 5 port side tanks. Vessel personnel entered tanks 4 and 5 port and marked leaking rivets with paint prior to lay up. The exact number of leaks could not be determined, as estimates ranged from no more than 12 to a maximum of 500 leaky rivets. It is held that the actual number was much closer to the lower estimate. The statements by Mr. Harvey Hayes that he assisted in marking up to 500 leaking rivets in side tanks and of Dennis N. Hale that he observed approximately 1000 rivets marked for repairs on the hull of the vessel above the side tank top level is not sufficiently reliable to support a finding of fact. The probability does exist, however, that Mr. Hayes did actually enter side tanks with another person and marked a small number of leaking rivets. Support for the rejection of the above statements is that

292

trained inspectors, surveyors and company personnel did not observe the supposedly marked rivets during the 1965 lay up season. It is possible that markings of side tank rivets were obliterated at the time that inspections were made. That the leaking into the port side tanks had been stopped or reduced and that Captain Hull was satisfied that the rivet problem had been corrected in drydock is accepted as fact. It is reasonable to assume that had there been any unusual leaking into side tanks or alarm over the condition of shell rivets, subsequent to his assuming command, Captain Crawley would have reported this fact to company officials. There is no evidence to substantiate any inference that leaky or faulty rivets caused or contributed to the cause of the casualty.

The forecast issued by the U.S. Weather Bureau for the southern two-thirds of Lake Huron at 1200 (12:00 P.M.) EST 28 November 1966 to cover the ensuing eighteen hour period was not sufficient to cause apprehension on the part of shipmasters. Vessels could generally expect protection in the lee of the Michigan shore. The weather information broadcast at 1800 (6:00 P.M.), which forecast winds of gale force from the north, was not interpreted by vessel masters as presenting conditions clearly dangerous to their operations. For this reason, most of the upbound vessels located in the Port Huron-Harbor Beach area continued northward until the wind force and action of the seas turned them around and forced their return to refuge in the Port Huron area. The winds were somewhat stronger and were from different directions than those expected. The sea conditions were much worse than would ordinarily be anticipated with the existing winds.

Whether a ship should or should not proceed in heavy weather conditions is a command decision. There is no clear showing that either the master of the SS Daniel J. Morrell or the masters of the other vessels who proceeded into the face of the storm were negligent for doing so.

The procedure of preparing forecasts every 6 hours does not in itself give sufficient advance warning to mariners since the seas build up so rapidly on the Great Lakes. It is believed that actual sea condition reports and sea condition forecasts issued by the U.S. Weather Bureau would contribute to the safety of vessels transiting the Great Lakes.

There was no evidence to indicate the reboilering, repowering, or vessel alterations since initial construction either caused or contributed to the cause of the casualty. No evidence was received to support a finding that previous loading, unloading or ballasting procedures contributed to the casualty.

Based on estimated positions of vessels in the area, the radar target observed by the master of the Benson Ford between 0100 and 0130 (1:00 A.M. and 1:30 A.M.) off the starboard beam was probably the Edward Y. Townsend.

Had the two screen bulkheads located in the cargo holds been of watertight construction, it is possible that one or both sections of the vessel would have remained afloat.

Loading manuals are not as a rule furnished to masters of Great Lakes bulk carriers and consequently masters cannot readily determine the effect of a particular loading or ballasting condition upon longitudinal bending moments. In the instant case it is felt that there was a shift in the normal loading pattern of the ballast caused by leakage from the ballast tanks and this effect was probably unknown to Captain Crawley. This effect is indeterminate because it is not clear whether the ballast tanks were refilled periodically to replenish the water which had leaked into the holds.

RECOMMENDATIONS

Based on the foregoing, it is recommended that:

The required forward and after life rafts on Great Lakes vessels be of the inflatable type to provide for easy launching and protection of personnel against the weather.

The capacity of the forward and after life rafts be sufficient to provide protection for all persons normally quartered in each part of the vessel.

To improve reliability of radio communication under conditions where the connection with the source of power aft is severed, that:

a. The Federal Regulations be changed to require an emergency source of power forward on Great Lakes vessels which have berthing and/or working spaces located both forward and aft, or

b. That consideration be given to recommending to the Federal Communications Commission, Washington, D.C. that an emergency radio with a self-contained source of power be required, and

c. That there be provided a datum marker buoy with the capacity of transmitting on 2182 kc. and capable of being either manually activated or automatically released and activated at a predetermined depth upon the sinking of the vessel. This could be stored with one of the required life rafts or attached with a pressure-release device to the side of the pilot house.

Special examinations of the hull structures of all Great Lakes vessels built prior to 1948 be conducted in order that a determination might be made as to whether weaknesses in hull plating or supporting structure have developed since the date of construction. NOTE: New ship steel specifications were adopted in 1948.

The owner or operator of each Great Lakes bulk carrier be required to furnish the master a loading manual which shows the effect of various loaded and ballasted conditions upon longitudinal bending moments. The effects of dynamic forces of free water in cargo holds should be included.

Consideration be given to change 46 CFR 113.25 to provide, for typical Great Lakes bulk carriers, regardless of date of construction, which have manned spaces separated by cargo holds, that:

a. The general alarm system shall be operated by means of manually operated contact makers located in the wheelhouse and in the engine room or at another suitable location in the after section of the vessel.

b. A separate source of power for the general alarm system be installed in the circuit at each end of the vessel and the installation be

296

made so that if the circuit be broken the forward alarms and the after alarms may be operated independently.

Further evaluation be made of the necessity to install tarpaulins over sliding plate type hatch covers which are properly secured, to determine whether or not the master of a Great Lakes vessel may be authorized by regulation to sail without tarpaulins in place during all seasons when the vessel is not carrying cargo.

Vessel owners and operators be encouraged to initiate a positive vessel reporting system. Reports at 24 hour intervals would be desirable. If the vessel does not report within one hour of the scheduled time the company should take positive action to determine the status of the vessel.

Consideration be given to requiring cargo hold compartmentation on newly constructed Great Lakes vessels so that in the event any one main cargo hold should be flooded the vessel will have sufficient buoyancy to remain afloat.

A recommendation be made to the U.S. Weather Bureau that some system be instituted to make possible the inclusion of on scene and forecasted sea conditions into regular marine weather broadcasts.

Since the screw joining the two major component groups of many signal pistols is not installed to prevent its working loose and dropping out, it is recommended that 46 CFR 160.028 be reviewed to require that when such screws are installed there be provision, such as use of lock nuts or peening of the ends, to prevent the screw from backing out.

The Master of the SS Daniel J. Morrell, Arthur I. Crawley, being deceased, it is recommended that no action be taken regarding his omitting the use of tarpaulins over the sliding plate hatch covers.

CHARLES TIGHE

Rear Admiral, U.S. Coast Guard

Chairman

W. A. BRUSO

Captain, U.S. Coast Guard

Member

ROBERT P. CHIRNSIDE

Commander, U.S. Coast Guard

Member

WILFRED R. BLEAKLEY, Jr.

Commander, U.S. Coast Guard

Member

RICHARD J. AKRIDGE

Lieutenant, U.S. Coast Guard

Member and Recorder

OTHER ITEMS OF INTEREST

<u>HOSPITAL REPORT</u>

Ashtabula General Hospital

HALE, Dennis/Dr. H.O. Tidd

Admitted: 12-5-66

<u>HISTORY</u>

This 26 year old white Seaman was transferred to the Ashtabula General Hospital from a hospital in Michigan where he had been under the care of Dr. Oakes. He is admitted here for further treatment and recuperation from injuries and exposure suffered in the sinking of a Great Lakes vessel. The history will be taken large from the narrative summary which Dr. Oakes kindly furnished.

He was admitted to the hospital in Michigan at 4:00 P.M. on November 30, 1966, with cold exposure and a rectal body temperature of 94.6°. His extremities and body were cold, blotchy, and purple, but there was no actual frozen tissue. The patient was warmed up to 97.4° in 90 minutes, and in five hours had a rebound temperature of 101°. His admission blood pressure was 120/64, this had risen to 152/80 within an hour after admission. Admitting hemoglobin was 18.9 gm. With a hemotocrit of 58%; a red count of 5.70 million; white count of 41,852 with a differential of 6 stabs., 68 segs., II lymphs., and 3 monos.

Initial Impression: Cold exposure, dehydration.

The patient was treated with IV fluids, 5% Dextrose in Water, soluable vitamins and Acromycin and a Tetanus Toxoid booster was given.

Past history: It was stated that the patient was in the United States Army from 1957-1959 in France, that he had had pneumonia, three day measles and chickenpox. The only surgical procedure he had had performed was a cyst taken off of his forehead.

He denied asthma or rheumatic fever, hepatitis, polio or arthritis. He had an allergy to Penicillin only.

Family history: Mother died when the patient was born, of hemorrhage.

Father, living, age 60, has had a lung removed for cancer.

He has one sister, two brothers, two step-sisters and three step-brothers.

The patient has been on sheet wadding and Ace bandage dressings to the feet and legs, has been on a low-salt diet, and has been continued on oral Acromycin, 250 mgm. 4 times a day until discharge this morning.

PHYSICAL EXAMINATION

A well-developed, slightly obese adult male appearing well-oriented, having no complaints, with the exception of numbness in the 5th and medial half of the 4th fingers, bilaterally, and lack of feeling in his feet.

FENT: Not remarkable. Tonsils present, small.

Neck: Supple

Lungfields: Clear to percussion & auscultation.

Heart: Regular sinus rhythm, no murmurs.

Abdomen: No masses. Liver, kidneys and spleen – not palpable.

300

Extremities: Skin: There is a sutured laceration of the right lateral neck. There is an abrasion of the left upper posterolateral thorax. In the left hand there are two healed blood blisters on the palmar surface of the middle and ring finger and one which is in the healing stage on the 2nd or forefinger. In the right upper extremity there is an abrasion of the right distal medial forearm. There are small abrasions and avulsions present on the right hand, and there is a dressing on the 5th finger which the patient says is for a severe "scraped finger". This dressing is not disturbed at the present time. Ace bandages were removed from both lower extremities, and there is a 1+ pitting edema of the right foot, and a 2+ pitting edema of the left foot. Pulses are active and equal. On the right foot there are abrasions on the medial surface of the foot, and a few healing blisters. On the left foot there are abrasions of the left ankle with small lacerations. There is partial avulsion of the 2nd toenail, there are healing contusions about the shins, bilaterally, and there is an abrasion above the left knee on the internal surface.

DEPARTMENT OF TRANSPORTATION

UNITED STATES COAST GUARD

MAILING ADDRESS: (G-MVI-1/83)
U.S. COAST GUARD
WASHINGTON, D.C. 20590
PHONE: 202-426-1464

16711
2 2 SEP 1977

Mr. Dennis N. Hale
5892 Buckeye Lane
Mentor-on-the-Lake, Ohio 44060

Dear Mr. Hale:

The President has asked me to respond to your letter of 3 April 1977, which expressed your concern for the safety of merchant seamen on Great Lakes vessels. I assure you, Mr. Hale, that the Coast Guard shares your concern. The loss of the EDMUND FITZGERALD has been the subject of a detailed investigation and positive steps have been initiated to improve vessel and personnel safety on the Great Lakes.

I had an opportunity to review the Coast Guard's response to an inquiry made on your behalf, by the Honorable William Stanton. That response addressed the issues which you raised in your letter to the President and supplied a compilation of action taken by the Coast Guard within recent years to enhance the safety of the Great Lakes merchant fleet. I am enclosing a copy of that letter.

I apologize for the delay in providing this response. However, when the aforementioned letter to Congressman Stanton was written the final action on the Marine Board of Investigation into the loss of the EDMUND FITZGERALD had not been completed. The recent publication of that action and the Marine Board's report outlines the Coast Guard's position and intended response to the problems made manifest by the casualty. I am enclosing a copy of this report and hope you find our action responsive to the concerns which you have expressed.

I appreciate your concern in this matter and hope you will find the information provided beneficial. If the Coast Guard can be of further assistance please feel free to write.

Sincerely,

O. W. SILER
Admiral, U. S. Coast Guard
Commandant

Encl: (1) COMDT (G-CC/104) ltr 16711 of 2 JUN 77 with enclosure
(2) Marine Casualty Report No. USCG 16732/64216

My son served on the Morrell during the summer of 1966 while on vacation from college. He knew most of the crew. He and I are concerned with these problems.

302

Your recent letter to President Carter has been forwarded to the Department of Transportation for a response.

I am asking the appropriate Departmental officials to investigate this matter for me and to prepare a responsive letter on my behalf. You will receive a reply as quickly as possible. Thank you for taking the time to write.

Sincerely,

BROCK ADAMS
Secretary of Transportation

MAY - 4 1977

Reply to Hale's note to President Jimmy Carter

Morrell's stern underwater upon discovery.   Drawing by Bob McGreevy

HENRY M. JACKSON, WASH., CHAIRMAN

FRANK CHURCH, IDAHO
LEE METCALF, MONT.
J. BENNETT JOHNSTON, LA.
JAMES ABOUREZK, S. DAK.
FLOYD K. HASKELL, COLO.
JOHN GLENN, OHIO
RICHARD STONE, FLA.
DALE BUMPERS, ARK.

PAUL J. FANNIN, ARIZ.
CLIFFORD P. HANSEN, WYO.
MARK O. HATFIELD, OREG.
JAMES A. McCLURE, IDAHO
DEWEY F. BARTLETT, OKLA.

GRENVILLE GARSIDE, SPECIAL COUNSEL AND STAFF DIRECTOR
WILLIAM J. VAN NESS, CHIEF COUNSEL

United States Senate

COMMITTEE ON
INTERIOR AND INSULAR AFFAIRS
WASHINGTON, D.C. 20510

April 21, 1977

Dennis N. Hale
5892 Buckeye Lane
Mentor-on-the-Lake, Ohio 44060

Dear Mr. Hale:

Thank you for your recent correspondence regarding the tragic sinking of the ore vessel "Edmund Fitzgerald" last year, and the need to improve shipping pilotage safety precautions.

I believe that we must direct appropriate authorities, such as the Coast Guard, to establish eligibility requirements for the issuance of a license to pilot any steam vessel in the Great Lakes and in territorial sea waters. In addition to upgrading pilotage standards, we must look to other aspects of the problems of navigational safety, such as equipment and training. Federal programs to divert water from the Great Lakes during periods of peaking water levels may also be advisable.

The Secretary of Transportation will be studying all of these possibilities in preparation for his annual report to the Congress on the state of transportation in the United States, and I look forward to reviewing this document as it pertains to inland and Great Lake shipping.

Thank you again for sharing with me your concerns on this matter.

Best regards.

Sincerely,

John Glenn
United States Senator

JG:jbg

DEPARTMENT OF TRANSPORTATION   Mailing Address

UNITED STATES COAST GUARD   U.S. Coast Guard (G-CMC/81)

Washington, D.C.

EXCERPT FROM FEDERAL REGISTER, VOL. 41, No. 110-Monday, June 7, 1976

The University of Victoria has published a report on hypothermia research, the short title of which is "MAN IN COLD WATER" dated June 30, 1975. This report estimates the survival time for a man in 44 degree F. water to be 2.44 hours when lightly clad, 4.10 hours when heavily clad and 8.53 hours when wearing a survival suit.

Conclusion: By these statistics, Dennis Hale should no longer be alive. He survived 38 hours of freezing temperatures, constantly drenched in heavy seas, clad only in his underwear and a pea jacket!

ABOVE: Morrell pilothouse and nameboard as it was discovered
BELOW: Dishes in the Morrell stern section
- Copyright David Trotter

Index

A

Alta Loma School 102, 108, 114, 232
Ashtabula 11, 22, 23, 28, 72, 119, 121, 124, 125, 140, 143, 149, 150, 162, 164, 165, 166, 167, 169, 171, 175, 185, 187, 188, 189, 190, 195, 203, 206, 226, 271
Ashtabula General Hospital 188,

B

Bad Axe, Michigan 228
Bakersfield, California 117
Balcomb, Norm 166, 200
Bar Le Duc, France 163
Bethlehem 21
Bethlehem Steel 10, 21, 22, 24, 76, 151, 170, 180, 196, 197, 244, 245, 247, 268, 272, 280
Blough, Roger (ship) 215
Blue Water Bridge 25
Bradley, Carl D. (ship) 18
Bragg, Norman 31
Brown, John (ship) 227
Buffalo 19

C

Campbell, Stu 26, 157
Cedarville 18
Checker Ice-Cream Company 60, 61
CKLW 24
Clark, Freddie 105
Clark, Nancy 5, 221
Cleary, John J. Jr 31, 32, 34, 63, 64, 65, 66, 74, 79, 100, 157, 239, 264, 266
Cleveland, Ohio 10, 39, 105, 151, 238, 246, 268, 269
Cleveland Hopkins Airport 184
Cleveland Plain Dealer 60
Columbus, Ohio 220, 283
Conneaut, Ohio 14
Connelly, Captain Thomas 193, 247, 249, 250, 251, 252, 256
Consolidated (Mullen) Coal Dock 23
Coplin, Larry 206
Crawley, Capt. Arthur 21, 22, 23, 26, 34, 35, 193, 239, 245, 247, 249, 250, 256, 263, , 276, 293, 295
Culver City Speedway 109, 110

D

E

F

G

H

I

J

K

Kadar, Skip 228
Kapets, Phil 26
Kapok 212
Kinsman Independent (ship) 194
Knotts Berry Farm 104, 105
Kushmaniuk, Victor 228

L

L. H. Mullen Company 147, 148, 149
Lackawanna 12, 13, 18, 19, 21, 22, 27, 197
Lagosi, Bella 116
Lake Erie 14
Lake Huron 3, 7, 22, 25, 36, 67, 152, 188, 194, 195, 226, 229, 238, 241, 247, 248, 249, 252, 253, 255, 257, 258, 259, 260, 261, 271, 280, 286, 290, 293
Lake Superior 22
Lake Superior State College 206, 207
Lightship, Lake Huron 25, 248, 252, 253, 255, 257, 258, 259, 261
Linkletter, Art 101, 103
Long Beach 108, 109
Los Angeles 86, 87, 101, 105, 109, 118, 120, 122, 130, 131, 133, 135, 139, 182
Los Angeles Coliseum 109

M

MacLeod, Duncan 34
Mahsem, Joe 27
Mansky, Fred (ship) 194
Mark Little Restaurant and Lounge 168
Mays, Frank 216, 217, 218, 235
McEachin, Fr. Cornelius 176
McGreevy, Robert 226
Mehringer, Tom 228
Miles Standish School 43, 55
Morgan, Brian 4, 225, 226
Muscle Beach 107, 147, 150

N

National Geographic 228, 232
Newman, Captain Zernie 257, 258

O

Oakes, Dr. Robert 174

P

Perrine, Joe 171

310

Dennis Hale with the bell from the Edmund Fitzgerald at the Great Lakes
Shipwreck Museum at Whitefish Point, MI.

You've read the book. Now experience the amazing survival story of Dennis Hale in person. His motivational speaking style captivates the audience as he recounts his time aboard the *Daniel J. Morrell*. Many people say their lives have been changed since hearing about his 38-hour ordeal on the liferaft.

For lecture information, autographed photos, and additional materials please contact:

Dennis Hale
PO Box 104
Rock Creek, OH 44084

DENNISHALE@WINDSTREAM.NET

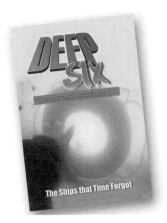